대화로 배우는 한국어

English(영어)
translation(번역판)

- 대화 (noun) : dialogue; conversation; talk
  Talking with and facing another person, or this kind of talk.

- 로 : no equivalent expression
  A postpositional particle that indicates a method or way to do something.

- 배우다 (verb) : learn
  To obtain new knowledge.

- -는 : no equivalent expression
  An ending of a word that makes the preceding statement function as an adnominal phrase and implies that an event or action is happening in the present.

- 한국어 (noun) : Korean; Korean language
  The language used by the Korean people.

※ 이 책의 폰트는 '함초롬 바탕체'를 사용하였습니다.

< 저자(author) >

㈜한글2119연구소

- 연구개발전담부서
- ISO 9001 : 품질경영시스템 인증
- ISO 14001 : 환경경영시스템 인증
- 이메일(e-mail) : gjh0675@naver.com

< 동영상(video) 자료(material) >

HANPUK_english(translation)
https://www.youtube.com/@HANPUK_English

제 2024153361 호

연구개발전담부서 인정서

1. 전담부서명: 연구개발전담부서

[소속기업명: (주)한글2119연구소]

2. 소 재 지: 인천광역시 부평구 마장로264번길 33
상가동 제지하층 제2호 (산곡동, 뉴서울아파트)

3. 신고 연월일: 2024년 05월 02일

과학기술정보통신부

「기초연구진흥 및 기술개발지원에 관한 법률」 제14조의 2제1항 및 같은 법 시행령 제27조제1항에 따라 위와 같이 기업의 연구개발전담부서로 인정합니다.

2024년 5월 13일

한국산업기술진흥협회장

G-CERTI *certificate*

hereby certifies that

Hangul 2119 Research Institute Co., Ltd.

Rm. 2, Lower level, Sangga-dong, 33, Majang-ro 264beon-gil,
Bupyeong-gu, Incheon, Korea

meets the Standard Requirements & Scope as following

ISO 9001:2015
Quality Management Systems

Creation of Media Content, Publication
of Korean Paper and Electronic Textbooks, Production
and Release of Albums for Korean Language Education

Certificate No:	GIS-6934-QC	**Code**	: 08, 39
Initial Date	: 2024-05-21	**Issue Date**	: 2024-05-21
Expiry Date	: 2027-05-20	**Valid Period**	: 2024-05-21 ~ 2027-05-20

Signed for and on behalf of GCERTI
President I.K.Cho

G-CERTI *certificate*

hereby certifies that

Hangul 2119 Research Institute Co., Ltd.

Rm. 2, Lower level, Sangga-dong, 33, Majang-ro 264beon-gil,
Bupyeong-gu, Incheon, Korea

meets the Standard Requirements & Scope as following

ISO 14001:2015
Environmental Management Systems

Creation of Media Content, Publication
of Korean Paper and Electronic Textbooks, Production and
Release of Albums for Korean Language Education

Certificate No	: GIS-6934-EC	**Code**	: 08, 39
Initial Date	: 2024-05-21	**Issue Date**	: 2024-05-21
Expiry Date	: 2027-05-20	**Valid Period**	: 2024-05-21 ~ 2027-05-20

Signed for and on behalf of GCERTI
President I.K.Cho

< 목차(table of contents) >

< 대화(dialogue) > - 1

배고플 텐데 왜 밥을 많이 남겼어?
배고플 텐데 왜 바블 마니 남겨써?
baegopeul tende wae babeul mani namgyeosseo?

사실은 조금 전에 간식으로 빵을 먹었거든요.
사시른 조금 저네 간시그로 빵을 머걷꺼드뇨.
sasireun jogeum jeone gansigeuro ppangeul meogeotgeodeunyo.

< 설명(explanation) / 번역(translation)>

배고프+[ㄹ 텐데] 왜 밥+을 많이 남기+었+어?
배고플 텐데 남겼어

• **배고프다 (adjective)** : 배 속이 빈 것을 느껴 음식이 먹고 싶다.
hungry
Feeling that one's stomach is empty and wanting to eat food.

• -ㄹ 텐데 : 앞에 오는 말에 대하여 말하는 사람의 강한 추측을 나타내면서 그와 관련되는 내용을 이어 말할 때 쓰는 표현.
-l tende (no equivalent expression)
An expression used to indicate the speaker's strong guess about the preceding statement and add the relevant content.

• **왜 (adverb)** : 무슨 이유로. 또는 어째서.
why
For what reason; how come.

• **밥 (noun)** : 쌀과 다른 곡식에 물을 붓고 물이 없어질 때까지 끓여서 익힌 음식.
steamed rice; rice
A dish made by boiling rice and other grains until the water has cooked away.

• 을 : 동작이 직접적으로 영향을 미치는 대상을 나타내는 조사.
eul (no equivalent expression)
A postpositional particle used to indicate the subject that an action has a direct influence on.

• **많이 (adverb)** : 수나 양, 정도 등이 일정한 기준보다 넘게.
much; in large numbers; in large amounts
In a state in which a number, amount, degree, etc., are larger than a certain standard.

• **남기다 (verb)** : 다 쓰지 않고 나머지가 있게 하다.
leave
To leave part of something without using it up.

• -었- : 어떤 사건이 과거에 완료되었거나 그 사건의 결과가 현재까지 지속되는 상황을 나타내는 어미.
-eot- (no equivalent expression)
An ending of a word used to indicate that an event was completed in the past or its result continues in the present.

• -어 : (두루낮춤으로) 어떤 사실을 서술하거나 **물음**, 명령, 권유를 나타내는 종결 어미.
-eo (no equivalent expression)
(informal addressee-lowering) A sentence-final ending used to describe a certain fact, **ask a question**, give an order, or advise.

사실+은 조금 전+에 간식+으로 빵+을 먹+었+거든요.

• **사실 (noun)** : 겉으로 드러나지 않은 일을 솔직하게 말할 때 쓰는 말.
truth is
An expression used to frankly tell someone something that is not seen nor known.

• 은 : 문장 속에서 어떤 대상이 화제임을 나타내는 조사.
eun (no equivalent expression)
A postpositional particle used to indicate that a certain subject is the topic of a sentence.

• **조금 (noun)** : 짧은 시간 동안.
a while
A duration of short time.

• **전 (noun)** : 일정한 때보다 앞.
earlier time
A time before a specific point in time.

• 에 : 앞말이 시간이나 때임을 나타내는 조사.
in; at
A postpositional particle to indicate that the preceding statement refers to the time.

• **간식 (noun)** : 식사와 식사 사이에 간단히 먹는 음식.
snack
Food that one eats between meals.

• 으로 : 신분이나 자격을 나타내는 조사.
euro (no equivalent expression)
A postpositional particle that indicates a status or capacity.

• **빵 (noun)** : 밀가루를 반죽하여 발효시켜 찌거나 구운 음식.
bread
Food made by baking or steaming fermented dough.

• 을 : 동작이 직접적으로 영향을 미치는 대상을 나타내는 조사.
eul (no equivalent expression)
A postpositional particle used to indicate the subject that an action has a direct influence on.

• **먹다 (verb)** : 음식 등을 입을 통하여 배 속에 들여보내다.
eat; have; consume; take
To put food into one's mouth and take it in one's stomach.

• -었- : 사건이 과거에 일어났음을 나타내는 어미.
-eot- (no equivalent expression)
An ending of a word used to indicate that an event happened in the past.

• -거든요 : (두루높임으로) 앞의 내용에 대해 말하는 사람이 생각한 이유나 원인, 근거를 나타내는 표현.
-geodeunnyo (no equivalent expression)
(informal addressee-raising) An expression used to indicate the speaker's reasoning or the basis for the preceding content.

< 대화(dialogue) > - 2

제가 지금 돈이 얼마 없거든요. 회비를 다음에 드려도 될까요?
제가 지금 도니 얼마 업꺼드뇨. 회비를 다으메 드려도 될까요?
jega jigeum doni eolma eopgeodeunyo. hoebireul daeume deuryeodo doelkkayo?

네. 그럼 다음 주 모임에 오실 때 주세요.
네. 그럼 다음 주 모이메 오실 때 주세요.
ne. geureom daeum ju moime osil ttae juseyo.

< 설명(explanation) / 번역(translation) >

제+가 지금 돈+이 얼마 없+거든요.

회비+를 다음+에 드리+[어도 되]+ㄹ까요?

드려도 될까요

• **제 (pronoun)** : 말하는 사람이 자신을 낮추어 가리키는 말인 '저'에 조사 '가'가 붙을 때의 형태.
I
A form of '저' (I), the humble form used by the speaker to show humility, when the postpositional particle '가' is attached to it.

• 가 : 어떤 상태나 상황에 놓인 대상이나 동작의 주체를 나타내는 조사.
ga (no equivalent expression)
A postpositional particle referring to a subject under a certain state or situation, or the subject of an act.

• **지금 (adverb)** : 말을 하고 있는 바로 이때에. 또는 그 즉시에.
now; immediately
At the present moment as one speaks, or that instant.

• **돈 (noun)** : 물건을 사고팔 때나 일한 값으로 주고받는 동전이나 지폐.
money
A coin or bill that is exchanged when trading goods or labor.

• 이 : 어떤 상태나 상황의 대상이나 동작의 주체를 나타내는 조사.
i (no equivalent expression)
A postpositional particle referring to a subject under a certain state or situation, or the agent of an action.

• **얼마 (noun)** : 밝힐 필요가 없는 적은 수량, 값, 정도.
some; some amount; some degree
A small number, amount, degree, or low price that one does not need to specify.

• **없다 (adjective)** : 어떤 물건을 가지고 있지 않거나 자격이나 능력 등을 갖추지 않은 상태이다.
lacking
Not having something or not possessing a credential, ability, etc.

• -거든요 : (두루높임으로) 앞으로 이어질 내용의 전제를 이야기하면서 뒤에 이야기가 계속 이어짐을 나타내는 표현.
-geodeunnyo (no equivalent expression)
(informal addressee-raising) An expression used to express the premise of the following content, indicating that the story continues later.

• **회비 (noun)** : 모임에서 사용하기 위하여 그 모임의 회원들이 내는 돈.
membership fee; dues
Money paid by members of an association to be spent on its activities.

• 를 : 동작이 직접적으로 영향을 미치는 대상을 나타내는 조사.
reul (no equivalent expression)
A postpositional particle used to indicate the subject that an act has a direct influence on.

• **다음 (noun)** : 시간이 지난 뒤.
next time; being later
A state in which a certain time has passed since something happened.

• 에 : 앞말이 시간이나 때임을 나타내는 조사.
in; at
A postpositional particle to indicate that the preceding statement refers to the time.

• **드리다 (verb)** : (높임말로) 주다. 무엇을 다른 사람에게 건네어 가지게 하거나 사용하게 하다.
give; offer
(honorific) To give; to hand something over to someone or allow someone to use it.

• -어도 되다 : 어떤 행동에 대한 허락이나 허용을 나타낼 때 쓰는 표현.
-eodo doeda (no equivalent expression)
An expression used to indicate that a certain act is allowed or accepted.

• -ㄹ까요 : (두루높임으로) 듣는 사람에게 의견을 묻거나 제안함을 나타내는 표현.
-lkkayo (no equivalent expression)
(informal addressee-raising) An expression used to ask for the listener's opinion or propose something.

네.

그럼 다음 주 모임+에 오+시+[ㄹ 때] 주+세요.
오실 때

• **네 (interjection)** : 윗사람의 물음이나 명령 등에 긍정하여 대답할 때 쓰는 말.
yes; yes sir; yes ma'am
An exclamation uttered when the speaker affirmatively answers the call or order of his/her superior.

• **그럼 (adverb)** : 앞의 내용을 받아들이거나 그 내용을 바탕으로 하여 새로운 주장을 할 때 쓰는 말.
then
A word used when accepting the preceding statement or making a new suggestion based on it.

• **다음 (noun)** : 이번 차례의 바로 뒤.
next; following
The thing that comes right after this time or turn in sequence.

• **주 (noun)** : 월요일부터 일요일까지의 칠 일 동안.
week
The seven-day period from Monday to Sunday.

• **모임 (noun)** : 어떤 일을 하기 위하여 여러 사람이 모이는 일.
meeting; gathering
A meeting of many people to do something.

• 에 : 앞말이 목적지이거나 어떤 행위의 진행 방향임을 나타내는 조사.
to; at
A postpositional particle to indicate that the preceding statement refers to a destination or the course of a certain action.

• **오다 (verb)** : 어떤 목적이 있는 모임에 참석하기 위해 다른 곳에 있다가 이곳으로 위치를 옮기다.
come
To move from another place to here to attend a gathering that has a certain purpose.

- -시- : 어떤 동작이나 상태의 주체를 높이는 뜻을 나타내는 어미.
  -si- (no equivalent expression)
  An ending of a word used for the subject honorifics of an action or state.

- -ㄹ 때 : 어떤 행동이나 상황이 일어나는 동안이나 그 시기 또는 그러한 일이 일어난 경우를 나타내는 표현.
  -l ttae (no equivalent expression)
  An expression used to indicate the duration, period, or occasion of a certain act or situation.

- **주다 (verb)** : 물건 등을 남에게 건네어 가지거나 쓰게 하다.
  give
  To give an item to someone else so he/she can have or use it.

- -세요 : (두루높임으로) 설명, 의문, 명령, **요청**의 뜻을 나타내는 종결 어미.
  -seyo (no equivalent expression)
  (informal addressee-raising) A sentence-final ending used to describe, ask a question, order, and **request**.

< 대화(dialogue) > - 3

내가 급한 사정이 생겨서 못 가게 된 공연 티켓이 있는데 네가 갈래?
내가 그판 사정이 생겨서 몬 가게 된 공연 티케시 인는데 네가 갈래?
naega geupan sajeongi saenggyeoseo mot gage doen gongyeon tikesi inneunde nega gallae?

정말? 그러면 나야 고맙지.
정말? 그러면 나야 고맙찌.
jeongmal? geureomyeon naya gomapji.

< 설명(explanation) / 번역(translation) >

내+가 급하+ㄴ 사정+이 생기+어서 못 가+[게 되]+ㄴ 공연 티켓+이 있+는데
급한 생겨서 가게 된

네+가 가+ㄹ래?
갈래

• **내 (pronoun)** : '나'에 조사 '가'가 붙을 때의 형태.
I
A form of '나' (I), when the postpositional particle '가' is attached to it.

• 가 : 어떤 상태나 상황에 놓인 대상이나 동작의 주체를 나타내는 조사.
ga (no equivalent expression)
A postpositional particle referring to a subject under a certain state or situation, or the subject of an act.

• **급하다 (adjective)** : 사정이나 형편이 빨리 처리해야 할 상태에 있다.
urgent
Having to do something quickly.

• -ㄴ : 앞의 말이 관형어의 기능을 하게 만들고 현재의 상태를 나타내는 어미.
-n (no equivalent expression)
An ending of a word that makes the preceding statement function as an adnominal phrase and refers to the present state.

• **사정 (noun)** : 일의 형편이나 이유.
situation; circumstances
The situation or reason for an incident.

• 이 : 어떤 상태나 상황의 대상이나 동작의 주체를 나타내는 조사.
i (no equivalent expression)
A postpositional particle referring to a subject under a certain state or situation, or the agent of an action.

• **생기다 (verb)** : 사고나 일, 문제 등이 일어나다.
occur; take place
For an incident, matter, trouble, etc., to happen.

• -어서 : 이유나 근거를 나타내는 연결 어미.
-eoseo (no equivalent expression)
A connective ending used for a reason or cause.

• **못 (adverb)** : 동사가 나타내는 동작을 할 수 없게.
not
The word that negates the action represented by the verb.

• **가다 (verb)** : 어떤 목적을 가진 모임에 참석하기 위해 이동하다.
go
To move to attend a certain meeting that has a specific purpose.

• -게 되다 : 앞의 말이 나타내는 상태나 상황이 됨을 나타내는 표현.
-ge doeda (no equivalent expression)
An expression used to indicate that something will become the state or situation mentioned in the preceding statement.

• -ㄴ : 앞의 말이 관형어의 기능을 하게 만들고 사건이나 동작이 완료되어 그 상태가 유지되고 있음을 나타내는 어미.
-n (no equivalent expression)
An ending of a word that makes the preceding statement function as an adnominal phrase and indicates that an event or action has been completed and its state continues.

• **공연 (noun)** : 음악, 무용, 연극 등을 많은 사람들 앞에서 보이는 것.
performance; show
Performing music, dance or a play in front of many people.

• **티켓 (noun)** : 입장권, 승차권 등의 표.
ticket
A ticket such as an admission ticket, boarding pass, etc.

• 이 : 어떤 상태나 상황의 대상이나 동작의 주체를 나타내는 조사.
i (no equivalent expression)
A postpositional particle referring to a subject under a certain state or situation, or the agent of an action.

• **있다 (adjective)** : 어떤 물건을 가지고 있거나 자격이나 능력 등을 갖춘 상태이다.
no equivalent expression
Having a certain object, qualification, ability, etc.

• -는데 : 뒤의 말을 하기 위하여 그 대상과 관련이 있는 상황을 미리 말함을 나타내는 연결 어미.
-neunde (no equivalent expression)
A connective ending used to talk in advance about a situation to follow.

• **네 (pronoun)** : '너'에 조사 '가'가 붙을 때의 형태.
you
A form of '너' (you), when the postpositional particle '가' is attached to it.

• 가 : 어떤 상태나 상황에 놓인 대상이나 동작의 주체를 나타내는 조사.
ga (no equivalent expression)
A postpositional particle referring to a subject under a certain state or situation, or the subject of an act.

• **가다 (verb)** : 어떤 목적을 가진 모임에 참석하기 위해 이동하다.
go
To move to attend a certain meeting that has a specific purpose.

• -ㄹ래 : (두루낮춤으로) 앞으로 어떤 일을 하려고 하는 자신의 의사를 나타내거나 그 일에 대하여 듣는 사람의 의사를 물어봄을 나타내는 종결 어미.
-llae (no equivalent expression)
(informal addressee-lowering) A sentence-final ending used to indicate the speaker's intention to do something in the future, or to ask for the listener's thoughts about that.

정말?

그러면 나+야 고맙+지.

• **정말 (noun)** : 거짓이 없는 사실. 또는 사실과 조금도 틀림이 없는 말.
fact
A truth without falsehood, or words without any lack of conformity to truth.

• **그러면 (adverb)** : 앞의 내용이 뒤의 내용의 조건이 될 때 쓰는 말.
if so
A conjunctive adverb used when the following statement is conditional upon the preceding one.

• **나 (pronoun)** : 말하는 사람이 친구나 아랫사람에게 자기를 가리키는 말.
I
A pronoun used to indicate oneself to a friend or a younger person.

• 야 : 강조의 뜻을 나타내는 조사.
ya (no equivalent expression)
A postpositional particle used to emphasize the preceding word.

• **고맙다 (adjective)** : 남이 자신을 위해 무엇을 해주어서 마음이 흐뭇하고 보답하고 싶다.
thankful; grateful
Pleased and wanting to return a favor to someone.

• -지 : (두루낮춤으로) 말하는 사람이 자신에 대한 이야기나 자신의 생각을 친근하게 말할 때 쓰는 종결 어미.
-ji (no equivalent expression)
(informal addressee-lowering) A sentence-final ending used when the speaker talks about himself/herself or his/her thoughts in a friendly manner.

< 대화(dialogue) > - 4

저녁때 손님이 오신다고 불고기에다가 잡채까지 준비하게요?
저녁때 손니미 오신다고 불고기에다가 잡채까지 준비하게요?
jeonyeokttae sonnimi osindago bulgogiedaga japchaekkaji junbihageyo?

그럼, 그 정도는 준비해야지.
그럼, 그 정도는 준비해야지.
geureom, geu jeongdoneun junbihaeyaji.

< 설명(explanation) / 번역(translation) >

저녁때 손님+이 오+시+ㄴ다고 불고기+에다가 잡채+까지 준비하+게요?
오신다고

• **저녁때 (noun)** : 저녁밥을 먹는 때.
dinner time
The time when dinner is eaten.

• **손님 (noun)** : (높임말로) 다른 곳에서 찾아온 사람.
visitor; caller; guest
(honorific) A person who comes to visit someone.

• 이 : 어떤 상태나 상황의 대상이나 동작의 주체를 나타내는 조사.
i (no equivalent expression)
A postpositional particle referring to a subject under a certain state or situation, or the agent of an action.

• **오다 (verb)** : 무엇이 다른 곳에서 이곳으로 움직이다.
come
For something to move from another place to here.

• -시- : 어떤 동작이나 상태의 주체를 높이는 뜻을 나타내는 어미.
-si- (no equivalent expression)
An ending of a word used for the subject honorifics of an action or state.

• -ㄴ다고 : 어떤 행위의 목적, 의도를 나타내거나 어떤 상황의 이유, 원인을 나타내는 연결 어미.
-ndago (no equivalent expression)
A connective ending used when implying the purpose or intention of a certain action, or the reason or cause of a certain situation.

• **불고기 (noun)** : 얇게 썰어 양념한 돼지고기나 쇠고기를 불에 구운 한국 전통 음식.
bulgogi (no equivalent expression)
barbequed beef: Traditional Korean food made by roasting seasoned slices of pork or beef.

• 에다가 : 더해지는 대상을 나타내는 조사.
edaga (no equivalent expression)
A postpositional particle referring to an entity that is added to.

• **잡채 (noun)** : 여러 가지 채소와 고기 등을 가늘게 썰어 기름에 볶은 것을 당면과 섞어 만든 음식.
japchae (no equivalent expression)
A Korean dish made by mixing sweet potato noodles with thin slices of stir-fried various vegetables, meat, etc.

• 까지 : 현재의 상태나 정도에서 그 위에 더함을 나타내는 조사.
kkaji (no equivalent expression)
A postpositional particle referring to an addition to the present state or degree.

• **준비하다 (verb)** : 미리 마련하여 갖추다.
prepare
To have something in place with advance preparations.

• -게요 : (두루높임으로) 앞의 내용이 그러하다면 뒤의 내용은 어떠할 것이라고 추측해 물음을 나타내는 표현.
-geyo (no equivalent expression)
(informal addressee-raising) An expression used to guess what the following statement would be like, if the preceding statement is such, and ask about it.

그럼, 그 정도+는 준비하+여야지.
준비해야지

• **그럼 (interjection)** : 말할 것도 없이 당연하다는 뜻으로 대답할 때 쓰는 말.
of course
An exclamation used when the speaker gives an answer meaning that something is absolutely right.

• **그 (determiner)** : 앞에서 이미 이야기한 대상을 가리킬 때 쓰는 말.
that; the
A term referring to something mentioned earlier.

• **정도 (noun)** : 사물의 성질이나 가치를 좋고 나쁨이나 더하고 덜한 정도로 나타내는 분량이나 수준.
degree
A quantity or level that represents the nature or value of something in terms of the degree of goodness or intensity.

• 는 : 강조의 뜻을 나타내는 조사.
neun (no equivalent expression)
A postpositional particle used to indicate an emphasis.

• **준비하다 (verb)** : 미리 마련하여 갖추다.
prepare
To have something in place with advance preparations.

• -여야지 : (두루낮춤으로) 말하는 사람의 결심이나 의지를 나타내는 종결 어미.
-yeoyaji (no equivalent expression)
(informal addressee-lowering) A sentence-final ending used to indicate the speaker's determination or will.

< 대화(dialogue) > - 5

장사가 잘됐으면 제가 그만뒀게요?
장사가 잘돼쓰면 제가 그만뒬께요?
jangsaga jaldwaesseumyeon jega geumandwotgeyo?

요즘은 장사하는 사람들이 다 어렵다고 하더라고요.
요즈믄 장사하는 사람드리 다 어렵따고 하더라고요.
yojeumeun jangsahaneun saramdeuri da eoryeopdago hadeoragoyo.

< 설명(explanation) / 번역(translation) >

장사+가 잘되+었으면 제+가 그만두+었+게요?
잘됐으면 그만뒀게요

• **장사 (noun)** : 이익을 얻으려고 물건을 사서 팖. 또는 그런 일.
business
The act of buying products to sell for profit, or such business.

• 가 : 어떤 상태나 상황에 놓인 대상이나 동작의 주체를 나타내는 조사.
ga (no equivalent expression)
A postpositional particle referring to a subject under a certain state or situation, or the subject of an act.

• **잘되다 (verb)** : 어떤 일이나 현상이 좋게 이루어지다.
go well; work well; work out
For a certain matter or phenomenon to go on in a desirable way.

• -었으면 : 현재 그렇지 않음을 표현하기 위해 실제 상황과 반대되는 가정을 할 때 쓰는 표현.
-eotsseumyeon (no equivalent expression)
An expression used to assume an opposite situation to say that it is not the case now.

• **제 (pronoun)** : 말하는 사람이 자신을 낮추어 가리키는 말인 '저'에 조사 '가'가 붙을 때의 형태.
I
A form of '저' (I), the humble form used by the speaker to show humility, when the postpositional particle '가' is attached to it.

• 가 : 어떤 상태나 상황에 놓인 대상이나 동작의 주체를 나타내는 조사.
ga (no equivalent expression)
A postpositional particle referring to a subject under a certain state or situation, or the subject of an act.

• **그만두다 (verb)** : 하던 일을 중간에 그치고 하지 않다.
stop
To stop and to not do what one has been doing.

• -었- : 어떤 사건이 과거에 완료되었거나 그 사건의 결과가 현재까지 지속되는 상황을 나타내는 어미.
-eot- (no equivalent expression)
An ending of a word used to indicate that an event was completed in the past or its result continues in the present.

• -게요 : (두루높임으로) 앞의 내용이 사실이라면 당연히 뒤의 내용이 이루어지겠지만 실제로는 그렇지 않음을 나타내는 표현.
-geyo (no equivalent expression)
(informal addressee-raising) An expression used to indicate the following content would obviously be realized if the preceding content were true, but actually it is not.

요즘+은 장사하+는 사람+들+이 다 어렵+다고 하+더라고요.

• **요즘 (noun)** : 아주 가까운 과거부터 지금까지의 사이.
nowadays; these days
A period from a while ago to the present.

• 은 : 문장 속에서 어떤 대상이 화제임을 나타내는 조사.
eun (no equivalent expression)
A postpositional particle used to indicate that a certain subject is the topic of a sentence.

• **장사하다 (verb)** : 이익을 얻으려고 물건을 사서 팔다.
do business; sell
To buy products to resell for profit.

• -는 : 앞의 말이 관형어의 기능을 하게 만들고 사건이나 동작이 현재 일어남을 나타내는 어미.
-neun (no equivalent expression)
An ending of a word that makes the preceding statement function as an adnominal phrase and implies that an event or action is happening in the present.

• **사람 (noun)** : 특별히 정해지지 않은 자기 외의 남을 가리키는 말.
other; other person
The word that refers to an unspecified person other than oneself.

• 들 : '복수'의 뜻을 더하는 접미사.
-deul (no equivalent expression)
A suffix used to mean plural.

• 이 : 어떤 상태나 상황의 대상이나 동작의 주체를 나타내는 조사.
i (no equivalent expression)
A postpositional particle referring to a subject under a certain state or situation, or the agent of an action.

• **다 (adverb)** : 남거나 빠진 것이 없이 모두.
all; everything
With nothing left over or missing.

• **어렵다 (adjective)** : 곤란한 일이나 고난이 많다.
difficult; hard
Being in serious trouble or suffering great hardship.

• -다고 : 다른 사람에게서 들은 내용을 간접적으로 전달하거나 주어의 생각, 의견 등을 나타내는 표현.
-dago (no equivalent expression)
An expression used to pass along what the speaker heard from another person, or to present the subject's thoughts, opinions, etc.

• **하다 (verb)** : 무엇에 대해 말하다.
say
To talk about something.

• -더라고요 : (두루높임으로) 과거에 경험하여 새로 알게 된 사실에 대해 지금 상대방에게 옮겨 전할 때 쓰는 표현.
-deoragoyo (no equivalent expression)
(informal addressee-raising) An expression used to refer to and convey in the present a fact the speaker learned through a past experience to the listener.

< 대화(dialogue) > - 6

우리 가족 중에서 누가 가장 늦게 일어나게요?
우리 가족 중에서 누가 가장 늗께 이러나게요?
uri gajok jungeseo nuga gajang neutge ireonageyo?

보나 마나 너겠지, 뭐.
보나 마나 너겓찌, 뭐.
bona mana neogetji, mwo.

< 설명(explanation) / 번역(translation) >

우리 가족 중+에서 누(구)+가 가장 늦+게 일어나+게요?
누가

• **우리 (pronoun)** : 말하는 사람이 자기보다 높지 않은 사람에게 자기와 관련된 것을 친근하게 나타낼 때 쓰는 말.
uri (no equivalent expression)
we: A pronoun used when the speaker intimately refers to something related to him/her while speaking to the person junior to himself/herself.

• **가족 (noun)** : 주로 한 집에 모여 살고 결혼이나 부모, 자식, 형제 등의 관계로 이루어진 사람들의 집단. 또는 그 구성원.
family
A group of people who mainly live together in the same house and are related by marriage or as parents, children, siblings, etc., or the members of such a group.

• **중 (noun)** : 여럿 가운데.
no equivalent expression
A bound noun used to refer to something out of many.

• 에서 : 여럿으로 이루어진 일정한 범위의 안.
eseo (no equivalent expression)
A state of being within a certain range of things.

• **누구 (pronoun)** : 모르는 사람을 가리키는 말.
no equivalent expression
A pronoun used to indicate a person that one does not know.

• 가 : 어떤 상태나 상황에 놓인 대상이나 동작의 주체를 나타내는 조사.
ga (no equivalent expression)
A postpositional particle referring to a subject under a certain state or situation, or the subject of an act.

• **가장 (adverb)** : 여럿 가운데에서 제일로.
best
In a way that is better than any other.

• **늦다 (adjective)** : 기준이 되는 때보다 뒤져 있다.
late; later
Later than a point in time that serves as the baseline.

• -게 : 앞의 말이 뒤에서 가리키는 일의 목적이나 결과, 방식, 정도 등이 됨을 나타내는 연결 어미.
-ge (no equivalent expression)
A connective ending used when the preceding statement is the purpose, result, method, amount, etc., of something mentioned in the following statement.

• **일어나다 (verb)** : 잠에서 깨어나다.
get up
To wake up.

• -게요 : (두루높임으로) 듣는 사람에게 한 번 추측해서 대답해 보라고 물을 때 쓰는 표현.
-geyo (no equivalent expression)
(informal addressee-raising) An expression used when asking the listener to try to guess and answer.

보+[나 마나] 너+(이)+겠+지, 뭐.
너겠지

• **보다 (verb)** : 눈으로 대상의 존재나 겉모습을 알다.
see; look at; notice
To perceive with eyes the existence or appearance of an object.

• -나 마나 : 그렇게 하나 그렇게 하지 않으나 다름이 없는 상황임을 나타내는 표현.
-na mana (no equivalent expression)
An expression used to indicate that whether a certain thing is done or not makes no difference.

• **너 (pronoun)** : 듣는 사람이 친구나 아랫사람일 때, 그 사람을 가리키는 말.
no equivalent expression
A pronoun used to indicate the listener when he/she is the same age or younger.

• 이다 : 주어가 지시하는 대상의 속성이나 부류를 지정하는 뜻을 나타내는 서술격 조사.
ida (no equivalent expression)
A predicate particle indicating the meaning of the attribute or category of the thing that the subject of the sentence refers to.

• -겠- : 미래의 일이나 추측을 나타내는 어미.
-get- (no equivalent expression)
An ending of a word referring to a future event or assumption.

• -지 : (두루낮춤으로) 말하는 사람이 자신에 대한 이야기나 자신의 생각을 친근하게 말할 때 쓰는 종결 어미.
-ji (no equivalent expression)
(informal addressee-lowering) A sentence-final ending used when the speaker talks about himself/herself or his/her thoughts in a friendly manner.

• **뭐 (interjection)** : 사실을 말할 때, 상대의 생각을 가볍게 반박하거나 새롭게 일깨워 주는 뜻으로 하는 말.
well; you know
An exclamation used to refute the other party's opinion lightly or to inform him/her of a new piece of information.

< 대화(dialogue) > - 7

저 앞 도로에서 무슨 일이 생겼나 봐요. 길이 이렇게 막히게요.
저 압 도로에서 무슨 이리 생견나 봐요. 기리 이러케 마키게요.
jeo ap doroeseo museun iri saenggyeonna bwayo. giri ireoke makigeyo.

사고라도 난 모양이네.
사고라도 난 모양이네.
sagorado nan moyangine.

< 설명(explanation) / 번역(translation) >

저 앞 도로+에서 무슨 일+이 생기+었+[나 보]+아요.
생겼나 봐요

길+이 이렇+게 막히+게요.

• **저 (determiner)** : 말하는 사람과 듣는 사람에게서 멀리 떨어져 있는 대상을 가리킬 때 쓰는 말.
that
A word used to indicate a person who is far away from the speaker and the listener.

• **앞 (noun)** : 향하고 있는 쪽이나 곳.
front
The direction or place one is facing.

• **도로 (noun)** : 사람이나 차가 잘 다닐 수 있도록 만들어 놓은 길.
road
A path built for cars and people to travel.

• 에서 : 앞말이 행동이 이루어지고 있는 장소임을 나타내는 조사.
eseo (no equivalent expression)
A postpositional particle used to indicate that the preceding word refers to a place where a certain action is being done.

• **무슨 (determiner)** : 확실하지 않거나 잘 모르는 일, 대상, 물건 등을 물을 때 쓰는 말.
what
An expression used to ask about a business, subject or object that one is not sure of or does not exactly know.

• **일 (noun)** : 어떤 내용을 가진 상황이나 사실.
matter; affair
A certain situation or fact.

• 이 : 어떤 상태나 상황의 대상이나 동작의 주체를 나타내는 조사.
i (no equivalent expression)
A postpositional particle referring to a subject under a certain state or situation, or the agent of an action.

• **생기다 (verb)** : 사고나 일, 문제 등이 일어나다.
occur; take place
For an incident, matter, trouble, etc., to happen.

• -었- : 어떤 사건이 과거에 완료되었거나 그 사건의 결과가 현재까지 지속되는 상황을 나타내는 어미.
-eot- (no equivalent expression)
An ending of a word used to indicate that an event was completed in the past or its result continues in the present.

• -나 보다 : 앞의 말이 나타내는 사실을 추측함을 나타내는 표현.
-na boda (no equivalent expression)
An expression used to guess about a fact mentioned in the preceding statement.

• -아요 : (두루높임으로) 어떤 사실을 서술하거나 질문, 명령, 권유함을 나타내는 종결 어미.
-ayo (no equivalent expression)
(informal addressee-raising) A sentence-final ending used to **describe** a certain fact, ask a question, give an order, or advise.

• **길 (noun)** : 사람이나 차 등이 지나다닐 수 있게 땅 위에 일정한 너비로 길게 이어져 있는 공간.
road; street; way
A long stretch of ground space with a fixed width meant for people or cars to travel along.

• 이 : 어떤 상태나 상황의 대상이나 동작의 주체를 나타내는 조사.
i (no equivalent expression)
A postpositional particle referring to a subject under a certain state or situation, or the agent of an action.

• **이렇다 (adjective)** : 상태, 모양, 성질 등이 이와 같다.
so; like this
(for a state, appearance, nature to be) Like this.

• -게 : 앞의 말이 뒤에서 가리키는 일의 목적이나 결과, 방식, 정도 등이 됨을 나타내는 연결 어미.
-ge (no equivalent expression)
A connective ending used when the preceding statement is the purpose, result, method, amount, etc., of something mentioned in the following statement.

• **막히다 (verb)** : 길에 차가 많아 차가 제대로 가지 못하게 되다.
be jammed
For cars to not run easily because there are many cars on the road.

• -게요 : (두루높임으로) 앞 문장의 내용에 대한 근거를 제시할 때 쓰는 표현.
-geyo (no equivalent expression)
(informal addressee-raising) An expression used when presenting the reason for the preceding statement.

사고+라도 나+[ㄴ 모양이]+네.
난 모양이네

• **사고 (noun)** : 예상하지 못하게 일어난 좋지 않은 일.
accident
An unfortunate affair that happens unexpectedly.

• 라도 : 유사한 것을 예로 들어 설명할 때 쓰는 조사.
rado (no equivalent expression)
A postpositional word used when explaining something by giving an example of a similar thing.

• **나다 (verb)** : 어떤 현상이나 사건이 일어나다.
happen; occur
For a phenomenon or event to happen.

• -ㄴ 모양이다 : 다른 사실이나 상황으로 보아 현재 어떤 일이 일어났거나 어떤 상태라고 추측함을 나타내는 표현.
-n moyangida (no equivalent expression)
An expression used to guess that something is in progress or in a certain state, considering another fact or situation.

• -네 : (아주낮춤으로) 지금 깨달은 일에 대하여 말함을 나타내는 종결 어미.
-ne (no equivalent expression)
(formal, highly addressee-lowering) A sentence-final ending used when talking about something that one just learned.

< 대화(dialogue) > - 8

다음 달에 적금을 타면 뭐 하게요?
다음 다레 적끄믈 타면 뭐 하게요?
daeum dare jeokgeumeul tamyeon mwo hageyo?

그걸로 딸아이 피아노 사 주려고 해요.
그걸로 따라이 피아노 사 주려고 해요.
geugeollo ttarai piano sa juryeogo haeyo.

< 설명(explanation) / 번역(translation) >

다음 달+에 적금+을 타+면 뭐 하+게요?

• **다음 (noun)** : 어떤 차례에서 바로 뒤.
next; following
Something that comes right after another in a sequence of time, place, turn, etc.

• **달 (noun)** : 일 년을 열둘로 나누어 놓은 기간.
month
A period in a year divided by twelve.

• 에 : 앞말이 시간이나 때임을 나타내는 조사.
in; at
A postpositional particle to indicate that the preceding statement refers to the time.

• **적금 (noun)** : 은행에 일정한 돈을 일정한 기간 동안 낸 다음에 찾는 저금.
term deposit
A type of savings where deposits are made with the bank over a certain period before withdrawal.

• 을 : 동작이 직접적으로 영향을 미치는 대상을 나타내는 조사.
eul (no equivalent expression)
A postpositional particle used to indicate the subject that an action has a direct influence on.

• **타다 (verb)** : 몫이나 상으로 주는 돈이나 물건을 받다.
receive
To receive money or an object as one's share or as a prize.

• -면 : 뒤에 오는 말에 대한 근거나 조건이 됨을 나타내는 연결 어미.
-myeon (no equivalent expression)
A connective ending used when the preceding statement becomes the reason or condition of the following statement.

• **뭐 (pronoun)** : 모르는 사실이나 사물을 가리키는 말.
what
A pronoun used to refer to a fact or object that one does not know of.

• **하다 (verb)** : 어떤 행동이나 동작, 활동 등을 행하다.
do; perform
To perform a certain move, action, activity, etc.

• -게요 : (두루높임으로) 상대의 의도를 물을 때 쓰는 표현.
-geyo (no equivalent expression)
(informal addressee-raising) An expression used when asking about the other person's intentions.

그것(그거)+ㄹ로 딸아이 피아노 사+[(아) 주]+[려고 하]+여요.
그걸로 사 주려고 해요

• **그것 (pronoun)** : 앞에서 이미 이야기한 대상을 가리키는 말.
no equivalent expression
A pronoun used to indicate the previously-mentioned object.

• ㄹ로 : 어떤 일의 수단이나 도구를 나타내는 조사.
ro (no equivalent expression)
A postpositional particle that indicates a tool or means for something.

• **딸아이 (noun)** : 남에게 자기 딸을 이르는 말.
daughter
A term used to address one's daughter in front of others.

• **피아노 (noun)** : 검은색과 흰색 건반을 손가락으로 두드리거나 눌러서 소리를 내는 큰 악기.
piano
A musical instrument that produces sound when its black and white keys are tapped or pressed with fingers.

• **사다 (verb)** : 돈을 주고 어떤 물건이나 권리 등을 자기 것으로 만들다.
buy; purchase; get
To get ownership of an item, right, etc., by paying for it.

• -아 주다 : 남을 위해 앞의 말이 나타내는 행동을 함을 나타내는 표현.
-a juda (no equivalent expression)
An expression used to indicate that one does the act mentioned in the preceding statement for someone.

• -려고 하다 : 앞의 말이 나타내는 행동을 할 의도나 의향이 있음을 나타내는 표현.
-ryeogo hada (no equivalent expression)
An expression used to indicate that one has the intention or wish to do the act mentioned in the preceding statement.

• -여요 : (두루높임으로) 어떤 사실을 서술하거나 질문, 명령, 권유함을 나타내는 종결 어미.
-yeoyo (no equivalent expression)
(informal addressee-raising) A sentence-final ending used to **describe** a certain fact, ask a question, give an order, or advise.

< 대화(dialogue) > - 9

누가 책상을 치우라고 시켰어요?
누가 책상을 치우라고 시켜써요?
nuga chaeksangeul chiurago sikyeosseoyo?

제가 영수에게 치우게 했습니다.
제가 영수에게 치우게 핻씀니다.
jega yeongsuege chiuge haetseumnida.

< 설명(explanation) / 번역(translation) >

누(구)+가 책상+을 치우+라고 시키+었+어요?
누가 시켰어요

• **누구 (pronoun)** : 모르는 사람을 가리키는 말.
no equivalent expression
A pronoun used to indicate a person that one does not know.

• 가 : 어떤 상태나 상황에 놓인 대상이나 동작의 주체를 나타내는 조사.
ga (no equivalent expression)
A postpositional particle referring to a subject under a certain state or situation, or the subject of an act.

• **책상 (noun)** : 책을 읽거나 글을 쓰거나 사무를 볼 때 앞에 놓고 쓰는 상.
desk
A table at which one reads a book, writes, or handles office work.

• 을 : 동작이 직접적으로 영향을 미치는 대상을 나타내는 조사.
eul (no equivalent expression)
A postpositional particle used to indicate the subject that an action has a direct influence on.

• **치우다 (verb)** : 물건을 다른 데로 옮기다.
move
To move an object to another place.

• -라고 : 다른 사람에게 들은 명령이나 권유 등의 내용을 간접적으로 전할 때 쓰는 표현.
-rago (no equivalent expression)
An expression used to indirectly convey the order, recommendation, etc., heard from another person.

• **시키다 (verb)** : 어떤 일이나 행동을 하게 하다.
order
To make a person do something.

• -었- : 사건이 과거에 일어났음을 나타내는 어미.
-eot- (no equivalent expression)
An ending of a word used to indicate that an event happened in the past.

• -어요 : (두루높임으로) 어떤 사실을 서술하거나 질문, 명령, 권유함을 나타내는 종결 어미.
-eoyo (no equivalent expression)
(informal addressee-raising) A sentence-final ending used to describe a certain fact, ask a question, give an order, or advise. **<question>**

제+가 영수+에게 치우+[게 하]+였+습니다.
치우게 했습니다

• **제 (pronoun)** : 말하는 사람이 자신을 낮추어 가리키는 말인 '저'에 조사 '가'가 붙을 때의 형태.
I
A form of '저' (I), the humble form used by the speaker to show humility, when the postpositional particle '가' is attached to it.

• 가 : 어떤 상태나 상황에 놓인 대상이나 동작의 주체를 나타내는 조사.
ga (no equivalent expression)
A postpositional particle referring to a subject under a certain state or situation, or the subject of an act.

• **영수 (noun)** : person's name

• 에게 : 어떤 행동이 미치는 대상임을 나타내는 조사.
ege (no equivalent expression)
A postpositional particle referring to the subject that is influenced by a certain action.

• **치우다 (verb)** : 물건을 다른 데로 옮기다.
move
To move an object to another place.

• -게 하다 : 남에게 어떤 행동을 하도록 시키거나 물건이 어떤 작동을 하게 만듦을 나타내는 표현.
-ge hada (no equivalent expression)
An expression used to order someone to do a certain thing or to make something work.

• -였- : 사건이 과거에 일어났음을 나타내는 어미.
-yeot- (no equivalent expression)
An ending of a word used to indicate that an event happened in the past.

• -습니다 : (아주높임으로) 현재의 동작이나 상태, 사실을 정중하게 설명함을 나타내는 종결 어미.
-seupnida (no equivalent expression)
(formal, highly addressee-raising) A sentence-final ending used to explain the present action, state, or fact politely.

< 대화(dialogue) > - 10

어머니가 아직도 여행을 못 가게 하셔?
어머니가 아직또 여행을 몯 가게 하셔?
eomeoniga ajikdo yeohaengeul mot gage hasyeo?

응. 끝까지 허락을 안 해 주실 모양이야.
응. 끋까지 허라글 안 해 주실 모양이야.
eung. kkeutkkaji heorageul an hae jusil moyangiya.

< 설명(explanation) / 번역(translation) >

어머니+가 아직+도 여행+을 못 가+[게 하]+시+어?
가게 하셔

- **어머니 (noun)** : 자기를 낳아 준 여자를 이르거나 부르는 말.
  mother
  A word used to refer to or address the woman who has given birth to you.

- 가 : 어떤 상태나 상황에 놓인 대상이나 동작의 주체를 나타내는 조사.
  ga (no equivalent expression)
  A postpositional particle referring to a subject under a certain state or situation, or the subject of an act.

- **아직 (adverb)** : 어떤 일이나 상태 또는 어떻게 되기까지 시간이 더 지나야 함을 나타내거나, 어떤 일이나 상태가 끝나지 않고 계속 이어지고 있음을 나타내는 말.
  yet; still
  An adverb used to indicate that more time is needed to reach a certain state, or that something or a certain state has not ended, but is going on.

- 도 : 놀라움, 감탄, 실망 등의 감정을 강조함을 나타내는 조사.
  do (no equivalent expression)
  A postpositional particle used to emphasize emotions such as a surprise, exclamation, disappointment, etc.

- **여행 (noun)** : 집을 떠나 다른 지역이나 외국을 두루 구경하며 다니는 일.
  travel; trip
  The act of going away from home, and visiting other places or foreign countries and doing sightseeing.

• 을 : 그 행동의 목적이 되는 일을 나타내는 조사.
eul (no equivalent expression)
A postpositional particle used to indicate the work that is the objective of a certain action.

• **못 (adverb)** : 동사가 나타내는 동작을 할 수 없게.
not
The word that negates the action represented by the verb.

• **가다 (verb)** : 어떤 목적을 가지고 일정한 곳으로 움직이다.
go
To move to a certain place with a specific purpose.

• -게 하다 : 다른 사람의 어떤 행동을 허용하거나 허락함을 나타내는 표현.
-ge hada (no equivalent expression)
An expression used to accept or allow a certain act of another person.

• -시- : 어떤 동작이나 상태의 주체를 높이는 뜻을 나타내는 어미.
-si- (no equivalent expression)
An ending of a word used for the subject honorifics of an action or state.

• -어 : (두루낮춤으로) 어떤 사실을 서술하거나 물음, 명령, 권유를 나타내는 종결 어미.
-eo (no equivalent expression)
(informal addressee-lowering) A sentence-final ending used to describe a certain fact, ask a **question**, give an order, or advise.

응.

끝+까지 허락+을 안 하+[여 주]+시+[ㄹ 모양이]+야.

해 주실 모양이야

• **응 (interjection)** : 상대방의 물음이나 명령 등에 긍정하여 대답할 때 쓰는 말.
yes; right
An exclamation uttered when the speaker gives an affirmative answer to someone's question, order, etc.

• **끝 (noun)** : 시간에서의 마지막 때.
end; final
The end of a lapse of time.

• 까지 : 어떤 범위의 끝임을 나타내는 조사.
kkaji (no equivalent expression)
A postpositional particle referring to the end of a certain range.

• **허락 (noun)** : 요청하는 일을 하도록 들어줌.
approval; consent; permission
The act of accepting another's request.

• 을 : 동작이 직접적으로 영향을 미치는 대상을 나타내는 조사.
eul (no equivalent expression)
A postpositional particle used to indicate the subject that an action has a direct influence on.

• **안 (adverb)** : 부정이나 반대의 뜻을 나타내는 말.
not
An adverb that has the meaning of negation or opposite.

• **하다 (verb)** : 어떤 행동이나 동작, 활동 등을 행하다.
do; perform
To perform a certain move, action, activity, etc.

• -여 주다 : 남을 위해 앞의 말이 나타내는 행동을 함을 나타내는 표현.
-yeo juda (no equivalent expression)
An expression used to indicate that one does the act mentioned in the preceding statement for someone.

• -시- : 어떤 동작이나 상태의 주체를 높이는 뜻을 나타내는 어미.
-si- (no equivalent expression)
An ending of a word used for the subject honorifics of an action or state.

• -ㄹ 모양이다 : 다른 사실이나 상황으로 보아 앞으로 어떤 일이 일어나거나 어떤 상태일 것이라고 추측함을 나타내는 표현.
-l moyangida (no equivalent expression)
An expression used to guess that something could happen or be in a certain state in the future, considering another fact or situation.

• -야 : (두루낮춤으로) 어떤 사실에 대하여 서술하거나 물음을 나타내는 종결 어미.
-ya (no equivalent expression)
(informal addressee-lowering) A sentence-final ending used to **describe** a certain fact or ask a question.

< 대화(dialogue) > - 11

할머니는 집에 계세요?
할머니는 지베 계세요(게세요)?
halmeonineun jibe gyeseyo(geseyo)?

응. 그런데 주무시고 계시니 깨우지 말고 좀 기다려.
응. 그런데 주무시고 계시니(게시니) 깨우지 말고 좀 기다려.
eung. geureonde jumusigo gyesini(gesini) kkaeuji malgo jom gidaryeo.

< 설명(explanation) / 번역(translation) >

할머니+는 집+에 계시+어요?
계세요

• **할머니 (noun)** : 아버지의 어머니, 또는 어머니의 어머니를 이르거나 부르는 말.
grandmother; granny
A word used to refer to or address the mother of one's father or mother.

• 는 : 문장 속에서 어떤 대상이 화제임을 나타내는 조사.
neun (no equivalent expression)
A postpositional particle used to indicate that a certain subject is the topic of a sentence.

• **집 (noun)** : 사람이나 동물이 추위나 더위 등을 막고 그 속에 들어 살기 위해 지은 건물.
house
A structure built by a human or animal to serve as protection from cold, heat, etc., and as a place to live in.

• 에 : 앞말이 어떤 장소나 자리임을 나타내는 조사.
on; in; at
A postpositional particle to indicate that the preceding statement refers to a certain place or space.

• **계시다 (verb)** : (높임말로) 높은 분이나 어른이 어느 곳에 있다.
be
(honorific) For one's senior or superior to be somewhere.

• -어요 : (두루높임으로) 어떤 사실을 서술하거나 질문, 명령, 권유함을 나타내는 종결 어미.
-eoyo (no equivalent expression)
(informal addressee-raising) A sentence-final ending used to describe a certain fact, **ask a question**, give an order, or advise.

응.

그런데 주무시+[고 계시]+니 깨우+[지 말]+고 좀 기다리+어.
기다려

• **응 (interjection)** : 상대방의 물음이나 명령 등에 긍정하여 대답할 때 쓰는 말.
yes; right
An exclamation uttered when the speaker gives an affirmative answer to someone's question, order, etc.

• **그런데 (adverb)** : 이야기를 앞의 내용과 관련시키면서 다른 방향으로 바꿀 때 쓰는 말.
by the way
A word used to change the direction of a story while relating it to the preceding statement.

• **주무시다 (verb)** : (높임말로) 자다.
sleep
(honorific) To sleep.

• -고 계시다 : (높임말로) 앞의 말이 나타내는 행동이 계속 진행됨을 나타내는 표현.
-go gyesida (no equivalent expression)
(honorific) An expression used to indicate that the act mentioned in the preceding statement continues to occur.

• -니 : 뒤에 오는 말에 대하여 앞에 오는 말이 원인이나 근거, 전제가 됨을 나타내는 연결 어미.
-ni (no equivalent expression)
A connective ending used when the preceding statement is the cause, reason, or premise for the following statement.

• **깨우다 (verb)** : 잠들거나 취한 상태 등에서 벗어나 온전한 정신 상태로 돌아오게 하다.
wake up
To make one get out of a sleeping, drunk state, etc., and come back to one's sound mental state.

• -지 말다 : 앞의 말이 나타내는 행동을 하지 못하게 함을 나타내는 표현.
-ji malda (no equivalent expression)
An expression used to prohibit the act mentioned in the preceding statement.

• -고 : 앞의 말과 뒤의 말이 차례대로 일어남을 나타내는 연결 어미.
-go (no equivalent expression)
A connective ending used when the preceding statement and the following statement happen in order.

• **좀 (adverb)** : 시간이 짧게.
a little
For a short while.

• **기다리다 (verb)** : 사람, 때가 오거나 어떤 일이 이루어질 때까지 시간을 보내다.
wait
To spend time until a person or time comes or a certain event is realized.

• -어 : (두루낮춤으로) 어떤 사실을 서술하거나 물음, 명령, 권유를 나타내는 종결 어미.
-eo (no equivalent expression)
(informal addressee-lowering) A sentence-final ending used to describe a certain fact, ask a question, **give an order**, or advise.

< 대화(dialogue) > - 12

여기서 산 가방을 환불하고 싶은데 어떻게 하면 되나요?
여기서 산 가방을 환불하고 시픈데 어떠케 하면 되나요?
yeogiseo san gabangeul hwanbulhago sipeunde eotteoke hamyeon doenayo?

네, 손님. 영수증은 가지고 계신가요?
네, 손님. 영수증은 가지고 계신가요(게신가요)?
ne, sonnim. yeongsujeungeun gajigo gyesingayo(gesingayo)?

< 설명(explanation) / 번역(translation) >

여기+서 사+ㄴ 가방+을 환불하+[고 싶]+은데 어떻게 하+[면 되]+나요?
산

• **여기 (pronoun)** : 말하는 사람에게 가까운 곳을 가리키는 말.
here; this
A pronoun used to indicate a place close to the speaker.

• 서 : 앞말이 행동이 이루어지고 있는 장소임을 나타내는 조사.
seo (no equivalent expression)
A postpositional particle used to indicate that the preceding word refers to a place where a certain act is being done.

• **사다 (verb)** : 돈을 주고 어떤 물건이나 권리 등을 자기 것으로 만들다.
buy; purchase; get
To get ownership of an item, right, etc., by paying for it.

• -ㄴ : 앞의 말이 관형어의 기능을 하게 만들고 사건이나 동작이 과거에 일어났음을 나타내는 어미.
-n (no equivalent expression)
An ending of a word that makes the preceding statement function as an adnominal phrase and indicates an event or action having occurred in the past.

• **가방 (noun)** : 물건을 넣어 손에 들거나 어깨에 멜 수 있게 만든 것.
bag
A container for storing a person's belongings, which can be held with a hand or hung on a shoulder.

• 을 : 동작이 직접적으로 영향을 미치는 대상을 나타내는 조사.
eul (no equivalent expression)
A postpositional particle used to indicate the subject that an action has a direct influence on.

• **환불하다** (verb) : 이미 낸 돈을 되돌려주다.
refund; give money back
To give back money that has been paid.

• -고 싶다 : 앞의 말이 나타내는 행동을 하기를 원함을 나타내는 표현.
-go sipda (no equivalent expression)
An expression used to state that the speaker wants to do the act mentioned in the preceding statement.

• -은데 : 뒤의 말을 하기 위하여 그 대상과 관련이 있는 상황을 미리 말함을 나타내는 연결 어미.
-eunde (no equivalent expression)
A connective ending used to talk in advance about a situation to follow.

• **어떻게** (adverb) : 어떤 방법으로. 또는 어떤 방식으로.
how
In what method; in what way.

• **하다** (verb) : 어떤 방식으로 행위를 이루다.
do
To complete an action in a certain way.

• -면 되다 : 조건이 되는 어떤 행동을 하거나 어떤 상태만 갖추어지면 문제가 없거나 충분함을 나타내는 표현.
-myeon doeda (no equivalent expression)
An expression used to indicate that, as long as one does or reaches a certain act or state, there is no problem or it is enough.

• -나요 : (두루높임으로) 앞의 내용에 대해 상대방에게 물어볼 때 쓰는 표현.
-nayo (no equivalent expression)
(informal addressee-raising) An expression used to ask the listener about the preceding content.

네, 손님.

영수증+은 가지+[고 계시]+ㄴ가요?

가지고 계신가요

• **네 (interjection)** : 윗사람의 물음이나 명령 등에 긍정하여 대답할 때 쓰는 말.
yes; yes sir; yes ma'am
An exclamation uttered when the speaker affirmatively answers the call or order of his/her superior.

• **손님 (noun)** : (높임말로) 여관이나 음식점 등의 가게에 찾아온 사람.
guest; customer
(honorific) A person who visits an inn, restaurant, etc.

• **영수증 (noun)** : 돈이나 물건을 주고받은 사실이 적힌 종이.
receipt
A piece of paper on which the details of transaction of money or goods are written.

• 은 : 문장 속에서 어떤 대상이 화제임을 나타내는 조사.
eun (no equivalent expression)
A postpositional particle used to indicate that a certain subject is the topic of a sentence.

• **가지다 (verb)** : 무엇을 손에 쥐거나 몸에 지니다.
have; hold
To carry or keep something, or hold it in one's hands.

• -고 계시다 : (높임말로) 앞의 말이 나타내는 행동의 결과가 계속됨을 나타내는 표현.
-go gyesida (no equivalent expression)
(honorific) An expression used to indicate that the result of the act denoted in the preceding statement continues to exist.

• -ㄴ가요 : (두루높임으로) 현재의 사실에 대한 물음을 나타내는 종결 어미.
-ngayo (no equivalent expression)
(informal addressee-raising) A sentence-final ending referring to a question about a fact of the present.

< 대화(dialogue) > - 13

숙제는 다 하고 나서 놀아라.
숙쩨는 다 하고 나서 노라라.
sukjeneun da hago naseo norara.

벌써 다 했어요. 저 놀다 올게요.
벌써 다 해써요. 저 놀다 올께요.
beolsseo da haesseoyo. jeo nolda olgeyo.

< 설명(explanation) / 번역(translation) >

숙제+는 다 하+[고 나]+(아)서 놀+아라.

하고 나서

• **숙제 (noun)** : 학생들에게 복습이나 예습을 위하여 수업 후에 하도록 내 주는 과제.
homework
An assignment given to students to do after class for a review or preview.

• 는 : 문장 속에서 어떤 대상이 화제임을 나타내는 조사.
neun (no equivalent expression)
A postpositional particle used to indicate that a certain subject is the topic of a sentence.

• **다 (adverb)** : 남거나 빠진 것이 없이 모두.
all; everything
With nothing left over or missing.

• **하다 (verb)** : 어떤 행동이나 동작, 활동 등을 행하다.
do; perform
To perform a certain move, action, activity, etc.

• -고 나다 : 앞에 오는 말이 나타내는 행동이 끝났음을 나타내는 표현.
-go nada (no equivalent expression)
An expression used to indicate that the act denoted in the preceding statement has finished.

• -아서 : 앞의 말과 뒤의 말이 순차적으로 일어남을 나타내는 연결 어미.
-aseo (no equivalent expression)
A connective ending used to indicate that the preceding event and the following one happened sequentially.

• **놀다 (verb)** : 놀이 등을 하면서 재미있고 즐겁게 지내다.
play; have fun
To have a good time while playing.

• -아라 : (아주낮춤으로) 명령을 나타내는 종결 어미.
-ara (no equivalent expression)
(formal, highly addressee-lowering) A sentence-final ending used to indicate a statement as a command.

벌써 다 하+였+어요.
했어요

저 놀+다 오+ㄹ게요.
올게요

• **벌써 (adverb)** : 이미 오래전에.
long ago
Already a long time ago.

• **다 (adverb)** : 남거나 빠진 것이 없이 모두.
all; everything
With nothing left over or missing.

• **하다 (verb)** : 어떤 행동이나 동작, 활동 등을 행하다.
do; perform
To perform a certain move, action, activity, etc.

• -였- : 어떤 사건이 과거에 완료되었거나 그 사건의 결과가 현재까지 지속되는 상황을 나타내는 어미.
-yeot- (no equivalent expression)
An ending of a word used to indicate that an event was completed in the past or its result continues in the present.

• -어요 : (두루높임으로) 어떤 사실을 서술하거나 질문, 명령, 권유함을 나타내는 종결 어미.
-eoyo (no equivalent expression)
(informal addressee-raising) A sentence-final ending used to **describe** a certain fact, ask a question, give an order, or advise.

• **저 (pronoun)** : 말하는 사람이 듣는 사람에게 자신을 낮추어 가리키는 말.
I; me
The humble form used by the speaker to refer to himself/herself for the purpose of showing humility to the listener.

• **놀다 (verb)** : 놀이 등을 하면서 재미있고 즐겁게 지내다.
play; have fun
To have a good time while playing.

• -다 : 어떤 행동이나 상태 등이 중단되고 다른 행동이나 상태로 바뀜을 나타내는 연결 어미.
-da (no equivalent expression)
A connective ending used when an action or state, etc., is stopped and changed to another action or state.

• **오다 (verb)** : 무엇이 다른 곳에서 이곳으로 움직이다.
come
For something to move from another place to here.

• -ㄹ게요 : (두루높임으로) 말하는 사람이 어떤 행동을 할 것을 듣는 사람에게 약속하거나 의지를 나타내는 표현.
-lgeyo (no equivalent expression)
(informal addressee-raising) An expression used when the speaker promises or notifies the listener that he/she will do something.

< 대화(dialogue) > - 14

이번 달리기 대회에서 시우가 일 등 할 줄 알았는데.
이번 달리기 대회에서 시우가 일 등 할 쭐 아란는데.
ibeon dalligi daehoeeseo siuga il deung hal jul aranneunde.

그러게, 너무 욕심을 부리다 넘어지고 만 거지.
그러게, 너무 욕씨믈 부리다 너머지고 만 거지.
geureoge, neomu yoksimeul burida neomeojigo man geoji.

< 설명(explanation) / 번역(translation) >

이번 달리기 대회+에서 시우+가 일 등 하+[ㄹ 줄] 알+았+는데.
할 줄

• **이번 (noun)** : 곧 돌아올 차례. 또는 막 지나간 차례.
this time
A turn soon to come, or one that just passed.

• **달리기 (noun)** : 일정한 거리를 누가 빨리 뛰는지 겨루는 경기.
running race
A race in which people compete to run a certain distance faster than others.

• **대회 (noun)** : 여러 사람이 실력이나 기술을 겨루는 행사.
competition; contest
An event where many people compete with each other over their abilities or skills.

• 에서 : 앞말이 행동이 이루어지고 있는 장소임을 나타내는 조사.
eseo (no equivalent expression)
A postpositional particle used to indicate that the preceding word refers to a place where a certain action is being done.

• **시우 (noun)** : person's name

• 가 : 어떤 상태나 상황에 놓인 대상이나 동작의 주체를 나타내는 조사.
ga (no equivalent expression)
A postpositional particle referring to a subject under a certain state or situation, or the subject of an act.

• **일 (determiner)** : 첫 번째의.
first
Corresponding to the first one in a sequence.

• **등 (noun)** : 등급이나 등수를 나타내는 단위.
deung (no equivalent expression)
A bound noun indicating a level or rank.

• **하다 (verb)** : 어떠한 결과를 이루어 내다.
get; become
To achieve certain results.

• -ㄹ 줄 : 어떤 사실이나 상태에 대해 알고 있거나 모르고 있음을 나타내는 표현.
-l jul (no equivalent expression)
An expression used to indicate that one either knows or does not know a certain fact or state.

• **알다 (verb)** : 어떤 사실을 그러하다고 여기거나 생각하다.
know; think
To consider or assume a fact as being of a certain quality.

• -았- : 사건이 과거에 일어났음을 나타내는 어미.
-at- (no equivalent expression)
An ending of a word used to indicate that an event happened in the past.

• -는데 : (두루낮춤으로) 듣는 사람의 반응을 기대하며 어떤 일에 대해 감탄함을 나타내는 종결 어미.
-neunde (no equivalent expression)
(informal addressee-lowering) A sentence-final ending used to admire something while anticipating the listener's response.

그러게, 너무 욕심+을 부리+다 넘어지+[고 말(마)]+[ㄴ 것(거)]+(이)+지.

넘어지고 만 거지

• **그러게 (interjection)** : 상대방의 말에 찬성하거나 동의하는 뜻을 나타낼 때 쓰는 말.
right; I know; yeah
An exclamation used to indicate that the speaker supports or agrees with the words of the other party.

• **너무 (adverb)** : 일정한 정도나 한계를 훨씬 넘어선 상태로.
too
To an excessive degree.

• **욕심 (noun)** : 무엇을 지나치게 탐내거나 가지고 싶어 하는 마음.
desire; greed
An excessive longing to get or have something.

• 을 : 동작이 직접적으로 영향을 미치는 대상을 나타내는 조사.
eul (no equivalent expression)
A postpositional particle used to indicate the subject that an action has a direct influence on.

• **부리다 (verb)** : 바람직하지 못한 행동이나 성질을 계속 드러내거나 보이다.
persist; wield
To often show or reveal an undesirable act or personality.

• -다 : 앞에 오는 말이 뒤에 오는 말의 원인이나 근거가 됨을 나타내는 연결 어미.
-da (no equivalent expression)
A connective ending used when the preceding statement is the cause or reason for the following statement.

• **넘어지다 (verb)** : 서 있던 사람이나 물체가 중심을 잃고 한쪽으로 기울어지며 쓰러지다.
fall down; trip over; tumble over
For a standing person or object to lose balance and fall down.

• -고 말다 : 앞에 오는 말이 가리키는 행동이 안타깝게도 끝내 일어났음을 나타내는 표현.
-go malda (no equivalent expression)
An expression used to state that it is regrettable that the act mentioned in the preceding statement finally occurred.

• -ㄴ 것 : 명사가 아닌 것을 문장에서 명사처럼 쓰이게 하거나 '이다' 앞에 쓰일 수 있게 할 때 쓰는 표현.
-n geot (no equivalent expression)
An expression used to enable a non-noun word to be used as a noun in a sentence or to be used in front of '이다' (be).

• 이다 : 주어가 지시하는 대상의 속성이나 부류를 지정하는 뜻을 나타내는 서술격 조사.
ida (no equivalent expression)
A predicate particle indicating the meaning of the attribute or category of the thing that the subject of the sentence refers to.

• -지 : (두루낮춤으로) 말하는 사람이 자신에 대한 이야기나 자신의 생각을 친근하게 말할 때 쓰는 종결 어미.
-ji (no equivalent expression)
(informal addressee-lowering) A sentence-final ending used when the speaker talks about himself/herself or his/her thoughts in a friendly manner.

< 대화(dialogue) > - 15

감독님, 저희 모두가 마지막 경기에 거는 기대가 큽니다.
감동님, 저히 모두가 마지막 경기에 거는 기대가 큼니다.
gamdongnim, jeohi moduga majimak gyeonggie geoneun gidaega keumnida.

네. 마지막 경기는 꼭 승리하고 말겠습니다.
네. 마지막 경기는 꼭 승니하고 말겓씀니다.
ne. majimak gyeonggineun kkok seungnihago malgetseumnida.

< 설명(explanation) / 번역(translation) >

감독+님, 저희 모두+가 마지막 경기+에 걸(거)+는 기대+가 크+ㅂ니다.
거는 큽니다

• **감독 (noun)** : 공연, 영화, 운동 경기 등에서 일의 전체를 지휘하며 책임지는 사람.
director; coach
A person who is responsible for and directs the entire process at a concert, in making a movie, preparing for and playing a sport, etc.

• 님 : '높임'의 뜻을 더하는 접미사.
-nim (no equivalent expression)
A suffix used to mean "honorific."

• **저희 (pronoun)** : 말하는 사람이 자기보다 높은 사람에게 자기를 포함한 여러 사람들을 가리키는 말.
our
A word used by the speaker to refer to a group of people including himself/herself when speaking to another person who is superior to him/her.

• **모두 (noun)** : 남거나 빠진 것이 없는 전체.
all
Everything without anything missing or remaining.

• 가 : 어떤 상태나 상황에 놓인 대상이나 동작의 주체를 나타내는 조사.
ga (no equivalent expression)
A postpositional particle referring to a subject under a certain state or situation, or the subject of an act.

• **마지막 (noun)** : 시간이나 순서의 맨 끝.
last
The very end of a time or order.

• **경기 (noun)** : 운동이나 기술 등의 능력을 서로 겨룸.
game; match
Sports or skill-based competitions.

• 에 : 앞말이 어떤 행위나 감정 등의 대상임을 나타내는 조사.
with; for; against
A postpositional particle to indicate that the preceding statement is the subject that is influenced by a certain action, emotion, etc.

• **걸다 (verb)** : 앞으로의 일에 대한 희망 등을 품거나 기대하다.
expect; hope
To have hope or expectation about something that will happen in the future.

• -는 : 앞의 말이 관형어의 기능을 하게 만들고 사건이나 동작이 현재 일어남을 나타내는 어미.
-neun (no equivalent expression)
An ending of a word that makes the preceding statement function as an adnominal phrase and implies that an event or action is happening in the present.

• **기대 (noun)** : 어떤 일이 이루어지기를 바라며 기다림.
expectation
Waiting and hoping for something to happen.

• 가 : 어떤 상태나 상황에 놓인 대상이나 동작의 주체를 나타내는 조사.
ga (no equivalent expression)
A postpositional particle referring to a subject under a certain state or situation, or the subject of an act.

• **크다 (adjective)** : 어떤 일의 규모, 범위, 정도, 힘 등이 보통 수준을 넘다.
big
The size, scope, degree, power, etc., of an incident exceeding an ordinary level.

• -ㅂ니다 : (아주높임으로) 현재의 동작이나 상태, 사실을 정중하게 설명함을 나타내는 종결 어미.
-pnida (no equivalent expression)
(formal, highly addressee-raising) A sentence-final ending used to explain the present action, state, or fact politely.

네.

마지막 경기+는 꼭 승리하+[고 말]+겠+습니다.

• **네 (interjection)** : 윗사람의 물음이나 명령 등에 긍정하여 대답할 때 쓰는 말.
yes; yes sir; yes ma'am
An exclamation uttered when the speaker affirmatively answers the call or order of his/her superior.

• **마지막 (noun)** : 시간이나 순서의 맨 끝.
last
The very end of a time or order.

• **경기 (noun)** : 운동이나 기술 등의 능력을 서로 겨룸.
game; match
Sports or skill-based competitions.

• 는 : 문장 속에서 어떤 대상이 화제임을 나타내는 조사.
neun (no equivalent expression)
A postpositional particle used to indicate that a certain subject is the topic of a sentence.

• **꼭 (adverb)** : 어떤 일이 있어도 반드시.
without fail; at any cost; certainly
By all means under any circumstances.

• **승리하다 (verb)** : 전쟁이나 경기 등에서 이기다.
win a victory
To win a war, game, etc.

• -고 말다 : 앞에 오는 말이 가리키는 일을 이루고자 하는 말하는 사람의 강한 의지를 나타내는 표현.
-go malda (no equivalent expression)
An expression used to indicate the strong will of the speaker to accomplish the goal denoted in the preceding statement.

• -겠- : 말하는 사람의 의지를 나타내는 어미.
-get- (no equivalent expression)
An ending of a word referring to the speaker's will.

• -습니다 : (아주높임으로) 현재의 동작이나 상태, 사실을 정중하게 설명함을 나타내는 종결 어미.
-seupnida (no equivalent expression)
(formal, highly addressee-raising) A sentence-final ending used to explain the present action, state, or fact politely.

< 대화(dialogue) > - 16

시간이 지나고 보니 모든 순간이 다 소중한 것 같아.
시가니 지나고 보니 모든 순가니 다 소중한 걷 가타.
sigani jinago boni modeun sungani da sojunghan geot gata.

무슨 일 있어? 갑자기 왜 그런 말을 해?
무슨 일 이써? 갑짜기 왜 그런 마를 해?
museun il isseo? gapjagi wae geureon mareul hae?

< 설명(explanation) / 번역(translation) >

시간+이 지나+[고 보]+니 모든 순간+이 다 소중하+[ㄴ 것 같]+아.
소중한 것 같아

• **시간 (noun)** : 자연히 지나가는 세월.
time
Time that passes naturally.

• 이 : 어떤 상태나 상황의 대상이나 동작의 주체를 나타내는 조사.
i (no equivalent expression)
A postpositional particle referring to a subject under a certain state or situation, or the agent of an action.

• **지나다 (verb)** : 시간이 흘러 그 시기에서 벗어나다.
pass; elapse
To get out of a period as time passes.

• -고 보다 : 앞의 말이 나타내는 행동을 하고 난 후에 뒤의 말이 나타내는 사실을 새로 깨달음을 나타내는 표현.
-go boda (no equivalent expression)
An expression used to state that the speaker did the act mentioned in the preceding statement, then realized the fact in the following statement.

• -니 : 앞에서 이야기한 내용과 관련된 다른 사실을 이어서 설명할 때 쓰는 연결 어미.
-ni (no equivalent expression)
A connective ending used when adding another fact related to the preceding statement.

• **모든 (determiner)** : 빠지거나 남는 것 없이 전부인.
every
All without exception or without anything or anyone left.

• **순간 (noun)** : 아주 짧은 시간 동안.
moment
A very short period.

• 이 : 어떤 상태나 상황의 대상이나 동작의 주체를 나타내는 조사.
i (no equivalent expression)
A postpositional particle referring to a subject under a certain state or situation, or the agent of an action.

• **다 (adverb)** : 남거나 빠진 것이 없이 모두.
all; everything
With nothing left over or missing.

• **소중하다 (adjective)** : 매우 귀중하다.
valuable
Very precious.

• -ㄴ 것 같다 : 추측을 나타내는 표현.
-n geot gatda (no equivalent expression)
An expression used to indicate that the statement is a guess.

• -아 : (두루낮춤으로) 어떤 사실을 서술하거나 물음, 명령, 권유를 나타내는 종결 어미.
-a (no equivalent expression)
(informal addressee-lowering) A sentence-final ending used to **describe** a certain fact, ask a question, give an order, or advise.

무슨 일 있+어?

갑자기 왜 그런 말+을 하+여?
해

• **무슨 (determiner)** : 확실하지 않거나 잘 모르는 일, 대상, 물건 등을 물을 때 쓰는 말.
what
An expression used to ask about a business, subject or object that one is not sure of or does not exactly know.

• **일 (noun)** : 해결하거나 처리해야 할 문제나 사항.
business; engagement
A problem or thing that one should resolve or deal with.

• **있다 (adjective)** : 어떤 사람에게 무슨 일이 생긴 상태이다.
no equivalent expression
Something happening to someone.

• -어 : (두루낮춤으로) 어떤 사실을 서술하거나 물음, 명령, 권유를 나타내는 종결 어미.
-eo (no equivalent expression)
(informal addressee-lowering) A sentence-final ending used to describe a certain fact, **ask a question**, give an order, or advise.

• **갑자기 (adverb)** : 미처 생각할 틈도 없이 빨리.
suddenly; all of a sudden
Quickly, not allowing someone to think.

• **왜 (adverb)** : 무슨 이유로. 또는 어째서.
why
For what reason; how come.

• **그런 (determiner)** : 상태, 모양, 성질 등이 그러한.
like that
A state, appearance, characteristic, etc. being as such.

• **말 (noun)** : 생각이나 느낌을 표현하고 전달하는 사람의 소리.
speech; words
Human voice through which thoughts or feelings are expressed and conveyed.

• 을 : 동작이 직접적으로 영향을 미치는 대상을 나타내는 조사.
eul (no equivalent expression)
A postpositional particle used to indicate the subject that an action has a direct influence on.

• **하다 (verb)** : 어떤 행동이나 동작, 활동 등을 행하다.
do; perform
To perform a certain move, action, activity, etc.

• -여 : (두루낮춤으로) 어떤 사실을 서술하거나 물음, 명령, 권유를 나타내는 종결 어미.
-yeo (no equivalent expression)
(informal addressee-lowering) A sentence-final ending used to describe a certain fact, **ask a question**, give an order, or advise.

< 대화(dialogue) > - 17

날씨가 추우니까 따뜻한 게 먹고 싶네.
날씨가 추우니까 따뜨탄 게 먹꼬 심네.
nalssiga chuunikka ttatteutan ge meokgo simne.

그럼 오늘 점심은 삼계탕을 먹으러 갈까?
그럼 오늘 점시믄 삼계탕을(삼게탕을) 머그러 갈까?
geureom oneul jeomsimeun samgyetangeul(samgetangeul) meogeureo galkka?

< 설명(explanation) / 번역(translation) >

날씨+가 춥(추우)+니까 따뜻하+[ㄴ 것(거)]+이 먹+[고 싶]+네.

추우니까 **따뜻한 게**

• **날씨 (noun)** : 그날그날의 기온이나 공기 중에 비, 구름, 바람, 안개 등이 나타나는 상태.
weather
The daily temperature or the conditions of rain, clouds, wind, fog, etc., in the atmosphere.

• 가 : 어떤 상태나 상황에 놓인 대상이나 동작의 주체를 나타내는 조사.
ga (no equivalent expression)
A postpositional particle referring to a subject under a certain state or situation, or the subject of an act.

• **춥다 (adjective)** : 대기의 온도가 낮다.
cold
(temperature) Low.

• -니까 : 뒤에 오는 말에 대하여 앞에 오는 말이 원인이나 근거, 전제가 됨을 강조하여 나타내는 연결 어미.
-nikka (no equivalent expression)
A connective ending used to emphasize that the preceding statement is the cause, reason, or premise for the following statement.

• **따뜻하다 (adjective)** : 아주 덥지 않고 기분이 좋은 정도로 온도가 알맞게 높다.
warm
Being an appropriate, pleasant temperature, which is not too high.

• -ㄴ 것 : 명사가 아닌 것을 문장에서 명사처럼 쓰이게 하거나 '이다' 앞에 쓰일 수 있게 할 때 쓰는 표현.
-n geot (no equivalent expression)
An expression used to enable a non-noun word to be used as a noun in a sentence or to be used in front of '이다' (be).

• 이 : 어떤 상태나 상황의 대상이나 동작의 주체를 나타내는 조사.
i (no equivalent expression)
A postpositional particle referring to a subject under a certain state or situation, or the agent of an action.

• **먹다 (verb)** : 음식 등을 입을 통하여 배 속에 들여보내다.
eat; have; consume; take
To put food into one's mouth and take it in one's stomach.

• -고 싶다 : 앞의 말이 나타내는 행동을 하기를 원함을 나타내는 표현.
-go sipda (no equivalent expression)
An expression used to state that the speaker wants to do the act mentioned in the preceding statement.

• -네 : (예사 낮춤으로) 단순한 서술을 나타내는 종결 어미.
-ne (no equivalent expression)
(formal, moderately addressee-lowering) A sentence-final ending referring to a simple description.

그럼 오늘 점심+은 삼계탕+을 먹+으러 가+ㄹ까?
갈까

• **그럼 (adverb)** : 앞의 내용을 받아들이거나 그 내용을 바탕으로 하여 새로운 주장을 할 때 쓰는 말.
then
A word used when accepting the preceding statement or making a new suggestion based on it.

• **오늘 (noun)** : 지금 지나가고 있는 이날.
today
The day that is passing at the present time.

• **점심 (noun)** : 아침과 저녁 식사 중간에, 낮에 하는 식사.
lunch
A meal eaten in the afternoon between breakfast and dinner.

• 은 : 문장 속에서 어떤 대상이 화제임을 나타내는 조사.
eun (no equivalent expression)
A postpositional particle used to indicate that a certain subject is the topic of a sentence.

• **삼계탕 (noun)** : 어린 닭에 인삼, 찹쌀, 대추 등을 넣고 푹 삶은 음식.
samgyetang; ginseng chicken soup
A dish made by boiling down a young chicken stuffed with ginseng, sticky rice, jujubes, etc.

• 을 : 동작이 직접적으로 영향을 미치는 대상을 나타내는 조사.
eul (no equivalent expression)
A postpositional particle used to indicate the subject that an action has a direct influence on.

• **먹다 (verb)** : 음식 등을 입을 통하여 배 속에 들여보내다.
eat; have; consume; take
To put food into one's mouth and take it in one's stomach.

• -으러 : 가거나 오거나 하는 동작의 목적을 나타내는 연결 어미.
-eureo (no equivalent expression)
A connective ending used to express the purpose of an action such as going and coming.

• **가다 (verb)** : 어떤 목적을 가지고 일정한 곳으로 움직이다.
go
To move to a certain place with a specific purpose.

• -ㄹ까 : (두루낮춤으로) 듣는 사람의 의사를 물을 때 쓰는 종결 어미.
-lkka (no equivalent expression)
(informal addressee-lowering) A sentence-final ending used to ask for the listener's opinion.

< 대화(dialogue) > - 18

아들이 자꾸 컴퓨터를 새로 사 달라고 해요.
아드리 자꾸 컴퓨터를 새로 사 달라고 해요.
adeuri jakku keompyuteoreul saero sa dallago haeyo.

그렇게 갖고 싶어 하는데 하나 사 줘요.
그러케 갇꼬 시퍼 하는데 하나 사 줘요.
geureoke gatgo sipeo haneunde hana sa jwoyo.

< 설명(explanation) / 번역(translation) >

아들+이 자꾸 컴퓨터+를 새로 사+[(아) 달]+라고 하+여요.

사 달라고 해요

• **아들 (noun)** : 남자인 자식.
son
One's male child.

• 이 : 어떤 상태나 상황의 대상이나 동작의 주체를 나타내는 조사.
i (no equivalent expression)
A postpositional particle referring to a subject under a certain state or situation, or the agent of an action.

• **자꾸 (adverb)** : 여러 번 계속하여.
frequently; repeatedly; again and again
Several times.

• **컴퓨터 (noun)** : 전자 회로를 이용하여 문서, 사진, 영상 등의 대량의 데이터를 빠르고 정확하게 처리하는 기계.
computer
A machine made from electronic circuits that quickly and accurately processes mass data such as documents, photographs, videos, etc.

• 를 : 동작이 직접적으로 영향을 미치는 대상을 나타내는 조사.
reul (no equivalent expression)
A postpositional particle used to indicate the subject that an act has a direct influence on.

• **새로 (adverb)** : 전과 달리 새롭게. 또는 새것으로.
freshly
Newly again, different from the past, or with a new thing.

• **사다 (verb)** : 돈을 주고 어떤 물건이나 권리 등을 자기 것으로 만들다.
buy; purchase; get
To get ownership of an item, right, etc., by paying for it.

• -아 달다 : 앞의 말이 나타내는 행동을 해 줄 것을 요구함을 나타내는 표현.
-a dalda (no equivalent expression)
An expression used to demand that the act mentioned in the preceding statement be carried out.

• -라고 : 다른 사람에게 들은 명령이나 권유 등의 내용을 간접적으로 전할 때 쓰는 표현.
-rago (no equivalent expression)
An expression used to indirectly convey the order, recommendation, etc., heard from another person.

• **하다 (verb)** : 무엇에 대해 말하다.
say
To talk about something.

• -여요 : (두루높임으로) 어떤 사실을 서술하거나 질문, 명령, 권유함을 나타내는 종결 어미.
-yeoyo (no equivalent expression)
(informal addressee-raising) A sentence-final ending used to **describe** a certain fact, ask a question, give an order, or advise.

그렇+게 갖+[고 싶어 하]+는데 하나 사+[(아) 주]+어요.
사 줘요

• **그렇다 (adjective)** : 상태, 모양, 성질 등이 그와 같다.
so; as such; like that
A state, appearance, characteristic, etc. being as such.

• -게 : 앞의 말이 뒤에서 가리키는 일의 목적이나 결과, 방식, 정도 등이 됨을 나타내는 연결 어미.
-ge (no equivalent expression)
A connective ending used when the preceding statement is the purpose, result, method, amount, etc., of something mentioned in the following statement.

• **갖다 (verb)** : 자기 것으로 하다.
own; possess; keep
To take possession of something.

• -고 싶어 하다 : 앞의 말이 나타내는 행동을 하기를 바라거나 그렇게 되기를 원함을 나타내는 표현.
-go sipeo hada (no equivalent expression)
An expression used to indicate that the speaker wants to do an action or fall into the state mentioned in the preceding statement.

• -는데 : 뒤의 말을 하기 위하여 그 대상과 관련이 있는 상황을 미리 말함을 나타내는 연결 어미.
-neunde (no equivalent expression)
A connective ending used to talk in advance about a situation to follow.

• **하나 (numeral)** : 숫자를 셀 때 맨 처음의 수.
one
The very first number when counting numbers.

• **사다 (verb)** : 돈을 주고 어떤 물건이나 권리 등을 자기 것으로 만들다.
buy; purchase; get
To get ownership of an item, right, etc., by paying for it.

• -아 주다 : 남을 위해 앞의 말이 나타내는 행동을 함을 나타내는 표현.
-a juda (no equivalent expression)
An expression used to indicate that one does the act mentioned in the preceding statement for someone.

• -어요 : (두루높임으로) 어떤 사실을 서술하거나 질문, 명령, 권유함을 나타내는 종결 어미.
-eoyo (no equivalent expression)
(informal addressee-raising) A sentence-final ending used to describe a certain fact, ask a question, **give an order**, or advise.

< 대화(dialogue) > - 19

출발했니? 언제쯤 도착할 것 같아?
출발핸니? 언제쯤 도차칼 껃 가타?
chulbalhaenni? eonjejjeum dochakal geot gata?

지금 가고 있으니까 십 분쯤 뒤에 도착할 거야.
지금 가고 이쓰니까 십 분쯤 뒤에 도차칼 꺼야.
jigeum gago isseunikka sip bunjjeum dwie dochakal geoya.

< 설명(explanation) / 번역(translation) >

출발하+였+니?
출발했니

언제+쯤 도착하+[ㄹ 것 같]+아?
도착할 것 같아

• **출발하다 (verb)** : 어떤 곳을 향하여 길을 떠나다.
depart; leave
To leave a place, heading for another place.

• -였- : 어떤 사건이 과거에 완료되었거나 그 사건의 결과가 현재까지 지속되는 상황을 나타내는 어미.
-yeot- (no equivalent expression)
An ending of a word used to indicate that an event was completed in the past or its result continues in the present.

• -니 : (아주낮춤으로) 물음을 나타내는 종결 어미.
-ni (no equivalent expression)
(formal, highly addressee-lowering) A sentence-final ending referring to a question.

• **언제 (pronoun)** : 알지 못하는 어느 때.
when; what time
Some time that one does not know.

• 쯤 : '정도'의 뜻을 더하는 접미사.
-jjeum (no equivalent expression)
A suffix used to mean an approximate amount.

• **도착하다 (verb)** : 목적지에 다다르다.
arrive; reach
To reach a destination.

• -ㄹ 것 같다 : 추측을 나타내는 표현.
-l geot gatda (no equivalent expression)
An expression used to indicate that the statement is a guess.

• -아 : (두루낮춤으로) 어떤 사실을 서술하거나 물음, 명령, 권유를 나타내는 종결 어미.
-a (no equivalent expression)
(informal addressee-lowering) A sentence-final ending used to describe a certain fact, **ask a question**, give an order, or advise.

지금 가+[고 있]+으니까 십 분+쯤 뒤+에 도착하+[ㄹ 것(거)]+(이)+야.
도착할 거야

• **지금 (adverb)** : 말을 하고 있는 바로 이때에. 또는 그 즉시에.
now; immediately
At the present moment as one speaks, or that instant.

• **가다 (verb)** : 한 곳에서 다른 곳으로 장소를 이동하다.
go; travel
To move from one place to another place.

• -고 있다 : 앞의 말이 나타내는 행동이 계속 진행됨을 나타내는 표현.
-go itda (no equivalent expression)
An expression used to state that the act mentioned in the preceding statement is continued.

• -으니까 : 뒤에 오는 말에 대하여 앞에 오는 말이 원인이나 근거, 전제가 됨을 강조하여 나타내는 연결 어미.
-eunikka (no equivalent expression)
A connective ending used to emphasize that the preceding statement is the cause, reason, or premise for the following statement.

• **십 (determiner)** : 열의.
ten
Amounting to ten.

• **분 (noun)** : 한 시간의 60분의 1을 나타내는 시간의 단위.
minute
A bound noun indicating a unit of time, which is one-sixtieth of an hour.

• 쯤 : '정도'의 뜻을 더하는 접미사.
-jjeum (no equivalent expression)
A suffix used to mean an approximate amount.

• **뒤 (noun)** : 시간이나 순서상으로 다음이나 나중.
next time; later time
A time or turn that comes next or later.

• 에 : 앞말이 시간이나 때임을 나타내는 조사.
in; at
A postpositional particle to indicate that the preceding statement refers to the time.

• **도착하다 (verb)** : 목적지에 다다르다.
arrive; reach
To reach a destination.

• -ㄹ 것 : 명사가 아닌 것을 문장에서 명사처럼 쓰이게 하거나 '이다' 앞에 쓰일 수 있게 할 때 쓰는 표현.
-l geot (no equivalent expression)
An expression used to enable a non-noun word to be used as a noun in the sentence or to be used in front of '이다' (be).

• 이다 : 주어가 지시하는 대상의 속성이나 부류를 지정하는 뜻을 나타내는 서술격 조사.
ida (no equivalent expression)
A predicate particle indicating the meaning of the attribute or category of the thing that the subject of the sentence refers to.

• -야 : (두루낮춤으로) 어떤 사실에 대하여 서술하거나 물음을 나타내는 종결 어미.
-ya (no equivalent expression)
(informal addressee-lowering) A sentence-final ending used to **describe** a certain fact or ask a question.

< 대화(dialogue) > - 20

넌 안경을 쓰고 있을 때 더 멋있어 보인다.
넌 안경을 쓰고 이쓸 때 더 머시써 보인다.
neon angyeongeul sseugo isseul ttae deo meosisseo boinda.

그래? 이제부터 계속 쓰고 다닐까 봐.
그래? 이제부터 계속(게속) 쓰고 다닐까 봐.
geurae? ijebuteo gyesok(gesok) sseugo danilkka bwa.

< 설명(explanation) / 번역(translation) >

너+는 안경+을 쓰+[고 있]+[을 때] 더 멋있+[어 보이]+ㄴ다.
넌 멋있어 보인다

• **너 (pronoun)** : 듣는 사람이 친구나 아랫사람일 때, 그 사람을 가리키는 말.
no equivalent expression
A pronoun used to indicate the listener when he/she is the same age or younger.

• 는 : 문장 속에서 어떤 대상이 화제임을 나타내는 조사.
neun (no equivalent expression)
A postpositional particle used to indicate that a certain subject is the topic of a sentence.

• **안경 (noun)** : 눈을 보호하거나 시력이 좋지 않은 사람이 잘 볼 수 있도록 눈에 쓰는 물건.
glasses; spectacles
An instrument that one wears over the eyes to proctect them or to supplement his/her eyesight for better vision.

• 을 : 동작이 직접적으로 영향을 미치는 대상을 나타내는 조사.
eul (no equivalent expression)
A postpositional particle used to indicate the subject that an action has a direct influence on.

• **쓰다 (verb)** : 얼굴에 어떤 물건을 걸거나 덮어쓰다.
wear; put on
To hang something on one's face or cover one's face with it.

• -고 있다 : 앞의 말이 나타내는 행동의 결과가 계속됨을 나타내는 표현.
-go itda (no equivalent expression)
An expression used to state that the result of the act mentioned in the preceding statement is continued.

• -을 때 : 어떤 행동이나 상황이 일어나는 동안이나 그 시기 또는 그러한 일이 일어난 경우를 나타내는 표현.
-eul ttae (no equivalent expression)
An expression used to indicate the duration, period, or occasion of a certain act or situation.

• **더 (adverb)** : 비교의 대상이나 어떤 기준보다 정도가 크게, 그 이상으로.
more
More or higher than something being compared or a certain threshold.

• **멋있다 (adjective)** : 매우 좋거나 훌륭하다.
nice; stylish; elegant
Very good or great.

• -어 보이다 : 겉으로 볼 때 앞의 말이 나타내는 것처럼 느껴지거나 추측됨을 나타내는 표현.
-eo boida (no equivalent expression)
An expression used to indicate that one feels or guesses something by appearance as mentioned in the preceding statement.

• -ㄴ다 : (아주낮춤으로) 현재 사건이나 사실을 서술함을 나타내는 종결 어미.
-nda (no equivalent expression)
(formal, highly addressee-lowering) A sentence-final ending used to describe an event or fact of the present.

그래?

이제+부터 계속 쓰+고 다니+[ㄹ까 보]+아.

다닐까 봐

• **그래 (interjection)** : 상대편의 말에 대한 감탄이나 가벼운 놀라움을 나타낼 때 쓰는 말.
really
An exclamation used to indicate that the speaker marvels at or is slightly surprised by the words of the other party.

• **이제 (noun)** : 말하고 있는 바로 이때.
now
This moment being spoken of.

• 부터 : 어떤 일의 시작이나 처음을 나타내는 조사.
buteo (no equivalent expression)
A postpositional particle that indicates the start or beginning of something.

• **계속** (adverb) : 끊이지 않고 잇따라.
continuously; successively
Continually without interruption.

• **쓰다** (verb) : 얼굴에 어떤 물건을 걸거나 덮어쓰다.
wear; put on
To hang something on one's face or cover one's face with it.

• -고 : 앞의 말이 나타내는 행동이나 그 결과가 뒤에 오는 행동이 일어나는 동안에 그대로 지속됨을 나타내는 연결 어미.
-go (no equivalent expression)
A connective ending used when an action or result of the preceding statement remains the same while the following action happens.

• **다니다** (verb) : 이리저리 오고 가다.
come and go
To come and go to places.

• -ㄹ까 보다 : 앞에 오는 말이 나타내는 행동을 할 의도가 있음을 나타내는 표현.
-lkka boda (no equivalent expression)
An expression used to indicate that the speaker has an intention to do the act mentioned in the preceding statement.

• -아 : (두루낮춤으로) 어떤 사실을 서술하거나 물음, 명령, 권유를 나타내는 종결 어미.
-a (no equivalent expression)
(informal addressee-lowering) A sentence-final ending used to **describe** a certain fact, ask a question, give an order, or advise.

< 대화(dialogue) > - 21

이건 어렸을 때 찍은 제 가족 사진이에요.
이건 어려쓸 때 찌근 제 가족 사지니에요.
igeon eoryeosseul ttae jjigeun je gajok sajinieyo.

시우 씨 어렸을 때는 키가 작고 통통했군요.
시우 씨 어려쓸 때는 키가 작꼬 통통핻꾸뇨.
siu ssi eoryeosseul ttaeneun kiga jakgo tongtonghaetgunyo.

< 설명(explanation) / 번역(translation) >

이것(이거)+은 어리+었+[을 때] 찍+은 저+의 가족 사진+이+에요.
이건 어렸을 때 제

• 이것(이거) (pronoun) : 말하는 사람에게 가까이 있거나 말하는 사람이 생각하고 있는 것을 가리키는 말.
this
The word that refers to something that is close to the speaker or something that the speaker is thinking of.

• 은 : 문장 속에서 어떤 대상이 화제임을 나타내는 조사.
eun (no equivalent expression)
A postpositional particle used to indicate that a certain subject is the topic of a sentence.

• 어리다 (adjective) : 나이가 적다.
young
Low in age.

• -었- : 사건이 과거에 일어났음을 나타내는 어미.
-eot- (no equivalent expression)
An ending of a word used to indicate that an event happened in the past.

• -을 때 : 어떤 행동이나 상황이 일어나는 동안이나 그 시기 또는 그러한 일이 일어난 경우를 나타내는 표현.
-eul ttae (no equivalent expression)
An expression used to indicate the duration, period, or occasion of a certain act or situation.

• **찍다 (verb)** : 어떤 대상을 카메라로 비추어 그 모양을 필름에 옮기다.
take
To transfer an image of an object to a film through a camera.

• -은 : 앞의 말이 관형어의 기능을 하게 만들고 사건이나 동작이 과거에 일어났음을 나타내는 어미.
-eun (no equivalent expression)
An ending of a word that makes the preceding word function as an adnominal phrase and indicates an event or action having occurred in the past.

• **저 (pronoun)** : 말하는 사람이 듣는 사람에게 자신을 낮추어 가리키는 말.
I; me
The humble form used by the speaker to refer to himself/herself for the purpose of showing humility to the listener.

• 의 : 앞의 말이 뒤의 말에 대하여 소유, 소속, 소재, 관계, 기원, 주체의 관계를 가짐을 나타내는 조사.
ui (no equivalent expression)
A postpositional particle used to indicate that the referent of the following word is owned by, belongs to, is related to, originates from, or is the object of what the preceding word indicates.

• **가족 (noun)** : 주로 한 집에 모여 살고 결혼이나 부모, 자식, 형제 등의 관계로 이루어진 사람들의 집단. 또는 그 구성원.
family
A group of people who mainly live together in the same house and are related by marriage or as parents, children, siblings, etc., or the members of such a group.

• **사진 (noun)** : 사물의 모습을 오래 보존할 수 있도록 사진기로 찍어 종이나 컴퓨터 등에 나타낸 영상.
picture; photo
An image of a certain object recorded by a camera, and then produced in a print format, in a file on the computer, etc. to preserve it for a long period of time.

• 이다 : 주어가 지시하는 대상의 속성이나 부류를 지정하는 뜻을 나타내는 서술격 조사.
ida (no equivalent expression)
A predicate particle indicating the meaning of the attribute or category of the thing that the subject of the sentence refers to.

• -에요 : (두루높임으로) 어떤 사실을 서술하거나 질문함을 나타내는 종결 어미.
-eyo (no equivalent expression)
(informal addressee-raising) A sentence-final ending used when **describing** a certain fact or asking a question.

시우 씨 어리+었+[을 때]+는 키+가 작+고 통통하+였+군요.
어렸을 때는 통통했군요

• **시우 (noun)** : person's name

• **씨 (noun)** : 그 사람을 높여 부르거나 이르는 말.
Mr.; Ms.; Mrs.
A bound noun used to address or call out to a certain person deferentially.

• **어리다 (adjective)** : 나이가 적다.
young
Low in age.

• -었- : 사건이 과거에 일어났음을 나타내는 어미.
-eot- (no equivalent expression)
An ending of a word used to indicate that an event happened in the past.

• -을 때 : 어떤 행동이나 상황이 일어나는 동안이나 그 시기 또는 그러한 일이 일어난 경우를 나타내는 표현.
-eul ttae (no equivalent expression)
An expression used to indicate the duration, period, or occasion of a certain act or situation.

• 는 : 어떤 대상이 다른 것과 대조됨을 나타내는 조사.
neun (no equivalent expression)
A postpositional particle used to indicate that a certain subject contrasts with something else.

• **키 (noun)** : 사람이나 동물이 바로 섰을 때의 발에서부터 머리까지의 몸의 길이.
height
The length of a person or animal in an upright position that is measured from the feet to the head.

• 가 : 어떤 상태나 상황에 놓인 대상이나 동작의 주체를 나타내는 조사.
ga (no equivalent expression)
A postpositional particle referring to a subject under a certain state or situation, or the subject of an act.

• **작다 (adjective)** : 길이, 넓이, 부피 등이 다른 것이나 보통보다 덜하다.
small; little
Lower than others or average in length, area, volume, etc.

• -고 : 두 가지 이상의 대등한 사실을 나열할 때 쓰는 연결 어미.
-go (no equivalent expression)
A connective ending used when listing more than two equal facts.

• **통통하다 (adjective)** : 키가 작고 살이 쪄서 몸이 옆으로 퍼져 있다.
chubby; stout
One's body being short and wide due to extra fat.

• -였- : 사건이 과거에 일어났음을 나타내는 어미.
-yeot- (no equivalent expression)
An ending of a word used to indicate that an event happened in the past.

• -군요 : (두루높임으로) 새롭게 알게 된 사실에 주목하거나 감탄함을 나타내는 표현.
-gunyo (no equivalent expression)
(informal addressee-raising) An expression used to indicate that the speaker notices or is impressed by a newly learned fact.

< 대화(dialogue) > - 22

꼼꼼한 지우 씨도 어제 큰 실수를 했나 봐요.
꼼꼼한 지우 씨도 어제 큰 실쑤를 핸나 봐요.
kkomkkomhan jiu ssido eoje keun silsureul haenna bwayo.

아무리 꼼꼼한 사람이라도 서두르면 실수하기 쉽지요.
아무리 꼼꼼한 사라미라도 서두르면 실쑤하기 쉽찌요.
amuri kkomkkomhan saramirado seodureumyeon silsuhagi swipjiyo.

< 설명(explanation) / 번역(translation) >

꼼꼼하+ㄴ 지우 씨+도 어제 크+ㄴ 실수+를 하+였+[나 보]+아요.
꼼꼼한 큰 했나 봐요

• **꼼꼼하다 (adjective)** : 빈틈이 없이 자세하고 차분하다.
meticulous; elaborate; careful
Paying much attention to detail, leaving nothing out, and being calm.

• -ㄴ : 앞의 말이 관형어의 기능을 하게 만들고 현재의 상태를 나타내는 어미.
-n (no equivalent expression)
An ending of a word that makes the preceding statement function as an adnominal phrase and refers to the present state.

• **지우 (noun)** : person's name

• **씨 (noun)** : 그 사람을 높여 부르거나 이르는 말.
Mr.; Ms.; Mrs.
A bound noun used to address or call out to a certain person deferentially.

• 도 : 이미 있는 어떤 것에 다른 것을 더하거나 포함함을 나타내는 조사.
do (no equivalent expression)
A postpositional particle used to indicate an addition or inclusion of another thing to something that already exists.

• **어제 (adverb)** : 오늘의 하루 전날에.
yesterday
On the day before today.

• **크다 (adjective)** : 어떤 일의 규모, 범위, 정도, 힘 등이 보통 수준을 넘다.
big
The size, scope, degree, power, etc., of an incident exceeding an ordinary level.

• -ㄴ : 앞의 말이 관형어의 기능을 하게 만들고 현재의 상태를 나타내는 어미.
-n (no equivalent expression)
An ending of a word that makes the preceding statement function as an adnominal phrase and refers to the present state.

• **실수 (noun)** : 잘 알지 못하거나 조심하지 않아서 저지르는 잘못.
mistake; blunder
A fault committed because one does not know something well or is not careful.

• 를 : 동작이 직접적으로 영향을 미치는 대상을 나타내는 조사.
reul (no equivalent expression)
A postpositional particle used to indicate the subject that an act has a direct influence on.

• **하다 (verb)** : 어떤 행동이나 동작, 활동 등을 행하다.
do; perform
To perform a certain move, action, activity, etc.

• -였- : 사건이 과거에 일어났음을 나타내는 어미.
-yeot- (no equivalent expression)
An ending of a word used to indicate that an event happened in the past.

• -나 보다 : 앞의 말이 나타내는 사실을 추측함을 나타내는 표현.
-na boda (no equivalent expression)
An expression used to guess about a fact mentioned in the preceding statement.

• -아요 : (두루높임으로) 어떤 사실을 서술하거나 질문, 명령, 권유함을 나타내는 종결 어미.
-ayo (no equivalent expression)
(informal addressee-raising) A sentence-final ending used to **describe** a certain fact, ask a question, give an order, or advise.

아무리 꼼꼼하+ㄴ 사람+이라도 서두르+면 실수하+[기가 쉽]+지요.
꼼꼼한

• **아무리 (adverb)** : 정도가 매우 심하게.
no matter how
To an extremely severe degree.

• **꼼꼼하다 (adjective)** : 빈틈이 없이 자세하고 차분하다.
meticulous; elaborate; careful
Paying much attention to detail, leaving nothing out, and being calm.

• -ㄴ : 앞의 말이 관형어의 기능을 하게 만들고 현재의 상태를 나타내는 어미.
-n (no equivalent expression)
An ending of a word that makes the preceding statement function as an adnominal phrase and refers to the present state.

• **사람 (noun)** : 생각할 수 있으며 언어와 도구를 만들어 사용하고 사회를 이루어 사는 존재.
human; man
A being that is capable of thinking, makes and uses languages and tools and lives by forming a society with others.

• 이라도 : 다른 경우들과 마찬가지임을 나타내는 조사.
irado (no equivalent expression)
A postpositional particle used when it is similar to other cases.

• **서두르다 (verb)** : 일을 빨리하려고 침착하지 못하고 급하게 행동하다.
hurry; rush
To not be calm but act in a hurried manner in order to do something quickly.

• -면 : 뒤에 오는 말에 대한 근거나 조건이 됨을 나타내는 연결 어미.
-myeon (no equivalent expression)
A connective ending used when the preceding statement becomes the reason or condition of the following statement.

• **실수하다 (verb)** : 잘 알지 못하거나 조심하지 않아서 잘못을 저지르다.
make a mistake; make a slip
To commit a fault because one does not know something well or is not careful.

• -기가 쉽다 : 앞의 말이 나타내는 행위를 하거나 그런 상태가 될 가능성이 많음을 나타내는 표현.
-giga swipda (no equivalent expression)
An expression used to state that the act or state mentioned in the preceding statement is likely to occur.

• -지요 : (두루높임으로) 말하는 사람이 자신에 대한 이야기나 자신의 생각을 친근하게 말할 때 쓰는 종결 어미.
-jiyo (no equivalent expression)
(informal addressee-raising) A sentence-final ending used when the speaker talks about himself/herself or his/her thoughts in a friendly manner.

< 대화(dialogue) > - 23

방이 되게 좁은 줄 알았는데 이렇게 보니 괜찮네.
방이 되게 조븐 줄 아란는데 이러케 보니 괜찬네.
bangi doege jobeun jul aranneunde ireoke boni gwaenchanne.

좁은 공간도 꾸미기 나름이야.
조븐 공간도 꾸미기 나르미야.
jobeun gonggando kkumigi nareumiya.

< 설명(explanation) / 번역(translation) >

방+이 되게 좁+[은 줄] 알+았+는데 이렇+게 보+니 괜찮+네.

• **방 (noun)** : 사람이 살거나 일을 하기 위해 벽을 둘러서 막은 공간.
room
A space enclosed by walls for residential or business purposes.

• 이 : 어떤 상태나 상황의 대상이나 동작의 주체를 나타내는 조사.
i (no equivalent expression)
A postpositional particle referring to a subject under a certain state or situation, or the agent of an action.

• **되게 (adverb)** : 아주 몹시.
very; really
Extremely.

• **좁다 (adjective)** : 면이나 바닥 등의 면적이 작다.
small
A surface, floor, etc., being small in size.

• -은 줄 : 어떤 사실이나 상태에 대해 알고 있거나 모르고 있음을 나타내는 표현.
-eun jul (no equivalent expression)
An expression used to indicate that one either knows or does not know a certain fact or state.

• **알다 (verb)** : 어떤 사실을 그러하다고 여기거나 생각하다.
know; think
To consider or assume a fact as being of a certain quality.

• -았- : 사건이 과거에 일어났음을 나타내는 어미.
-at- (no equivalent expression)
An ending of a word used to indicate that an event happened in the past.

• -는데 : 뒤의 말을 하기 위하여 그 대상과 관련이 있는 상황을 미리 말함을 나타내는 연결 어미.
-neunde (no equivalent expression)
A connective ending used to talk in advance about a situation to follow.

• **이렇다 (adjective)** : 상태, 모양, 성질 등이 이와 같다.
so; like this
(for a state, appearance, nature to be) Like this.

• -게 : 앞의 말이 뒤에서 가리키는 일의 목적이나 결과, 방식, 정도 등이 됨을 나타내는 연결 어미.
-ge (no equivalent expression)
A connective ending used when the preceding statement is the purpose, result, method, amount, etc., of something mentioned in the following statement.

• **보다 (verb)** : 대상의 내용이나 상태를 알기 위하여 살피다.
look at; take a look at; look in
To inspect an object to understand its content or state.

• -니 : 뒤에 오는 말에 대하여 앞에 오는 말이 원인이나 근거, 전제가 됨을 나타내는 연결 어미.
-ni (no equivalent expression)
A connective ending used when the preceding statement is the cause, reason, or premise for the following statement.

• **괜찮다 (adjective)** : 꽤 좋다.
nice; fine
Fairly good.

• -네 : (아주낮춤으로) 지금 깨달은 일에 대하여 말함을 나타내는 종결 어미.
-ne (no equivalent expression)
(formal, highly addressee-lowering) A sentence-final ending used when talking about something that one just learned.

좁+은 공간+도 꾸미+[기 나름이]+야.

• **좁다 (adjective)** : 면이나 바닥 등의 면적이 작다.
small
A surface, floor, etc., being small in size.

• -은 : 앞의 말이 관형어의 기능을 하게 만들고 현재의 상태를 나타내는 어미.
-eun (no equivalent expression)
An ending of a word that makes the preceding word function as an adnominal phrase and refers to the present state.

• **공간 (noun)** : 아무것도 없는 빈 곳이나 자리.
space
An empty place or site.

• 도 : 이미 있는 어떤 것에 다른 것을 더하거나 포함함을 나타내는 조사.
do (no equivalent expression)
A postpositional particle used to indicate an addition or inclusion of another thing to something that already exists.

• **꾸미다 (verb)** : 모양이 좋아지도록 손질하다.
decorate; adorn
To decorate for something to look better.

• -기 나름이다 : 어떤 일이 앞의 말이 나타내는 행동을 어떻게 하느냐에 따라 달라질 수 있음을 나타내는 표현.
-gi nareumida (no equivalent expression)
An expression used to indicate that something depends on how the act mentioned in the preceding statement is done.

• -야 : (두루낮춤으로) 어떤 사실에 대하여 서술하거나 물음을 나타내는 종결 어미.
-ya (no equivalent expression)
(informal addressee-lowering) A sentence-final ending used to **describe** a certain fact or ask a question.

< 대화(dialogue) > - 24

나물 반찬 말고 더 맛있는 거 없어요?
나물 반찬 말고 더 마신는 거 업써요?
namul banchan malgo deo masinneun geo eopseoyo?

반찬 투정하지 말고 빨리 먹기나 해.
반찬 투정하지 말고 빨리 먹끼나 해.
banchan tujeonghaji malgo ppalli meokgina hae.

< 설명(explanation) / 번역(translation) >

나물 반찬 말+고 더 맛있+[는 것(거)] 없+어요?

맛있는 거

• **나물 (noun)** : 먹을 수 있는 풀이나 나뭇잎, 채소 등을 삶거나 볶거나 또는 날것으로 양념하여 무친 반찬.
namul; seasoned vegetables
A variety of Korean side dishes made by seasoning boiled, fried or uncooked edible grass, leaves, vegetables, etc.

• **반찬 (noun)** : 식사를 할 때 밥에 곁들여 먹는 음식.
side dish
Food to eat with rice when having a meal.

• **말다 (verb)** : 앞의 것이 아니고 뒤의 것임을 나타내는 말.
not be
An expression used to indicate that something is the latter one, not the former one.

• -고 : 두 가지 이상의 대등한 사실을 나열할 때 쓰는 연결 어미.
-go (no equivalent expression)
A connective ending used when listing more than two equal facts.

• **더 (adverb)** : 비교의 대상이나 어떤 기준보다 정도가 크게, 그 이상으로.
more
More or higher than something being compared or a certain threshold.

• **맛있다 (adjective)** : 맛이 좋다.
tasty; delicious
Tasting good.

• -는 것 : 명사가 아닌 것을 문장에서 명사처럼 쓰이게 하거나 '이다' 앞에 쓰일 수 있게 할 때 쓰는 표현.
-neun geot (no equivalent expression)
An expression used to enable a non-noun word to be used as a noun in a sentence or to be used in front of '이다' (be).

• **없다 (adjective)** : 사람, 사물, 현상 등이 어떤 곳에 자리나 공간을 차지하고 존재하지 않는 상태이다.
being not
(for a person, thing, phenomenon, etc. to be) Not occupying a spot or space at a certain location.

• -어요 : (두루높임으로) 어떤 사실을 서술하거나 질문, 명령, 권유함을 나타내는 종결 어미.
-eoyo (no equivalent expression)
(informal addressee-raising) A sentence-final ending used to describe a certain fact, **ask a question**, give an order, or advise.

반찬 투정하+[지 말]+고 빨리 먹+[기나 하]+여.
먹기나 해

• **반찬 (noun)** : 식사를 할 때 밥에 곁들여 먹는 음식.
side dish
Food to eat with rice when having a meal.

• **투정하다 (verb)** : 무엇이 모자라거나 마음에 들지 않아 떼를 쓰며 조르다.
complain; grumble; growl
To badger someone for more of something or for a new one, when something is in shortage or is not satisfactory.

• -지 말다 : 앞의 말이 나타내는 행동을 하지 못하게 함을 나타내는 표현.
-ji malda (no equivalent expression)
An expression used to prohibit the act mentioned in the preceding statement.

• -고 : 앞의 말과 뒤의 말이 차례대로 일어남을 나타내는 연결 어미.
-go (no equivalent expression)
A connective ending used when the preceding statement and the following statement happen in order.

• **빨리 (adverb)** : 걸리는 시간이 짧게.
quickly
In a short duration of time.

• **먹다 (verb)** : 음식 등을 입을 통하여 배 속에 들여보내다.
eat; have; consume; take
To put food into one's mouth and take it in one's stomach.

• -기나 하다 : 마음에 차지는 않지만 듣는 사람이나 다른 사람이 앞의 말이 나타내는 행동을 하길 바랄 때 쓰는 표현.
-gina hada (no equivalent expression)
An expression used to indicate that the speaker does not like it, but wants the listener to do the act mentioned in the preceding statement.

• -여 : (두루낮춤으로) 어떤 사실을 서술하거나 물음, 명령, 권유를 나타내는 종결 어미.
-yeo (no equivalent expression)
(informal addressee-lowering) A sentence-final ending used to describe a certain fact, ask a question, **give an order**, or advise.

< 대화(dialogue) > - 25

수박 한 통에 이만 원이라고요? 좀 비싼데요.
수박 한 통에 이만 워니라고요? 좀 비싼데요.
subak han tonge iman woniragoyo? jom bissandeyo.

비싸기는요. 요즘 물가가 얼마나 올랐는데요.
비싸기느뇨. 요즘 물까가 얼마나 올란는데요.
bissagineunyo. yojeum mulgaga eolmana ollanneundeyo.

< 설명(explanation) / 번역(translation) >

수박 한 통+에 이만 원+이+라고요?

좀 비싸+ㄴ데요.
비싼데요

• **수박 (noun)** : 둥글고 크며 초록 빛깔에 검푸른 줄무늬가 있으며 속이 붉고 수분이 많은 과일.
watermelon
A big, green, round fruit with blackish blue stripes on it which contains red, watery flesh.

• **한 (determiner)** : 하나의.
one
One.

• **통 (noun)** : 배추나 수박, 호박 등을 세는 단위.
head
A unit used to count cabbages, watermelons, pumpkins, etc.

• 에 : 앞말이 기준이 되는 대상이나 단위임을 나타내는 조사.
per; for; against
A postpositional particle to indicate that the preceding statement is a unit or subject that is the standard for something.

• **이만** : 20,000

• **원 (noun)** : 한국의 화폐 단위.
won
A Korean monetary unit.

• 이다 : 주어가 지시하는 대상의 속성이나 부류를 지정하는 뜻을 나타내는 서술격 조사.
ida (no equivalent expression)
A predicate particle indicating the meaning of the attribute or category of the thing that the subject of the sentence refers to.

• -라고요 : (두루높임으로) 다른 사람의 말을 확인하거나 따져 물을 때 쓰는 표현.
-ragoyo (no equivalent expression)
(informal addressee-raising) An expression used to confirm or question another person's remark.

• **좀 (adverb)** : 분량이나 정도가 적게.
a little
In a small quantity or to a small degree.

• **비싸다 (adjective)** : 물건값이나 어떤 일을 하는 데 드는 비용이 보통보다 높다.
expensive; costly
The price of an object or the cost to do something being higher than the average.

• -ㄴ데요 : (두루높임으로) 의외라 느껴지는 어떤 사실을 감탄하여 말할 때 쓰는 표현.
-ndeyo (no equivalent expression)
(informal addressee-raising) An expression used to tell an unexpected fact with wonder.

비싸+기는요.

요즘 물가+가 얼마나 오르(올ㄹ)+았+는데요.

올랐는데요

• **비싸다 (adjective)** : 물건값이나 어떤 일을 하는 데 드는 비용이 보통보다 높다.
expensive; costly
The price of an object or the cost to do something being higher than the average.

• -기는요 : (두루높임으로) 상대방의 말을 가볍게 부정하거나 반박함을 나타내는 표현.
-gineunyo (no equivalent expression)
(informal addressee-raising) An expression used to lightly deny or refute the listener's remark.

- **요즘 (noun)** : 아주 가까운 과거부터 지금까지의 사이.
  nowadays; these days
  A period from a while ago to the present.

- **물가 (noun)** : 물건이나 서비스의 평균적인 가격.
  prices
  The average prices of goods or services.

- 가 : 어떤 상태나 상황에 놓인 대상이나 동작의 주체를 나타내는 조사.
  ga (no equivalent expression)
  A postpositional particle referring to a subject under a certain state or situation, or the subject of an act.

- **얼마나 (adverb)** : 상태나 느낌 등의 정도가 매우 크고 대단하게.
  how
  In a great and enormous degree in terms of a state or feeling.

- **오르다 (verb)** : 값, 수치, 온도, 성적 등이 이전보다 많아지거나 높아지다.
  rise; increase; go up
  For a value, number, temperature, performance, etc., to become larger or higher.

- -았- : 어떤 사건이 과거에 완료되었거나 그 사건의 결과가 현재까지 지속되는 상황을 나타내는 어미.
  -at- (no equivalent expression)
  An ending of a word used to indicate that an event was completed in the past or its result continues in the present.

- -는데요 : (두루높임으로) 어떤 상황을 전달하여 듣는 사람의 반응을 기대함을 나타내는 표현.
  -neundeyo (no equivalent expression)
  (informal addressee-raising) An expression used to tell a situation, expecting a response from the listener.

< 대화(dialogue) > - 26

왜 나한테 거짓말을 했어?
왜 나한테 거진마를 해써?
wae nahante geojinmareul haesseo?

그건 너와 멀어질까 봐 두려웠기 때문이야.
그건 너와 머러질까 봐 두려월끼 때무니야.
geugeon neowa meoreojilkka bwa duryeowotgi ttaemuniya.

< 설명(explanation) / 번역(translation) >

왜 나+한테 거짓말+을 하+였+어?
했어

• **왜** (adverb) : 무슨 이유로. 또는 어째서.
why
For what reason; how come.

• **나** (pronoun) : 말하는 사람이 친구나 아랫사람에게 자기를 가리키는 말.
I
A pronoun used to indicate oneself to a friend or a younger person.

• 한테 : 어떤 행동이 미치는 대상임을 나타내는 조사.
hante (no equivalent expression)
A postpositional particle referring to the subject that an act has an influence on.

• **거짓말** (noun) : 사실이 아닌 것을 사실인 것처럼 꾸며서 하는 말.
lie; falsehood
A remark which is not true, intended to make someone believe it is true.

• 을 : 동작이 직접적으로 영향을 미치는 대상을 나타내는 조사.
eul (no equivalent expression)
A postpositional particle used to indicate the subject that an action has a direct influence on.

• **하다** (verb) : 어떤 행동이나 동작, 활동 등을 행하다.
do; perform
To perform a certain move, action, activity, etc.

• -였- : 사건이 과거에 일어났음을 나타내는 어미.
-yeot- (no equivalent expression)
An ending of a word used to indicate that an event happened in the past.

• -어 : (두루낮춤으로) 어떤 사실을 서술하거나 물음, 명령, 권유를 나타내는 종결 어미.
-eo (no equivalent expression)
(informal addressee-lowering) A sentence-final ending used to describe a certain fact, **ask a question**, give an order, or advise.

그것(그거)+은 너+와 멀어지+[ㄹ까 보]+아 두렵(두려우)+었+[기 때문]+이+야.
그건 멀어질까 봐 두려웠기 때문이야

• **그것 (pronoun)** : 앞에서 이미 이야기한 대상을 가리키는 말.
no equivalent expression
A pronoun used to indicate the previously-mentioned object.

• 은 : 문장 속에서 어떤 대상이 화제임을 나타내는 조사.
eun (no equivalent expression)
A postpositional particle used to indicate that a certain subject is the topic of a sentence.

• **너 (pronoun)** : 듣는 사람이 친구나 아랫사람일 때, 그 사람을 가리키는 말.
no equivalent expression
A pronoun used to indicate the listener when he/she is the same age or younger.

• 와 : 무엇인가를 상대로 하여 어떤 일을 할 때 그 상대임을 나타내는 조사.
wa (no equivalent expression)
A postpositional particle that indicates the person who one is doing something with.

• **멀어지다 (verb)** : 친하던 사이가 다정하지 않게 되다.
become estranged; be alienated
For a close relationship to become less close.

• -ㄹ까 보다 : 앞에 오는 말이 나타내는 상황이 될 것을 걱정하거나 두려워함을 나타내는 표현.
-lkka boda (no equivalent expression)
An expression used to indicate that the speaker is worried or afraid that the situation mentioned in the preceding statement may happen.

• -아 : 앞에 오는 말이 뒤에 오는 말에 대한 원인이나 이유임을 나타내는 연결 어미.
-a (no equivalent expression)
A connective ending used when the preceding statement is the cause or reason for the following statement.

• **두렵다 (adjective)** : 걱정되고 불안하다.
afraid
Feeling anxious and uneasy.

• -었- : 사건이 과거에 일어났음을 나타내는 어미.
-eot- (no equivalent expression)
An ending of a word used to indicate that an event happened in the past.

• -기 때문 : 앞의 내용이 뒤에 오는 일의 원인이나 까닭임을 나타내는 표현.
-gi ttaemun (no equivalent expression)
An expression used to indicate that the preceding statement is the reason or cause for the following incident.

• 이다 : 주어가 지시하는 대상의 속성이나 부류를 지정하는 뜻을 나타내는 서술격 조사.
ida (no equivalent expression)
A predicate particle indicating the meaning of the attribute or category of the thing that the subject of the sentence refers to.

• -야 : (두루낮춤으로) 어떤 사실에 대하여 서술하거나 물음을 나타내는 종결 어미.
-ya (no equivalent expression)
(informal addressee-lowering) A sentence-final ending used to **describe** a certain fact or ask a question.

< 대화(dialogue) > - 27

이번 휴가 때 남자 친구에게 운전을 배우기로 했어.
이번 휴가 때 남자 친구에게 운저늘 배우기로 해써.
ibeon hyuga ttae namja chinguege unjeoneul baeugiro haesseo.

그러면 분명히 서로 싸우게 될 텐데…….
그러면 분명히 서로 싸우게 될 텐데…….
geureomyeon bunmyeonghi seoro ssauge doel tende…….

< 설명(explanation) / 번역(translation) >

이번 휴가 때 남자 친구+에게 운전+을 배우+[기로 하]+였+어.

배우기로 했어

• **이번 (noun)** : 곧 돌아올 차례. 또는 막 지나간 차례.
this time
A turn soon to come, or one that just passed.

• **휴가 (noun)** : 직장이나 군대 등의 단체에 속한 사람이 일정한 기간 동안 일터를 벗어나서 쉬는 일. 또는 그런 기간.
leave; break; vacation
A state in which a person belonging to an organization such as a company or an army leaves his/her workplace and takes a rest for a limited period of time; or such a period.

• **때 (noun)** : 어떤 시기 동안.
time
A state of being during a certain period.

• **남자 친구 (noun)** : 여자가 사랑하는 감정을 가지고 사귀는 남자.
boyfriend
A man that a woman dates with a feeling of love.

• 에게 : 어떤 행동의 주체이거나 비롯되는 대상임을 나타내는 조사.
ege (no equivalent expression)
A postpositional particle indicating the agent of a certain action or one from which an action comes from.

• **운전 (noun)** : 기계나 자동차를 움직이고 조종함.
driving; operation
The act of moving and handling a machine or car.

• 을 : 동작이 직접적으로 영향을 미치는 대상을 나타내는 조사.
eul (no equivalent expression)
A postpositional particle used to indicate the subject that an action has a direct influence on.

• **배우다 (verb)** : 새로운 기술을 익히다.
learn; acquire
To learn a new skill.

• -기로 하다 : 앞의 말이 나타내는 행동을 할 것을 결심하거나 약속함을 나타내는 표현.
-giro hada (no equivalent expression)
An expression used to decide or promise the performance of the act mentioned in the preceding statement.

• -였- : 어떤 사건이 과거에 완료되었거나 그 사건의 결과가 현재까지 지속되는 상황을 나타내는 어미.
-yeot- (no equivalent expression)
An ending of a word used to indicate that an event was completed in the past or its result continues in the present.

• -어 : (두루낮춤으로) 어떤 사실을 서술하거나 물음, 명령, 권유를 나타내는 종결 어미.
-eo (no equivalent expression)
(informal addressee-lowering) A sentence-final ending used to **describe** a certain fact, ask a question, give an order, or advise.

그러면 분명히 서로 싸우+[게 되]+[ㄹ 텐데]…….

싸우게 될 텐데

• **그러면 (adverb)** : 앞의 내용이 뒤의 내용의 조건이 될 때 쓰는 말.
if so
A conjunctive adverb used when the following statement is conditional upon the preceding one.

• **분명히 (adverb)** : 어떤 사실이 틀림이 없이 확실하게.
surely
(a fact being confirmed) Certainly and accurately.

• **서로 (adverb)** : 관계를 맺고 있는 둘 이상의 대상이 각기 그 상대에 대하여.
each other; one another
Toward each person who is one of two or more people who are related.

• **싸우다 (verb)** : 말이나 힘으로 이기려고 다투다.
fight; quarrel; dispute
To try to win by argument or force.

• -게 되다 : 앞의 말이 나타내는 상태나 상황이 됨을 나타내는 표현.
-ge doeda (no equivalent expression)
An expression used to indicate that something will become the state or situation mentioned in the preceding statement.

• -ㄹ 텐데 : 앞에 오는 말에 대하여 말하는 사람의 강한 추측을 나타내면서 그와 관련되는 내용을 이어 말할 때 쓰는 표현.
-l tende (no equivalent expression)
An expression used to indicate the speaker's strong guess about the preceding statement and add the relevant content.

< 대화(dialogue) > - 28

운동선수로서 뭐가 제일 힘들어?
운동선수로서 뭐가 제일 힘드러?
undongseonsuroseo mwoga jeil himdeureo?

글쎄, 체중을 조절하기 위한 끊임없는 노력이겠지.
글쎄, 체중을 조절하기 위한 끄니멈는 노려기겓찌.
geulsse, chejungeul jojeolhagi wihan kkeunimeomneun noryeogigetji.

< 설명(explanation) / 번역(translation) >

운동선수+로서 뭐+가 제일 힘들+어?

• **운동선수 (noun)** : 운동에 뛰어난 재주가 있어 전문적으로 운동을 하는 사람.
sportsman; athlete
A person who is good at sports or does it as a profession.

• 로서 : 어떤 지위나 신분, 자격을 나타내는 조사.
roseo (no equivalent expression)
A postpositional particle that indicates a status, position, or qualification.

• **뭐 (pronoun)** : 모르는 사실이나 사물을 가리키는 말.
what
A pronoun used to refer to a fact or object that one does not know of.

• 가 : 어떤 상태나 상황에 놓인 대상이나 동작의 주체를 나타내는 조사.
ga (no equivalent expression)
A postpositional particle referring to a subject under a certain state or situation, or the subject of an act.

• **제일 (adverb)** : 여럿 중에서 가장.
most
Best among many.

• **힘들다 (adjective)** : 어떤 일을 하는 것이 어렵거나 곤란하다.
hard; difficult; tough
Difficult or tough to do a certain act.

• -어 : (두루낮춤으로) 어떤 사실을 서술하거나 물음, 명령, 권유를 나타내는 종결 어미.
-eo (no equivalent expression)
(informal addressee-lowering) A sentence-final ending used to describe a certain fact, **ask a question**, give an order, or advise.

글쎄, 체중+을 조절하+[기 위한] 끊임없+는 노력+이+겠+지.

• **글쎄 (interjection)** : 상대방의 물음이나 요구에 대하여 분명하지 않은 태도를 나타낼 때 쓰는 말.
well; hm
An exclamation used when showing an uncertain attitude toward someone's question or demand.

• **체중 (noun)** : 몸의 무게.
weight
The weight of a person's body.

• 을 : 동작이 직접적으로 영향을 미치는 대상을 나타내는 조사.
eul (no equivalent expression)
A postpositional particle used to indicate the subject that an action has a direct influence on.

• **조절하다 (verb)** : 균형에 맞게 바로잡거나 상황에 알맞게 맞추다.
control
To correct to a balanced state or adjust to the circumstances.

• -기 위한 : 뒤에 오는 명사를 수식하면서 그 목적이나 의도를 나타내는 표현.
-gi wihan (no equivalent expression)
An expression used to indicate a purpose or intention, while modifying the following noun.

• **끊임없다 (adjective)** : 계속하거나 이어져 있던 것이 끊이지 아니하다.
incessant; unceasing; ceaseless
Something that has been continued or connected being not interrupted.

• -는 : 앞의 말이 관형어의 기능을 하게 만들고 사건이나 동작이 현재 일어남을 나타내는 어미.
-neun (no equivalent expression)
An ending of a word that makes the preceding statement function as an adnominal phrase and implies that an event or action is happening in the present.

• **노력 (noun)** : 어떤 목적을 이루기 위하여 힘을 들이고 애를 씀.
effort; endeavor; hard work
Making an effort and working hard to achieve something.

- 이다 : 주어가 지시하는 대상의 속성이나 부류를 지정하는 뜻을 나타내는 서술격 조사.
  ida (no equivalent expression)
  A predicate particle indicating the meaning of the attribute or category of the thing that the subject of the sentence refers to.

- -겠- : 미래의 일이나 추측을 나타내는 어미.
  -get- (no equivalent expression)
  An ending of a word referring to a future event or assumption.

- -지 : (두루낮춤으로) 말하는 사람이 자신에 대한 이야기나 자신의 생각을 친근하게 말할 때 쓰는 종결 어미.
  -ji (no equivalent expression)
  (informal addressee-lowering) A sentence-final ending used when the speaker talks about himself/herself or his/her thoughts in a friendly manner.

< 대화(dialogue) > - 29

요즘 부쩍 운동을 열심히 하시네요.
요즘 부쩍 운동을 열씸히 하시네요.
yojeum bujjeok undongeul yeolsimhi hasineyo.

건강을 유지하기 위해서 운동을 좀 해야겠더라고요.
건강을 유지하기 위해서 운동을 좀 해야겐떠라고요.
geongangeul yujihagi wihaeseo undongeul jom haeyagetdeoragoyo.

< 설명(explanation) / 번역(translation) >

요즘 부쩍 운동+을 열심히 하+시+네요.

• **요즘 (noun)** : 아주 가까운 과거부터 지금까지의 사이.
nowadays; these days
A period from a while ago to the present.

• **부쩍 (adverb)** : 어떤 사물이나 현상이 갑자기 크게 변화하는 모양.
greatly; dramatically
A word describing a sudden, big change in a certain object or phenomenon.

• **운동 (noun)** : 몸을 단련하거나 건강을 위하여 몸을 움직이는 일.
exercise
The act of moving one's body in order to train it or improve one's health.

• 을 : 동작이 직접적으로 영향을 미치는 대상을 나타내는 조사.
eul (no equivalent expression)
A postpositional particle used to indicate the subject that an action has a direct influence on.

• **열심히 (adverb)** : 어떤 일에 온 정성을 다하여.
hard; diligently; zealously
With all one's heart.

• **하다 (verb)** : 어떤 행동이나 동작, 활동 등을 행하다.
do; perform
To perform a certain move, action, activity, etc.

• -시- : 어떤 동작이나 상태의 주체를 높이는 뜻을 나타내는 어미.
-si- (no equivalent expression)
An ending of a word used for the subject honorifics of an action or state.

• -네요 : (두루높임으로) 말하는 사람이 직접 경험하여 새롭게 알게 된 사실에 대해 감탄함을 나타낼 때 쓰는 표현.
-neyo (no equivalent expression)
(informal addressee-raising) An expression used to indicate that the speaker is impressed by a fact he/she learned anew from a past personal experience.

건강+을 유지하+[기 위해서] 운동+을 좀 하+여야겠+더라고요.
해야겠더라고요

• **건강 (noun)** : 몸이나 정신이 이상이 없이 튼튼한 상태.
health; wellbeing
A state of body and mind that is robust with no illness.

• 을 : 동작이 직접적으로 영향을 미치는 대상을 나타내는 조사.
eul (no equivalent expression)
A postpositional particle used to indicate the subject that an action has a direct influence on.

• **유지하다 (verb)** : 어떤 상태나 상황 등을 그대로 이어 나가다.
keep; maintain
To keep a certain state, situation, etc., as it is.

• -기 위해서 : 어떤 일을 하는 목적인 의도를 나타내는 표현.
-gi wihaeseo (no equivalent expression)
An expression used to indicate the intention, which is the goal for doing a certain thing.

• **운동 (noun)** : 몸을 단련하거나 건강을 위하여 몸을 움직이는 일.
exercise
The act of moving one's body in order to train it or improve one's health.

• 을 : 동작이 직접적으로 영향을 미치는 대상을 나타내는 조사.
eul (no equivalent expression)
A postpositional particle used to indicate the subject that an action has a direct influence on.

• **좀 (adverb)** : 분량이나 정도가 적게.
a little
In a small quantity or to a small degree.

• **하다 (verb)** : 어떤 행동이나 동작, 활동 등을 행하다.
do; perform
To perform a certain move, action, activity, etc.

• -여야겠- : 앞의 말이 나타내는 행동에 대한 강한 의지를 나타내거나 그 행동을 할 필요가 있음을 완곡하게 말할 때 쓰는 표현.
-yeoyaget- (no equivalent expression)
An expression used to indicate a strong will for the act mentioned in the preceding statement, or to guess that doing the act may be necessary.

• -더라고요 : (두루높임으로) 과거에 경험하여 새로 알게 된 사실에 대해 지금 상대방에게 옮겨 전할 때 쓰는 표현.
-deoragoyo (no equivalent expression)
(informal addressee-raising) An expression used to refer to and convey in the present a fact the speaker learned through a past experience to the listener.

< 대화(dialogue) > - 30

해외여행을 떠나기 전에 무엇을 준비해야 할까요?
해외여행을 떠나기 저네 무어슬 준비해야 할까요?
haeoeyeohaengeul tteonagi jeone mueoseul junbihaeya halkkayo?

먼저 여권을 준비하고 환전도 해야 해요.
먼저 여꿔늘 준비하고 환전도 해야 해요.
meonjeo yeogwoneul junbihago hwanjeondo haeya haeyo.

< 설명(explanation) / 번역(translation) >

해외여행+을 떠나+[기 전에] 무엇+을 준비하+[여야 하]+ㄹ까요?
준비해야 할까요

• **해외여행 (noun)** : 외국으로 여행을 가는 일. 또는 그런 여행.
overseas travel; trip abroad
A trip to overseas destinations, or such a trip.

• 을 : 그 행동의 목적이 되는 일을 나타내는 조사.
eul (no equivalent expression)
A postpositional particle used to indicate the work that is the objective of a certain action.

• **떠나다 (verb)** : 어떤 일을 하러 나서다.
set forth
To set out to do something.

• -기 전에 : 뒤에 오는 말이 나타내는 행동이 앞에 오는 말이 나타내는 행동보다 앞서는 것을 나타내는 표현.
-gi jeone (no equivalent expression)
An expression used to state that a certain act occurs earlier than the act in the preceding statement.

• **무엇 (pronoun)** : 모르는 사실이나 사물을 가리키는 말.
what
A word indicating an unknown fact or thing.

• 을 : 동작이 직접적으로 영향을 미치는 대상을 나타내는 조사.
eul (no equivalent expression)
A postpositional particle used to indicate the subject that an action has a direct influence on.

• **준비하다 (verb)** : 미리 마련하여 갖추다.
prepare
To have something in place with advance preparations.

• -여야 하다 : 앞에 오는 말이 어떤 일을 하거나 어떤 상황에 이르기 위한 의무적인 행동이거나 필수적인 조건임을 나타내는 표현.
-yeoya hada (no equivalent expression)
An expression used to indicate that the preceding statement is the required act or condition to realize a certain incident or situation.

• -ㄹ까요 : (두루높임으로) 듣는 사람에게 의견을 묻거나 제안함을 나타내는 표현.
-lkkayo (no equivalent expression)
(informal addressee-raising) An expression used to ask for the listener's opinion or propose something.

먼저 여권+을 준비하+고 환전+도 하+[여야 하]+여요.
해야 해요

• **먼저 (adverb)** : 시간이나 순서에서 앞서.
earlier; first
Being or happening before something else in time or order.

• **여권 (noun)** : 다른 나라를 여행하는 사람의 신분이나 국적을 증명하고, 여행하는 나라에 그 사람의 보호를 맡기는 문서.
passport
An official document that proves a traveler's nationality or identity in a foreign country, and requests his/her protection for the country.

• 을 : 동작이 직접적으로 영향을 미치는 대상을 나타내는 조사.
eul (no equivalent expression)
A postpositional particle used to indicate the subject that an action has a direct influence on.

• **준비하다 (verb)** : 미리 마련하여 갖추다.
prepare
To have something in place with advance preparations.

• -고 : 두 가지 이상의 대등한 사실을 나열할 때 쓰는 연결 어미.
-go (no equivalent expression)
A connective ending used when listing more than two equal facts.

• **환전 (noun)** : 한 나라의 화폐를 다른 나라의 화폐와 맞바꿈.
foreign exchange; money exchange
The act of changing one country's currency into another's.

• 도 : 이미 있는 어떤 것에 다른 것을 더하거나 포함함을 나타내는 조사.
do (no equivalent expression)
A postpositional particle used to indicate an addition or inclusion of another thing to something that already exists.

• **하다 (verb)** : 어떤 행동이나 동작, 활동 등을 행하다.
do; perform
To perform a certain move, action, activity, etc.

• -여야 하다 : 앞에 오는 말이 어떤 일을 하거나 어떤 상황에 이르기 위한 의무적인 행동이거나 필수적인 조건임을 나타내는 표현.
-yeoya hada (no equivalent expression)
An expression used to indicate that the preceding statement is the required act or condition to realize a certain incident or situation.

• -여요 : (두루높임으로) 어떤 사실을 서술하거나 질문, 명령, 권유함을 나타내는 종결 어미.
-yeoyo (no equivalent expression)
(informal addressee-raising) A sentence-final ending used to **describe** a certain fact, ask a question, give an order, or advise.

< 대화(dialogue) > - 31

저 다음 달에 한국에 갑니다.
저 다음 다레 한구게 감니다.
jeo daeum dare hanguge gamnida.

어머, 그럼 우리 서울에서 볼 수 있겠네요?
어머, 그럼 우리 서우레서 볼 쑤 읻껜네요?
eomeo, geureom uri seoureseo bol su itgenneyo?

< 설명(explanation) / 번역(translation) >

저 다음 달+에 한국+에 가+ㅂ니다.
갑니다

• **저 (pronoun)** : 말하는 사람이 듣는 사람에게 자신을 낮추어 가리키는 말.
I; me
The humble form used by the speaker to refer to himself/herself for the purpose of showing humility to the listener.

• **다음 (noun)** : 어떤 차례에서 바로 뒤.
next; following
Something that comes right after another in a sequence of time, place, turn, etc.

• **달 (noun)** : 일 년을 열둘로 나누어 놓은 기간.
month
A period in a year divided by twelve.

• 에 : 앞말이 시간이나 때임을 나타내는 조사.
in; at
A postpositional particle to indicate that the preceding statement refers to the time.

• **한국 (noun)** : 아시아 대륙의 동쪽에 있는 나라. 한반도와 그 부속 섬들로 이루어져 있으며, 대한민국이라고도 부른다. 1950년에 일어난 육이오 전쟁 이후 휴전선을 사이에 두고 국토가 둘로 나뉘었다. 언어는 한국어이고, 수도는 서울이다.
Korea
A country located in East Asia; it consists of the Korean Peninsula and affiliated islands; divided into South Korea and North Korea since the 1953 ceasefire agreement, it is called either the Republic of Korea or South Korea; the official language is Korean and the capital is Seoul.

• 에 : 앞말이 목적지이거나 어떤 행위의 진행 방향임을 나타내는 조사.
to; at
A postpositional particle to indicate that the preceding statement refers to a destination or the course of a certain action.

• **가다 (verb)** : 한 곳에서 다른 곳으로 장소를 이동하다.
go; travel
To move from one place to another place.

• -ㅂ니다 : (아주높임으로) 현재의 동작이나 상태, 사실을 정중하게 설명함을 나타내는 종결 어미.
-pnida (no equivalent expression)
(formal, highly addressee-raising) A sentence-final ending used to explain the present action, state, or fact politely.

어머, 그럼 우리 서울+에서 보+[ㄹ 수 있]+겠+네요?

볼 수 있겠네요

• **어머 (interjection)** : 주로 여자들이 예상하지 못한 일로 갑자기 놀라거나 감탄할 때 내는 소리.
oh my goodness; why
An exclamation used when mainly women are suddenly surprised at or admire an unexpected matter.

• **그럼 (adverb)** : 앞의 내용을 받아들이거나 그 내용을 바탕으로 하여 새로운 주장을 할 때 쓰는 말.
then
A word used when accepting the preceding statement or making a new suggestion based on it..

• **우리 (pronoun)** : 말하는 사람이 자기와 듣는 사람 또는 이를 포함한 여러 사람들을 가리키는 말.
we
A pronoun used when the speaker refers to himself/herself and the listener or listeners, or a group of people including the speaker and listener or listeners.

• **서울 (noun)** : 한반도 중앙에 있는 특별시. 한국의 수도이자 정치, 경제, 산업, 사회, 문화, 교통의 중심지이다. 북한산, 관악산 등의 산에 둘러싸여 있고 가운데로는 한강이 흐른다.
Seoul
A metropolitan city located in the center of the Korean Peninsula, it is the capital of the Republic of Korea and the center of the country's politics, business, society, culture and transportation. It is surrounded by mountains such as Bukhansan Mountain and Gwanaksan Mountain and crossed by the Hangang River.

• 에서 : 앞말이 행동이 이루어지고 있는 장소임을 나타내는 조사.
eseo (no equivalent expression)
A postpositional particle used to indicate that the preceding word refers to a place where a certain action is being done.

• **보다 (verb)** : 사람을 만나다.
meet; see
To meet a person.

• -ㄹ 수 있다 : 어떤 행동이나 상태가 가능함을 나타내는 표현.
-l su itda (no equivalent expression)
An expression used to indicate that an act or state is possible.

• -겠- : 미래의 일이나 추측을 나타내는 어미.
-get- (no equivalent expression)
An ending of a word referring to a future event or assumption.

• -네요 : (두루높임으로) 말하는 사람이 추측하거나 짐작한 내용에 대해 듣는 사람에게 동의를 구하며 물을 때 쓰는 표현.
-neyo (no equivalent expression)
(informal addressee-raising) An expression used to ask the listener for a consent about the speaker's guess or assumption.

< 대화(dialogue) > - 32

매일 만드는 대로 요리했는데 오늘은 평소보다 맛이 없는 것 같아요.
매일 만드는 대로 요리핸는데 오느른 평소보다 마시 엄는 걷 가타요.
maeil mandeuneun daero yorihaenneunde oneureun pyeongsoboda masi eomneun geot gatayo.

아니에요. 맛있어요. 잘 먹을게요.
아니에요. 마시써요. 잘 머글께요.
anieyo. masisseoyo. jal meogeulgeyo.

< 설명(explanation) / 번역(translation) >

매일 만들(만드)+[는 대로] 요리하+였+는데
만드는 대로 요리했는데

오늘+은 평소+보다 맛+이 없+[는 것 같]+아요.

• **매일 (adverb)** : 하루하루마다 빠짐없이.
every day; every single day
Every day without exceptions.

• **만들다 (verb)** : 힘과 기술을 써서 없던 것을 생기게 하다.
make; create; produce; manufacture
To create something that did not exist, using one's power or skill.

• -는 대로 : 앞에 오는 말이 뜻하는 현재의 행동이나 상황과 같음을 나타내는 표현.
-neun daero (no equivalent expression)
An expression used to indicate that something is the same as the present act or state mentioned in the preceding statement.

• **요리하다 (verb)** : 음식을 만들다.
cook
To make food.

• -였- : 어떤 사건이 과거에 완료되었거나 그 사건의 결과가 현재까지 지속되는 상황을 나타내는 어미.
-yeot- (no equivalent expression)
An ending of a word used to indicate that an event was completed in the past or its result continues in the present.

• -는데 : 뒤의 말을 하기 위하여 그 대상과 관련이 있는 상황을 미리 말함을 나타내는 연결 어미.
-neunde (no equivalent expression)
A connective ending used to talk in advance about a situation to follow.

• **오늘 (noun)** : 지금 지나가고 있는 이날.
today
The day that is passing at the present time.

• 은 : 어떤 대상이 다른 것과 대조됨을 나타내는 조사.
eun (no equivalent expression)
A postpositional particle used to indicate that a certain subject contrasts with something else.

• **평소 (noun)** : 특별한 일이 없는 보통 때.
ordinary times
Ordinary times in which nothing special is happening.

• 보다 : 서로 차이가 있는 것을 비교할 때, 비교의 대상이 되는 것을 나타내는 조사.
boda (no equivalent expression)
A postpositional particle that indicates the subject of a comparison when comparing different things.

• **맛 (noun)** : 음식 등을 혀에 댈 때 느껴지는 감각.
taste
A sensation that is felt when touching one's tongue to food, etc.

• 이 : 어떤 상태나 상황의 대상이나 동작의 주체를 나타내는 조사.
i (no equivalent expression)
A postpositional particle referring to a subject under a certain state or situation, or the agent of an action.

• **없다 (adjective)** : 어떤 사실이나 현상이 현실로 존재하지 않는 상태이다.
lacking
(for a fact or phenomenon to be) Not existent in reality.

• -는 것 같다 : 추측을 나타내는 표현.
-neun geot gatda (no equivalent expression)
An expression used to indicate that the statement is a guess.

• -아요 : (두루높임으로) 어떤 사실을 서술하거나 질문, 명령, 권유함을 나타내는 종결 어미.
-ayo (no equivalent expression)
(informal addressee-raising) A sentence-final ending used to **describe** a certain fact, ask a question, give an order, or advise.

아니+에요.

맛있+어요.

잘 먹+을게요.

• **아니다 (adjective)** : 어떤 사실이나 내용을 부정하는 뜻을 나타내는 말.
not
Used to negate a fact or statement.

• -에요 : (두루높임으로) 어떤 사실을 서술하거나 질문함을 나타내는 종결 어미.
-eyo (no equivalent expression)
(informal addressee-raising) A sentence-final ending used when **describing** a certain fact or asking a question.

• **맛있다 (adjective)** : 맛이 좋다.
tasty; delicious
Tasting good.

• -어요 : (두루높임으로) 어떤 사실을 서술하거나 질문, 명령, 권유함을 나타내는 종결 어미.
-eoyo (no equivalent expression)
(informal addressee-raising) A sentence-final ending used to **describe** a certain fact, ask a question, give an order, or advise.

• **잘 (adverb)** : 충분히 만족스럽게.
well
In a sufficiently satisfactory manner.

• **먹다 (verb)** : 음식 등을 입을 통하여 배 속에 들여보내다.
eat; have; consume; take
To put food into one's mouth and take it in one's stomach.

• -을게요 : (두루높임으로) 말하는 사람이 어떤 행동을 할 것을 듣는 사람에게 약속하거나 의지를 나타내는 표현.
-eulgeyo (no equivalent expression)
(informal addressee-raising) An expression used used when the speaker promises or notifies the listener that he/she will do something.

< 대화(dialogue) > - 33

지아야, 여행 잘 다녀와. 전화하고.
지아야, 여행 잘 다녀와. 전화하고.
jiaya, yeohaeng jal danyeowa. jeonhwahago.

네, 호텔에 도착하는 대로 전화 드릴게요.
네, 호테레 도차카는 대로 전화 드릴께요.
ne, hotere dochakaneun daero jeonhwa deurilgeyo.

< 설명(explanation) / 번역(translation) >

지아+야, 여행 잘 다녀오+아.
다녀와

전화하+고.

• **지아 (noun)** : person's name

• 야 : 친구나 아랫사람, 동물 등을 부를 때 쓰는 조사.
ya (no equivalent expression)
A postpositional word used to address a friend, younger person, animal, etc.

• **여행 (noun)** : 집을 떠나 다른 지역이나 외국을 두루 구경하며 다니는 일.
travel; trip
The act of going away from home, and visiting other places or foreign countries and doing sightseeing.

• **잘 (adverb)** : 아무 탈 없이 편안하게.
well
Comfortably and without difficulties.

• **다녀오다 (verb)** : 어떤 일을 하기 위해 갔다가 오다.
come back; be back
To go somewhere to do something and come back.

• -아 : (두루낮춤으로) 어떤 사실을 서술하거나 물음, 명령, 권유를 나타내는 종결 어미.
-a (no equivalent expression)
(informal addressee-lowering) A sentence-final ending used to describe a certain fact, ask a question, **give an order**, or advise.

• **전화하다 (verb)** : 전화기를 통해 사람들끼리 말을 주고받다.
call; phone
To converse between people via telephone.

• -고 : (두루낮춤으로) 뒤에 올 또 다른 명령 표현을 생략한 듯한 느낌을 주면서 부드럽게 명령할 때 쓰는 종결 어미.
-go (no equivalent expression)
(informal addressee-lowering) A sentence-final ending used when ordering gently, as if giving a feeling of having omitted another ordering phrase that should follow.

네, 호텔+에 도착하+[는 대로] 전화 드리+ㄹ게요.
드릴게요

• **네 (interjection)** : 윗사람의 물음이나 명령 등에 긍정하여 대답할 때 쓰는 말.
yes; yes sir; yes ma'am
An exclamation uttered when the speaker affirmatively answers the call or order of his/her superior.

• **호텔 (noun)** : 시설이 잘 되어 있고 규모가 큰 고급 숙박업소.
hotel
A decent accommodation which is usually large-sized and well-equipped with facilities.

• 에 : 앞말이 목적지이거나 어떤 행위의 진행 방향임을 나타내는 조사.
to; at
A postpositional particle to indicate that the preceding statement refers to a destination or the course of a certain action.

• **도착하다 (verb)** : 목적지에 다다르다.
arrive; reach
To reach a destination.

• -는 대로 : 어떤 행동이나 상황이 나타나는 그때 바로, 또는 직후에 곧의 뜻을 나타내는 표현.
-neun daero (no equivalent expression)
An expression used to indicate someone does something upon or soon after the moment of a certain act or state.

• **전화 (noun)** : 전화기를 통해 사람들끼리 말을 주고받음. 또는 그렇게 하여 전달되는 내용.
call; phone call
The act of exchanging words between people via telephone, or such conversation.

• **드리다 (verb)** : 윗사람에게 어떤 말을 하거나 인사를 하다.
say; say hello
To say something or to greet an elder.

• -ㄹ게요 : (두루높임으로) 말하는 사람이 어떤 행동을 할 것을 듣는 사람에게 약속하거나 의지를 나타내는 표현.
-lgeyo (no equivalent expression)
(informal addressee-raising) An expression used when the speaker promises or notifies the listener that he/she will do something.

< 대화(dialogue) > - 34

우리 이번 주말에 영화 보기로 했지?
우리 이번 주마레 영화 보기로 핻찌?
uri ibeon jumare yeonghwa bogiro haetji?

응. 그런데 날씨가 좋으니까 영화를 보는 대신에 공원에 놀러 갈까?
응. 그런데 날씨가 조으니까 영화를 보는 대시네 공워네 놀러 갈까?
eung. geureonde nalssiga joeunikka yeonghwareul boneun daesine gongwone nolleo galkka?

< 설명(explanation) / 번역(translation) >

우리 이번 주말+에 영화 보+[기로 하]+였+지?
보기로 했지

• **우리 (pronoun)** : 말하는 사람이 자기와 듣는 사람 또는 이를 포함한 여러 사람들을 가리키는 말.
we
A pronoun used when the speaker refers to himself/herself and the listener or listeners, or a group of people including the speaker and listener or listeners.

• **이번 (noun)** : 곧 돌아올 차례. 또는 막 지나간 차례.
this time
A turn soon to come, or one that just passed.

• **주말 (noun)** : 한 주일의 끝.
weekend
The end of a week.

• 에 : 앞말이 시간이나 때임을 나타내는 조사.
in; at
A postpositional particle to indicate that the preceding statement refers to the time.

• **영화 (noun)** : 일정한 의미를 갖고 움직이는 대상을 촬영하여 영사기로 영사막에 비추어서 보게 하는 종합 예술.
film; movie
A composite art which captures moving objects on film with a certain message and then shows it on a screen by using a projector.

• **보다 (verb)** : 눈으로 대상을 즐기거나 감상하다.
watch; see; enjoy
To enjoy or appreciate an object with eyes.

• -기로 하다 : 앞의 말이 나타내는 행동을 할 것을 결심하거나 약속함을 나타내는 표현.
-giro hada (no equivalent expression)
An expression used to decide or promise the performance of the act mentioned in the preceding statement.

• -였- : 어떤 사건이 과거에 완료되었거나 그 사건의 결과가 현재까지 지속되는 상황을 나타내는 어미.
-yeot- (no equivalent expression)
An ending of a word used to indicate that an event was completed in the past or its result continues in the present.

• -지 : (두루낮춤으로) 이미 알고 있는 것을 다시 확인하듯이 물을 때 쓰는 종결 어미.
-ji (no equivalent expression)
(informal addressee-lowering) A sentence-final ending used to ask something that the speaker already knows to cross-check the information.

응.

그런데 날씨+가 좋+으니까 영화+를 보+[는 대신에] 공원+에 놀+러 가+ㄹ까?
갈까

• **응 (interjection)** : 상대방의 물음이나 명령 등에 긍정하여 대답할 때 쓰는 말.
yes; right
An exclamation uttered when the speaker gives an affirmative answer to someone's question, order, etc.

• **그런데 (adverb)** : 이야기를 앞의 내용과 관련시키면서 다른 방향으로 바꿀 때 쓰는 말.
by the way
A word used to change the direction of a story while relating it to the preceding statement.

• **날씨 (noun)** : 그날그날의 기온이나 공기 중에 비, 구름, 바람, 안개 등이 나타나는 상태.
weather
The daily temperature or the conditions of rain, clouds, wind, fog, etc., in the atmosphere.

• 가 : 어떤 상태나 상황에 놓인 대상이나 동작의 주체를 나타내는 조사.
ga (no equivalent expression)
A postpositional particle referring to a subject under a certain state or situation, or the subject of an act.

• **좋다 (adjective)** : 날씨가 맑고 화창하다.
nice
Sunny and clear.

• -으니까 : 뒤에 오는 말에 대하여 앞에 오는 말이 원인이나 근거, 전제가 됨을 강조하여 나타내는 연결 어미.
-eunikka (no equivalent expression)
A connective ending used to emphasize that the preceding statement is the cause, reason, or premise for the following statement.

• **영화 (noun)** : 일정한 의미를 갖고 움직이는 대상을 촬영하여 영사기로 영사막에 비추어서 보게 하는 종합 예술.
film; movie
A composite art which captures moving objects on film with a certain message and then shows it on a screen by using a projector.

• 를 : 동작이 직접적으로 영향을 미치는 대상을 나타내는 조사.
reul (no equivalent expression)
A postpositional particle used to indicate the subject that an act has a direct influence on.

• **보다 (verb)** : 눈으로 대상을 즐기거나 감상하다.
watch; see; enjoy
To enjoy or appreciate an object with eyes.

• -는 대신에 : 앞에 오는 말이 나타내는 행동이나 상태를 비슷하거나 맞먹는 다른 행동이나 상태로 바꾸는 것을 나타내는 표현.
-neun daesine (no equivalent expression)
An expression used to offer something similar to make up for a behavior or state mentioned in the preceding statement.

• **공원 (noun)** : 사람들이 놀고 쉴 수 있도록 풀밭, 나무, 꽃 등을 가꾸어 놓은 넓은 장소.
park
A large place with grass, trees and flowers where people can play and rest.

• 에 : 앞말이 목적지이거나 어떤 행위의 진행 방향임을 나타내는 조사.
to; at
A postpositional particle to indicate that the preceding statement refers to a destination or the course of a certain action.

• **놀다 (verb)** : 놀이 등을 하면서 재미있고 즐겁게 지내다.
play; have fun
To have a good time while playing.

- -러 : 가거나 오거나 하는 동작의 목적을 나타내는 연결 어미.
  -reo (no equivalent expression)
  A connective ending used to express the purpose of an action such as going and coming.

- **가다 (verb)** : 어떤 목적을 가지고 일정한 곳으로 움직이다.
  go
  To move to a certain place with a specific purpose.

- -ㄹ까 : (두루낮춤으로) 듣는 사람의 의사를 물을 때 쓰는 종결 어미.
  -lkka (no equivalent expression)
  (informal addressee-lowering) A sentence-final ending used to ask for the listener's opinion.

< 대화(dialogue) > - 35

열 시가 다 돼 가는데도 지우가 집에 안 들어오네요.
열 시가 다 돼 가는데도 지우가 지베 안 드러오네요.
yeol siga da dwae ganeundedo jiuga jibe an deureooneyo.

벌써 시간이 그렇게 됐네요. 제가 전화해 볼게요.
벌써 시가니 그러케 됀네요. 제가 전화해 볼께요.
beolsseo sigani geureoke dwaenneyo. jega jeonhwahae bolgeyo.

< 설명(explanation) / 번역(translation) >

열 시+가 다 되+[어 가]+는데도 지우+가 집+에 안 들어오+네요.
돼 가는데도

• **열 (determiner)** : 아홉에 하나를 더한 수의.
ten
Equal to 9 + 1.

• **시 (noun)** : 하루를 스물넷으로 나누었을 때 그 하나를 나타내는 시간의 단위.
o'clock
A bound noun indicating one of 24 hours of a day.

• 가 : 바뀌게 되는 대상이나 부정하는 대상임을 나타내는 조사.
ga (no equivalent expression)
A postpositional particle referring to the subject that is to be changed, or the subject that one denies.

• **다 (adverb)** : 행동이나 상태의 정도가 한정된 정도에 거의 가깝게.
almost
Nearly close to the limit in terms of the degree of behavior or state.

• **되다 (verb)** : 어떤 때나 시기, 상태에 이르다.
come; fall
To reach a certain timing or state.

• -어 가다 : 앞의 말이 나타내는 행동이나 상태가 계속 진행됨을 나타내는 표현.
-eo gada (no equivalent expression)
An expression used to indicate that the act or state mentioned in the preceding statement is continued.

• -는데도 : 앞에 오는 말이 나타내는 상황에 상관없이 뒤에 오는 말이 나타내는 상황이 일어남을 나타내는 표현.
-neundedo (no equivalent expression)
An expression used to indicate that the following situation will occur, regardless of the preceding situation.

• **지우 (noun)** : person's name

• 가 : 어떤 상태나 상황에 놓인 대상이나 동작의 주체를 나타내는 조사.
ga (no equivalent expression)
A postpositional particle referring to a subject under a certain state or situation, or the subject of an act.

• **집 (noun)** : 사람이나 동물이 추위나 더위 등을 막고 그 속에 들어 살기 위해 지은 건물.
house
A structure built by a human or animal to serve as protection from cold, heat, etc., and as a place to live in.

• 에 : 앞말이 목적지이거나 어떤 행위의 진행 방향임을 나타내는 조사.
to; at
A postpositional particle to indicate that the preceding statement refers to a destination or the course of a certain action.

• **안 (adverb)** : 부정이나 반대의 뜻을 나타내는 말.
not
An adverb that has the meaning of negation or opposite.

• **들어오다 (verb)** : 어떤 범위의 밖에서 안으로 이동하다.
come in; get in; enter
To move inside from outside within a certain range.

• -네요 : (두루높임으로) 말하는 사람이 직접 경험하여 새롭게 알게 된 사실에 대해 감탄함을 나타낼 때 쓰는 표현.
-neyo (no equivalent expression)
(informal addressee-raising) An expression used to indicate that the speaker is impressed by a fact he/she learned anew from a past personal experience.

벌써 시간+이 그렇+[게 되]+었+네요.

그렇게 됐네요

제+가 전화하+[여 보]+ㄹ게요.

전화해 볼게요

• **벌써 (adverb)** : 생각보다 빠르게.
so soon
More quickly than one thought.

• **시간 (noun)** : 어떤 일을 하도록 정해진 때. 또는 하루 중의 어느 한 때.
time
A time when one is supposed to do something, or a particular time of day.

• 이 : 어떤 상태나 상황의 대상이나 동작의 주체를 나타내는 조사.
i (no equivalent expression)
A postpositional particle referring to a subject under a certain state or situation, or the agent of an action.

• **그렇다 (adjective)** : 상태, 모양, 성질 등이 그와 같다.
so; as such; like that
A state, appearance, characteristic, etc. being as such.

• -게 되다 : 앞의 말이 나타내는 상태나 상황이 됨을 나타내는 표현.
-ge doeda (no equivalent expression)
An expression used to indicate that something will become the state or situation mentioned in the preceding statement.

• -었- : 어떤 사건이 과거에 완료되었거나 그 사건의 결과가 현재까지 지속되는 상황을 나타내는 어미.
-eot- (no equivalent expression)
An ending of a word used to indicate that an event was completed in the past or its result continues in the present.

• -네요 : (두루높임으로) 말하는 사람이 직접 경험하여 새롭게 알게 된 사실에 대해 감탄함을 나타낼 때 쓰는 표현.
-neyo (no equivalent expression)
(informal addressee-raising) An expression used to indicate that the speaker is impressed by a fact he/she learned anew from a past personal experience.

• **제 (pronoun)** : 말하는 사람이 자신을 낮추어 가리키는 말인 '저'에 조사 '가'가 붙을 때의 형태.
I
A form of '저' (I), the humble form used by the speaker to show humility, when the postpositional particle '가' is attached to it.

• 가 : 어떤 상태나 상황에 놓인 대상이나 동작의 주체를 나타내는 조사.
ga (no equivalent expression)
A postpositional particle referring to a subject under a certain state or situation, or the subject of an act.

• **전화하다 (verb)** : 전화기를 통해 사람들끼리 말을 주고받다.
call; phone
To converse between people via telephone.

• -여 보다 : 앞의 말이 나타내는 행동을 시험 삼아 함을 나타내는 표현.
-yeo boda (no equivalent expression)
An expression used to indicate that one does the act mentioned in the preceding statement, as a test.

• -ㄹ게요 : (두루높임으로) 말하는 사람이 어떤 행동을 할 것을 듣는 사람에게 약속하거나 의지를 나타내는 표현.
-lgeyo (no equivalent expression)
(informal addressee-raising) An expression used when the speaker promises or notifies the listener that he/she will do something.

< 대화(dialogue) > - 36

친구들이랑 여행 갈 건데 너도 갈래?
친구드리랑 여행 갈 건데 너도 갈래?
chingudeurirang yeohaeng gal geonde neodo gallae?

저도 가도 돼요? 어디로 가는데요? 혹시 제주도로 가요?
저도 가도 돼요? 어디로 가는데요? 혹씨 제주도로 가요?
jeodo gado dwaeyo? eodiro ganeundeyo? hoksi jejudoro gayo?

< 설명(explanation) / 번역(translation) >

친구+들+이랑 여행 가+[ㄹ 것(거)]+(이)+ㄴ데 너+도 가+ㄹ래?

갈 건데 **갈래**

• **친구 (noun)** : 사이가 가까워 서로 친하게 지내는 사람.
friend
A person that one is close to and in an amicable relationship with.

• 들 : '복수'의 뜻을 더하는 접미사.
-deul (no equivalent expression)
A suffix used to mean plural.

• 이랑 : 어떤 일을 함께 하는 대상임을 나타내는 조사.
irang (no equivalent expression)
A postpositional particle used to indicate the subject one is doing something with.

• **여행 (noun)** : 집을 떠나 다른 지역이나 외국을 두루 구경하며 다니는 일.
travel; trip
The act of going away from home, and visiting other places or foreign countries and doing sightseeing.

• **가다 (verb)** : 어떤 일을 하기 위해서 다른 곳으로 이동하다.
go; move
To move to another place to do a certain task.

• -ㄹ 것 : 명사가 아닌 것을 문장에서 명사처럼 쓰이게 하거나 '이다' 앞에 쓰일 수 있게 할 때 쓰는 표현.

-l geot (no equivalent expression)

An expression used to enable a non-noun word to be used as a noun in the sentence or to be used in front of '이다' (be).

• 이다 : 주어가 지시하는 대상의 속성이나 부류를 지정하는 뜻을 나타내는 서술격 조사.

ida (no equivalent expression)

A predicate particle indicating the meaning of the attribute or category of the thing that the subject of the sentence refers to.

• -ㄴ데 : 뒤의 말을 하기 위하여 그 대상과 관련이 있는 상황을 미리 말함을 나타내는 연결 어미.

-nde (no equivalent expression)

A connective ending used to talk in advance about a situation to follow.

• **너 (pronoun)** : 듣는 사람이 친구나 아랫사람일 때, 그 사람을 가리키는 말.

no equivalent expression

A pronoun used to indicate the listener when he/she is the same age or younger.

• 도 : 이미 있는 어떤 것에 다른 것을 더하거나 포함함을 나타내는 조사.

do (no equivalent expression)

A postpositional particle used to indicate an addition or inclusion of another thing to something that already exists.

• **가다 (verb)** : 어떤 일을 하기 위해서 다른 곳으로 이동하다.

go; move

To move to another place to do a certain task.

• -ㄹ래 : (두루낮춤으로) 앞으로 어떤 일을 하려고 하는 자신의 의사를 나타내거나 그 일에 대하여 듣는 사람의 의사를 물어봄을 나타내는 종결 어미.

-llae (no equivalent expression)

(informal addressee-lowering) A sentence-final ending used to indicate the speaker's intention to do something in the future, or to ask for the listener's thoughts about that.

저+도 가+[(아)도 되]+어요?

가도 돼요

어디+로 가+는데요?

혹시 제주도+로 가+(아)요?

가요

• **저 (pronoun)** : 말하는 사람이 듣는 사람에게 자신을 낮추어 가리키는 말.
I; me
The humble form used by the speaker to refer to himself/herself for the purpose of showing humility to the listener.

• 도 : 이미 있는 어떤 것에 다른 것을 더하거나 포함함을 나타내는 조사.
do (no equivalent expression)
A postpositional particle used to indicate an addition or inclusion of another thing to something that already exists.

• **가다 (verb)** : 어떤 일을 하기 위해서 다른 곳으로 이동하다.
go; move
To move to another place to do a certain task.

• -아도 되다 : 어떤 행동에 대한 허락이나 허용을 나타낼 때 쓰는 표현.
-ado deoda (no equivalent expression)
An expression used to indicate that a certain act is allowed or accepted.

• -어요 : (두루높임으로) 어떤 사실을 서술하거나 질문, 명령, 권유함을 나타내는 종결 어미.
-eoyo (no equivalent expression)
(informal addressee-raising) A sentence-final ending used to describe a certain fact, **ask a question**, give an order, or advise.

• **어디 (pronoun)** : 모르는 곳을 가리키는 말.
where
The word that means a place which one does not know.

• 로 : 움직임의 방향을 나타내는 조사.
ro (no equivalent expression)
A postpositional particle that indicates the direction of a movement.

• **가다 (verb)** : 어떤 일을 하기 위해서 다른 곳으로 이동하다.
go; move
To move to another place to do a certain task.

• -는데요 : (두루높임으로) 듣는 사람에게 어떤 대답을 요구할 때 쓰는 표현.
-neundeyo (no equivalent expression)
(informal addressee-raising) An expression used to demand an answer from the listener.

• **혹시 (adverb)** : 그러리라 생각하지만 분명하지 않아 말하기를 망설일 때 쓰는 말.
by any chance
The word that is used when one is hesitant to say something he/she thinks is possible but he/she is uncertain about.

• **제주도 (noun)** : 한국 서남해에 있는 화산섬. 한국에서 가장 큰 섬으로 화산 활동 지형의 특색이 잘 드러나 있어 관광 산업이 발달하였다. 해녀, 말, 귤이 유명하다.

Jejudo Island

A volcanic island off the southwestern coast of South Korea; as the country's largest island, it is home to a well-developed tourism industry that benefits from geographical features characteristic of volcanic activities; also well-known for woman divers, horses and tangerines.

• 로 : 움직임의 방향을 나타내는 조사.

ro (no equivalent expression)

A postpositional particle that indicates the direction of a movement.

• **가다 (verb)** : 어떤 일을 하기 위해서 다른 곳으로 이동하다.

go; move

To move to another place to do a certain task.

• -아요 : (두루높임으로) 어떤 사실을 서술하거나 질문, 명령, 권유함을 나타내는 종결 어미.

-ayo (no equivalent expression)

(informal addressee-raising) A sentence-final ending used to describe a certain fact, **ask a question**, give an order, or advise.

< 대화(dialogue) > - 37

요새 아르바이트하느라 힘들지 않니?
요새 아르바이트하느라 힘들지 안니?
yosae areubaiteuhaneura himdeulji anni?

네. 아르바이트를 하면 경험을 쌓는 동시에 돈도 벌 수 있어서 좋아요.
네. 아르바이트를 하면 경허믈 싼는 동시에 돈도 벌 쑤 이써서 조아요.
ne. areubaiteureul hamyeon gyeongheomeul ssanneun dongsie dondo beol su isseoseo joayo.

< 설명(explanation) / 번역(translation) >

요새 아르바이트하+느라 힘들+[지 않]+니?

• **요새 (noun)** : 얼마 전부터 이제까지의 매우 짧은 동안.
these days; nowadays; lately
An abbreviated word for these days, meaning an extremely short period from a while ago to the present.

• **아르바이트하다 (verb)** : 짧은 기간 동안 돈을 벌기 위해 자신의 본업 외에 임시로 하는 일을 하다.
do a part time job; have a side job; moonlight
To do a temporary job to make money or to make more money, besides one's main job or role.

• -느라 : 앞에 오는 말이 나타내는 행동이 뒤에 오는 말의 목적이나 원인이 됨을 나타내는 연결 어미.
-neura (no equivalent expression)
A connective ending used when the action of the preceding statement is the purpose or cause of the following statement.

• **힘들다 (adjective)** : 힘이 많이 쓰이는 면이 있다.
strenuous; laborious
Requiring much power or effort.

• -지 않다 : 앞의 말이 나타내는 행위나 상태를 부정하는 뜻을 나타내는 표현.
-ji anta (no equivalent expression)
An expression used to deny the act or state indicated in the preceding statement.

• -니 : (아주낮춤으로) 물음을 나타내는 종결 어미.
-ni (no equivalent expression)
(formal, highly addressee-lowering) A sentence-final ending referring to a question.

네.

아르바이트+를 하+면 경험+을 쌓+[는 동시에]

돈+도 벌(버)+[ㄹ 수 있]+어서 좋+아요.

벌 수 있어서

• **네 (interjection)** : 윗사람의 물음이나 명령 등에 긍정하여 대답할 때 쓰는 말.
yes; yes sir; yes ma'am
An exclamation uttered when the speaker affirmatively answers the call or order of his/her superior.

• **아르바이트 (noun)** : 돈을 벌기 위해 자신의 본업 외에 임시로 하는 일.
part-time job; side job; student job; moonlighting
A temporary job one has to make money or to make more money, besides one's main job or role.

• 를 : 동작이 직접적으로 영향을 미치는 대상을 나타내는 조사.
reul (no equivalent expression)
A postpositional particle used to indicate the subject that an act has a direct influence on.

• **하다 (verb)** : 어떤 행동이나 동작, 활동 등을 행하다.
do; perform
To perform a certain move, action, activity, etc.

• -면 : 뒤에 오는 말에 대한 근거나 조건이 됨을 나타내는 연결 어미.
-myeon (no equivalent expression)
A connective ending used when the preceding statement becomes the reason or condition of the following statement.

• **경험 (noun)** : 자신이 실제로 해 보거나 겪어 봄. 또는 거기서 얻은 지식이나 기능.
experience
Doing or going through something, or the knowledge or skills obtained in doing so.

• 을 : 동작이 직접적으로 영향을 미치는 대상을 나타내는 조사.
eul (no equivalent expression)
A postpositional particle used to indicate the subject that an action has a direct influence on.

• **쌓다** (verb) : 오랫동안 기술이나 경험, 지식 등을 많이 익히다.
accumulate; obtain
To acquire a lot of skills, experiences, knowledge, etc., over a long time.

• -는 동시에 : 앞에 오는 말과 뒤에 오는 말이 나타내는 행동이나 상태가 함께 일어남을 나타내는 표현.
-neun dongsie (no equivalent expression)
An expression used to indicate that a certain act or state mentioned in the preceding statement and following statement happens at the same time.

• **돈** (noun) : 물건을 사고팔 때나 일한 값으로 주고받는 동전이나 지폐.
money
A coin or bill that is exchanged when trading goods or labor.

• 도 : 이미 있는 어떤 것에 다른 것을 더하거나 포함함을 나타내는 조사.
do (no equivalent expression)
A postpositional particle used to indicate an addition or inclusion of another thing to something that already exists.

• **벌다** (verb) : 일을 하여 돈을 얻거나 모으다.
make; earn
To obtain or save money by doing some work.

• -ㄹ 수 있다 : 어떤 행동이나 상태가 가능함을 나타내는 표현.
-l su itda (no equivalent expression)
An expression used to indicate that an act or state is possible.

• -어서 : 이유나 근거를 나타내는 연결 어미.
-eoseo (no equivalent expression)
A connective ending used for a reason or cause.

• **좋다** (adjective) : 어떤 일이나 대상이 마음에 들고 만족스럽다.
fond of; in love with
Happy about and satisfied with a thing or object.

• -아요 : (두루높임으로) 어떤 사실을 서술하거나 질문, 명령, 권유함을 나타내는 종결 어미.
-ayo (no equivalent expression)
(informal addressee-raising) A sentence-final ending used to **describe** a certain fact, ask a question, give an order, or advise.

< 대화(dialogue) > - 38

저는 지금부터 청소를 할게요.
저는 지금부터 청소를 할께요.
jeoneun jigeumbuteo cheongsoreul halgeyo.

그럼, 시우 씨가 청소하는 동안 저는 장을 보러 다녀올게요.
그럼, 시우 씨가 청소하는 동안 저는 장을 보러 다녀올께요.
geureom, siu ssiga cheongsohaneun dongan jeoneun jangeul boreo danyeoolgeyo.

< 설명(explanation) / 번역(translation) >

저+는 지금+부터 청소+를 하+ㄹ게요.
할게요

• **저 (pronoun)** : 말하는 사람이 듣는 사람에게 자신을 낮추어 가리키는 말.
I; me
The humble form used by the speaker to refer to himself/herself for the purpose of showing humility to the listener.

• 는 : 문장 속에서 어떤 대상이 화제임을 나타내는 조사.
neun (no equivalent expression)
A postpositional particle used to indicate that a certain subject is the topic of a sentence.

• **지금 (noun)** : 말을 하고 있는 바로 이때.
now
The present moment as one speaks.

• 부터 : 어떤 일의 시작이나 처음을 나타내는 조사.
buteo (no equivalent expression)
A postpositional particle that indicates the start or beginning of something.

• **청소 (noun)** : 더럽고 지저분한 것을 깨끗하게 치움.
cleaning
An act of cleaning something dirty and messy.

• 를 : 동작이 직접적으로 영향을 미치는 대상을 나타내는 조사.
reul (no equivalent expression)
A postpositional particle used to indicate the subject that an act has a direct influence on.

• **하다 (verb)** : 어떤 행동이나 동작, 활동 등을 행하다.
do; perform
To perform a certain move, action, activity, etc.

• -ㄹ게요 : (두루높임으로) 말하는 사람이 어떤 행동을 할 것을 듣는 사람에게 약속하거나 의지를 나타내는 표현.
-lgeyo (no equivalent expression)
(informal addressee-raising) An expression used when the speaker promises or notifies the listener that he/she will do something.

그럼, 시우 씨+가 청소하+[는 동안] 저+는 장+을 보+러 다녀오+ㄹ게요.

다녀올게요

• **그럼 (adverb)** : 앞의 내용을 받아들이거나 그 내용을 바탕으로 하여 새로운 주장을 할 때 쓰는 말.
then
A word used when accepting the preceding statement or making a new suggestion based on it.

• **시우 (noun)** : person's name

• **씨 (noun)** : 그 사람을 높여 부르거나 이르는 말.
Mr.; Ms.; Mrs.
A bound noun used to address or call out to a certain person deferentially.

• 가 : 어떤 상태나 상황에 놓인 대상이나 동작의 주체를 나타내는 조사.
ga (no equivalent expression)
A postpositional particle referring to a subject under a certain state or situation, or the subject of an act.

• **청소하다 (verb)** : 더럽고 지저분한 것을 깨끗하게 치우다.
clean
To clean something dirty and messy.

• -는 동안 : 앞에 오는 말이 나타내는 행동이나 상태가 계속되는 시간 만큼을 나타내는 표현.
-neun dongan (no equivalent expression)
An expression used to indicate the time, for which the act or state mentioned in the preceding statement lasts.

• **저 (pronoun)** : 말하는 사람이 듣는 사람에게 자신을 낮추어 가리키는 말.
I; me
The humble form used by the speaker to refer to himself/herself for the purpose of showing humility to the listener.

- 는 : 문장 속에서 어떤 대상이 화제임을 나타내는 조사.
  neun (no equivalent expression)
  A postpositional particle used to indicate that a certain subject is the topic of a sentence.

- **장 (noun)** : 여러 가지 상품을 사고파는 곳.
  market
  A place where a variety of products are sold and bought.

- 을 : 동작이 직접적으로 영향을 미치는 대상을 나타내는 조사.
  eul (no equivalent expression)
  A postpositional particle used to indicate the subject that an action has a direct influence on.

- **보다 (verb)** : 시장에 가서 물건을 사다.
  purchase; buy; get
  To purchase something at a market.

- -러 : 가거나 오거나 하는 동작의 목적을 나타내는 연결 어미.
  -reo (no equivalent expression)
  A connective ending used to express the purpose of an action such as going and coming.

- **다녀오다 (verb)** : 어떤 일을 하기 위해 갔다가 오다.
  come back; be back
  To go somewhere to do something and come back.

- -ㄹ게요 : (두루높임으로) 말하는 사람이 어떤 행동을 할 것을 듣는 사람에게 약속하거나 의지를 나타내는 표현.
  -lgeyo (no equivalent expression)
  (informal addressee-raising) An expression used when the speaker promises or notifies the listener that he/she will do something.

< 대화(dialogue) > - 39

지우는 어디 갔어? 아까부터 안 보이네.
지우는 어디 가써? 아까부터 안 보이네.
jiuneun eodi gasseo? akkabuteo an boine.

글쎄, 급한 일이 있는 듯 뛰어가더라.
글쎄, 그판 이리 인는 듣 뛰어가더라.
geulsse, geupan iri inneun deut ttwieogadeora.

< 설명(explanation) / 번역(translation) >

지우+는 어디 가+았+어?
갔어

아까+부터 안 보이+네.

• **지우 (noun)** : person's name

• 는 : 문장 속에서 어떤 대상이 화제임을 나타내는 조사.
neun (no equivalent expression)
A postpositional particle used to indicate that a certain subject is the topic of a sentence.

• **어디 (pronoun)** : 모르는 곳을 가리키는 말.
where
The word that means a place which one does not know.

• **가다 (verb)** : 한 곳에서 다른 곳으로 장소를 이동하다.
go; travel
To move from one place to another place.

• -았- : 어떤 사건이 과거에 완료되었거나 그 사건의 결과가 현재까지 지속되는 상황을 나타내는 어미.
-at- (no equivalent expression)
An ending of a word used to indicate that an event was completed in the past or its result continues in the present.

• -어 : (두루낮춤으로) 어떤 사실을 서술하거나 물음, 명령, 권유를 나타내는 종결 어미.
-eo (no equivalent expression)
(informal addressee-lowering) A sentence-final ending used to describe a certain fact, **ask a question**, give an order, or advise.

• **아까 (noun)** : 조금 전.
a moment ago
A little while ago.

• 부터 : 어떤 일의 시작이나 처음을 나타내는 조사.
buteo (no equivalent expression)
A postpositional particle that indicates the start or beginning of something.

• **안 (adverb)** : 부정이나 반대의 뜻을 나타내는 말.
not
An adverb that has the meaning of negation or opposite.

• **보이다 (verb)** : 눈으로 대상의 존재나 겉모습을 알게 되다.
be viewed; be visible; be in sight
To come to know the presence or outward appearance of an object by looking at it.

• -네 : (아주낮춤으로) 지금 깨달은 일에 대하여 말함을 나타내는 종결 어미.
-ne (no equivalent expression)
(formal, highly addressee-lowering) A sentence-final ending used when talking about something that one just learned.

글쎄, 급하+ㄴ 일+이 있+[는 듯] 뛰어가+더라.
급한

• **글쎄 (interjection)** : 상대방의 물음이나 요구에 대하여 분명하지 않은 태도를 나타낼 때 쓰는 말.
well; hm
An exclamation used when showing an uncertain attitude toward someone's question or demand.

• **급하다 (adjective)** : 사정이나 형편이 빨리 처리해야 할 상태에 있다.
urgent
Having to do something quickly.

• -ㄴ : 앞의 말이 관형어의 기능을 하게 만들고 현재의 상태를 나타내는 어미.
-n (no equivalent expression)
An ending of a word that makes the preceding statement function as an adnominal phrase and refers to the present state.

• **일 (noun)** : 어떤 내용을 가진 상황이나 사실.
matter; affair
A certain situation or fact.

• 이 : 어떤 상태나 상황의 대상이나 동작의 주체를 나타내는 조사.
i (no equivalent expression)
A postpositional particle referring to a subject under a certain state or situation, or the agent of an action.

• **있다 (adjective)** : 어떤 일이 이루어지거나 벌어질 계획이다.
no equivalent expression
Something being planned to be realized or happen.

• -는 듯 : 뒤에 오는 말의 내용과 관련하여 짐작할 수 있거나 비슷하다고 여겨지는 상태나 상황을 나타낼 때 쓰는 표현.
-neun deut (no equivalent expression)
An expression used to guess that something said might be similar to the preceding state or situation.

• **뛰어가다 (verb)** : 어떤 곳으로 빨리 뛰어서 가다.
run; go running
To run and go to a certain place very fast.

• -더라 : (아주낮춤으로) 말하는 이가 직접 경험하여 새롭게 알게 된 사실을 지금 전달함을 나타내는 종결 어미.
-deora (no equivalent expression)
(formal, highly addressee-lowering) A sentence-final ending used to convey in the present a fact the speaker realized anew from the speaker's personal experience.

< 대화(dialogue) > - 40

지아 씨, 어디서 타는 듯한 냄새가 나요.
지아 씨, 어디서 타는 드탄 냄새가 나요.
jia ssi, eodiseo taneun deutan naemsaega nayo.

어머, 냄비를 불에 올려놓고 깜빡 잊어버렸네요.
어머, 냄비를 부레 올려노코 깜빡 이저버련네요.
eomeo, naembireul bure ollyeonoko kkamppak ijeobeoryeonneyo.

< 설명(explanation) / 번역(translation) >

지아 씨, 어디+서 타+[는 듯하]+ㄴ 냄새+가 나+(아)요.
타는 듯한 나요

• **지아 (noun)** : person's name

• **씨 (noun)** : 그 사람을 높여 부르거나 이르는 말.
Mr.; Ms.; Mrs.
A bound noun used to address or call out to a certain person deferentially.

• **어디 (pronoun)** : 정해져 있지 않거나 정확하게 말할 수 없는 어느 곳을 가리키는 말.
anywhere
The word that means a place which is not definite or impossible to specify.

• 서 : 앞말이 출발점의 뜻을 나타내는 조사.
seo (no equivalent expression)
A postpositional particle used to indicate that the preceding word refers to the starting point of something.

• **타다 (verb)** : 뜨거운 열을 받아 검은색으로 변할 정도로 지나치게 익다.
be overcooked
For food to be overcooked until it becomes blackish.

• -는 듯하다 : 앞에 오는 말의 내용을 추측함을 나타내는 표현.
-neun deutada (no equivalent expression)
An expression used to guess the content of the preceding statement.

• -ㄴ : 앞의 말이 관형어의 기능을 하게 만들고 현재의 상태를 나타내는 어미.
-n (no equivalent expression)
An ending of a word that makes the preceding statement function as an adnominal phrase and refers to the present state.

• **냄새 (noun)** : 코로 맡을 수 있는 기운.
smell; scent; odor
The trait of something the nose can sense.

• 가 : 어떤 상태나 상황에 놓인 대상이나 동작의 주체를 나타내는 조사.
ga (no equivalent expression)
A postpositional particle referring to a subject under a certain state or situation, or the subject of an act.

• **나다 (verb)** : 알아차릴 정도로 소리나 냄새 등이 드러나다.
be heard; smell
For a sound, smell, etc., to be revealed enough to be recognized.

• -아요 : (두루높임으로) 어떤 사실을 서술하거나 질문, 명령, 권유함을 나타내는 종결 어미.
-ayo (no equivalent expression)
(informal addressee-raising) A sentence-final ending used to **describe** a certain fact, ask a question, give an order, or advise.

어머, 냄비+를 불+에 올려놓+고 깜빡 잊어버리+었+네요.

잊어버렸네요

• **어머 (interjection)** : 주로 여자들이 예상하지 못한 일로 갑자기 놀라거나 감탄할 때 내는 소리.
oh my goodness; why
An exclamation used when mainly women are suddenly surprised at or admire an unexpected matter.

• **냄비 (noun)** : 음식을 끓이는 데 쓰는, 솥보다 작고 뚜껑과 손잡이가 있는 그릇.
sauce pan
A container, smaller than a caldron, which has a lid and two handles and is used in the kitchen to cook food.

• 를 : 동작이 직접적으로 영향을 미치는 대상을 나타내는 조사.
reul (no equivalent expression)
A postpositional particle used to indicate the subject that an act has a direct influence on.

• **불 (noun)** : 물질이 빛과 열을 내며 타는 것.
fire
The act of a substance burning while emitting light and heat.

• 에 : 앞말이 어떤 행위나 작용이 미치는 대상임을 나타내는 조사.
on; in; to
A postpositional particle to indicate that the preceding statement is the subject to which a certain action or operation is applied.

• **올려놓다 (verb)** : 어떤 물건을 무엇의 위쪽에 옮겨다 두다.
put something on
To place something on something.

• -고 : 앞의 말이 나타내는 행동이나 그 결과가 뒤에 오는 행동이 일어나는 동안에 그대로 지속됨을 나타내는 연결 어미.
-go (no equivalent expression)
A connective ending used when an action or result of the preceding statement remains the same while the following action happens.

• **깜빡 (adverb)** : 기억이나 의식 등이 잠깐 흐려지는 모양.
forgetfully
In a manner of one's memory or conciousness being dim or lost.

• **잊어버리다 (verb)** : 기억해야 할 것을 한순간 전혀 생각해 내지 못하다.
forget
To momentarily fail to recall something that one should remember.

• -었- : 어떤 사건이 과거에 완료되었거나 그 사건의 결과가 현재까지 지속되는 상황을 나타내는 어미.
-eot- (no equivalent expression)
An ending of a word used to indicate that an event was completed in the past or its result continues in the present.

• -네요 : (두루높임으로) 말하는 사람이 직접 경험하여 새롭게 알게 된 사실에 대해 감탄함을 나타낼 때 쓰는 표현.
-neyo (no equivalent expression)
(informal addressee-raising) An expression used to indicate that the speaker is impressed by a fact he/she learned anew from a past personal experience.

< 대화(dialogue) > - 41

너 왜 저녁을 다 안 먹고 남겼니?
너 왜 저녀글 다 안 먹꼬 남견니?
neo wae jeonyeogeul da an meokgo namgyeonni?

저는 먹는 만큼 살이 쪄서 식사량을 줄여야겠어요.
저는 멍는 만큼 사리 쪄서 식싸량을 주려야게써요.
jeoneun meongneun mankeum sari jjeoseo siksaryangeul juryeoyagesseoyo.

< 설명(explanation) / 번역(translation) >

너 왜 저녁+을 다 안 먹+고 남기+었+니?
남겼니

• **너 (pronoun)** : 듣는 사람이 친구나 아랫사람일 때, 그 사람을 가리키는 말.
no equivalent expression
A pronoun used to indicate the listener when he/she is the same age or younger.

• **왜 (adverb)** : 무슨 이유로. 또는 어째서.
why
For what reason; how come.

• **저녁 (noun)** : 저녁에 먹는 밥.
dinner
A meal eaten in the evening.

• 을 : 동작이 직접적으로 영향을 미치는 대상을 나타내는 조사.
eul (no equivalent expression)
A postpositional particle used to indicate the subject that an action has a direct influence on.

• **다 (adverb)** : 남거나 빠진 것이 없이 모두.
all; everything
With nothing left over or missing.

• **안 (adverb)** : 부정이나 반대의 뜻을 나타내는 말.
not
An adverb that has the meaning of negation or opposite.

• **먹다 (verb)** : 음식 등을 입을 통하여 배 속에 들여보내다.
eat; have; consume; take
To put food into one's mouth and take it in one's stomach.

• -고 : 앞의 말과 뒤의 말이 차례대로 일어남을 나타내는 연결 어미.
-go (no equivalent expression)
A connective ending used when the preceding statement and the following statement happen in order.

• **남기다 (verb)** : 다 쓰지 않고 나머지가 있게 하다.
leave
To leave part of something without using it up.

• -었- : 어떤 사건이 과거에 완료되었거나 그 사건의 결과가 현재까지 지속되는 상황을 나타내는 어미.
-eot- (no equivalent expression)
An ending of a word used to indicate that an event was completed in the past or its result continues in the present.

• -니 : (아주낮춤으로) 물음을 나타내는 종결 어미.
-ni (no equivalent expression)
(formal, highly addressee-lowering) A sentence-final ending referring to a question.

저+는 먹+[는 만큼] 살+이 찌+어서 식사량+을 줄이+어야겠+어요.

쪄서 **줄여야겠어요**

• **저 (pronoun)** : 말하는 사람이 듣는 사람에게 자신을 낮추어 가리키는 말.
I; me
The humble form used by the speaker to refer to himself/herself for the purpose of showing humility to the listener.

• 는 : 문장 속에서 어떤 대상이 화제임을 나타내는 조사.
neun (no equivalent expression)
A postpositional particle used to indicate that a certain subject is the topic of a sentence.

• **먹다 (verb)** : 음식 등을 입을 통하여 배 속에 들여보내다.
eat; have; consume; take
To put food into one's mouth and take it in one's stomach.

• -는 만큼 : 뒤에 오는 말이 앞에 오는 말과 비례하거나 비슷한 정도 혹은 수량임을 나타내는 표현.
-neun mankeum (no equivalent expression)
An expression used to indicate that the following content is proportional to the preceding content or of a similar level or quantity.

• **살 (noun)** : 사람이나 동물의 몸에서 뼈를 둘러싸고 있는 부드러운 부분.
flesh; weight
The tender part of the human or animal body that covers the bones.

• 이 : 어떤 상태나 상황의 대상이나 동작의 주체를 나타내는 조사.
i (no equivalent expression)
A postpositional particle referring to a subject under a certain state or situation, or the agent of an action.

• **찌다 (verb)** : 몸에 살이 붙어 뚱뚱해지다.
gain weight
To put more flesh on one's body and become fat.

• -어서 : 이유나 근거를 나타내는 연결 어미.
-eoseo (no equivalent expression)
A connective ending used for a reason or cause.

• **식사량 (noun)** : 음식을 먹는 양.
portion of food
The amount of food one eats.

• 을 : 동작이 직접적으로 영향을 미치는 대상을 나타내는 조사.
eul (no equivalent expression)
A postpositional particle used to indicate the subject that an action has a direct influence on.

• **줄이다 (verb)** : 수나 양을 원래보다 적게 하다.
cut; cut down on; reduce
To make a number or quantity smaller than original.

• -어야겠- : 앞의 말이 나타내는 행동에 대한 강한 의지를 나타내거나 그 행동을 할 필요가 있음을 완곡하게 말할 때 쓰는 표현.
-eoyaget- (no equivalent expression)
An expression used to indicate a strong will for the act mentioned in the preceding statement, or to guess that doing the act may be necessary.

• -어요 : (두루높임으로) 어떤 사실을 서술하거나 질문, 명령, 권유함을 나타내는 종결 어미.
-eoyo (no equivalent expression)
(informal addressee-raising) A sentence-final ending used to **describe** a certain fact, ask a question, give an order, or advise.

< 대화(dialogue) > - 42

이 늦은 시간에 라면을 먹어?
이 느즌 시가네 라며늘 머거?
i neujeun sigane ramyeoneul meogeo?

야근하느라 저녁도 못 먹는 바람에 배고파 죽겠어.
야근하느라 저녁또 몯 멍는 바라메 배고파 주께써.
yageunhaneura jeonyeokdo mot meongneun barame baegopa jukgesseo.

< 설명(explanation) / 번역(translation) >

이 늦+은 시간+에 라면+을 먹+어?

• 이 (determiner) : 말하는 사람에게 가까이 있거나 말하는 사람이 생각하고 있는 대상을 가리킬 때 쓰는 말.
this
The word that is used to refer to a person who is close to the speaker or something that the speaker is thinking of.

• 늦다 (adjective) : 적당한 때를 지나 있다. 또는 시기가 한창인 때를 지나 있다.
late; later
Being past the right time, or being past the peak of something.

• -은 : 앞의 말이 관형어의 기능을 하게 만들고 현재의 상태를 나타내는 어미.
-eun (no equivalent expression)
An ending of a word that makes the preceding word function as an adnominal phrase and refers to the present state.

• 시간 (noun) : 어떤 일을 하도록 정해진 때. 또는 하루 중의 어느 한 때.
time
A time when one is supposed to do something, or a particular time of day.

• 에 : 앞말이 시간이나 때임을 나타내는 조사.
in; at
A postpositional particle to indicate that the preceding statement refers to the time.

• **라면 (noun)** : 기름에 튀겨 말린 국수와 가루 스프가 들어 있어서 물에 끓이기만 하면 간편하게 먹을 수 있는 음식.

ramen; instant noodles

An easy-to-cook instant noodle dish made by just boiling previously-fried dry noodles and adding powdered soup to them.

• 을 : 동작이 직접적으로 영향을 미치는 대상을 나타내는 조사.

eul (no equivalent expression)

A postpositional particle used to indicate the subject that an action has a direct influence on.

• **먹다 (verb)** : 음식 등을 입을 통하여 배 속에 들여보내다.

eat; have; consume; take

To put food into one's mouth and take it in one's stomach.

• -어 : (두루낮춤으로) 어떤 사실을 서술하거나 물음, 명령, 권유를 나타내는 종결 어미.

-eo (no equivalent expression)

(informal addressee-lowering) A sentence-final ending used to describe a certain fact, **ask a question**, give an order, or advise.

야근하+느라고 저녁+도 못 먹+[는 바람에] 배고프(배고ㅍ)+[아 죽]+겠+어.

배고파 죽겠어

• **야근하다 (verb)** : 퇴근 시간이 지나 밤늦게까지 일하다.

work overtime

To work overtime till late at night.

• -느라고 : 앞에 오는 말이 나타내는 행동이 뒤에 오는 말의 목적이나 원인이 됨을 나타내는 연결 어미.

-neurago (no equivalent expression)

A connective ending used when the action of the preceding statement is the purpose or cause of the following statement.

• **저녁 (noun)** : 저녁에 먹는 밥.

dinner

A meal eaten in the evening.

• 도 : 극단적인 경우를 들어 다른 경우는 말할 것도 없음을 나타내는 조사.

do (no equivalent expression)

A postpositional particle used when giving an extreme case in order to show that it is obvious in another case.

• **못 (adverb)** : 동사가 나타내는 동작을 할 수 없게.
not
The word that negates the action represented by the verb.

• **먹다 (verb)** : 음식 등을 입을 통하여 배 속에 들여보내다.
eat; have; consume; take
To put food into one's mouth and take it in one's stomach.

• -는 바람에 : 앞의 말이 나타내는 행동이나 상태가 뒤에 오는 말의 원인이나 이유가 됨을 나타내는 표현.
-neun barame (no equivalent expression)
An expression used to indicate that an act or state mentioned in the preceding statement is the cause or reason for the following statement.

• **배고프다 (adjective)** : 배 속이 빈 것을 느껴 음식이 먹고 싶다.
hungry
Feeling that one's stomach is empty and wanting to eat food.

• -아 죽다 : 앞의 말이 나타내는 상태의 정도가 매우 심함을 나타내는 표현.
-a jukda (no equivalent expression)
An expression used to indicate that the state mentioned in the preceding statement is very severe.

• -겠- : 미래의 일이나 추측을 나타내는 어미.
-get- (no equivalent expression)
An ending of a word referring to a future event or assumption.

• -어 : (두루낮춤으로) 어떤 사실을 서술하거나 물음, 명령, 권유를 나타내는 종결 어미.
-eo (no equivalent expression)
(informal addressee-lowering) A sentence-final ending used to **describe** a certain fact, ask a question, give an order, or advise.

< 대화(dialogue) > - 43

겨울이 가면 봄이 오는 법이야. 힘들다고 포기하면 안 돼.
겨우리 가면 보미 오는 버비야. 힘들다고 포기하면 안 돼.
gyeouri gamyeon bomi oneun beobiya. himdeuldago pogihamyeon an dwae.

고마워. 네 말에 다시 힘이 나는 것 같아.
고마워. 네 마레 다시 히미 나는 걷 가타.
gomawo. ne mare dasi himi naneun geot gata.

< 설명(explanation) / 번역(translation) >

겨울+이 가+면 봄+이 오+[는 법이]+야.

힘들+다고 포기하+[면 안 되]+어.

포기하면 안 돼

• **겨울 (noun)** : 네 계절 중의 하나로 가을과 봄 사이의 추운 계절.
winter
One of four seasons which is the coldest, and comes between fall and spring.

• 이 : 어떤 상태나 상황의 대상이나 동작의 주체를 나타내는 조사.
i (no equivalent expression)
A postpositional particle referring to a subject under a certain state or situation, or the agent of an action.

• **가다 (verb)** : 시간이 지나거나 흐르다.
pass; flow
For time to pass or flow.

• -면 : 뒤에 오는 말에 대한 근거나 조건이 됨을 나타내는 연결 어미.
-myeon (no equivalent expression)
A connective ending used when the preceding statement becomes the reason or condition of the following statement.

• **봄 (noun)** : 네 계절 중의 하나로 겨울과 여름 사이의 계절.
spring
The season between winter and summer.

• 이 : 어떤 상태나 상황의 대상이나 동작의 주체를 나타내는 조사.
i (no equivalent expression)
A postpositional particle referring to a subject under a certain state or situation, or the agent of an action.

• **오다 (verb)** : 어떤 때나 계절 등이 닥치다.
come; arrive
For a time, season, etc., to come.

• -는 법이다 : 앞의 말이 나타내는 동작이나 상태가 이미 그렇게 정해져 있거나 그런 것이 당연하다는 뜻을 나타내는 표현.
-neun beobida (no equivalent expression)
An expression used to indicate that the act or state mentioned in the preceding statement has been decided already or is reasonable.

• -야 : (두루낮춤으로) 어떤 사실에 대하여 서술하거나 물음을 나타내는 종결 어미.
-ya (no equivalent expression)
(informal addressee-lowering) A sentence-final ending used to **describe** a certain fact or ask a question.

• **힘들다 (adjective)** : 마음이 쓰이거나 수고가 되는 면이 있다.
hard; difficult
Requiring much attention and effort.

• -다고 : 어떤 행위의 목적, 의도를 나타내거나 어떤 상황의 이유, 원인을 나타내는 연결 어미.
-dago (no equivalent expression)
A connective ending referring to the purpose or intention of a certain action, or the reason or cause of a certain situation.

• **포기하다 (verb)** : 하려던 일이나 생각을 중간에 그만두다.
give up
To stop doing something one intended to do or a thought.

• -면 안 되다 : 어떤 행동이나 상태를 금지하거나 제한함을 나타내는 표현.
-myeon an doeda (no equivalent expression)
An expression used to indicate that a certain act or state is banned or limited.

• -어 : (두루낮춤으로) 어떤 사실을 서술하거나 물음, 명령, 권유를 나타내는 종결 어미.
-eo (no equivalent expression)
(informal addressee-lowering) A sentence-final ending used to describe a certain fact, ask a question, **give an order**, or advise.

고맙(고마우)+어.
고마워

너+의 말+에 다시 힘+이 나+[는 것 같]+아.
네

- **고맙다 (adjective)** : 남이 자신을 위해 무엇을 해주어서 마음이 흐뭇하고 보답하고 싶다.
  thankful; grateful
  Pleased and wanting to return a favor to someone.

- -어 : (두루낮춤으로) 어떤 사실을 서술하거나 물음, 명령, 권유를 나타내는 종결 어미.
  -eo (no equivalent expression)
  (informal addressee-lowering) A sentence-final ending used to **describe** a certain fact, ask a question, give an order, or advise.

- **너 (pronoun)** : 듣는 사람이 친구나 아랫사람일 때, 그 사람을 가리키는 말.
  no equivalent expression
  A pronoun used to indicate the listener when he/she is the same age or younger.

- 의 : 앞의 말이 뒤의 말에 대하여 소유, 소속, 소재, 관계, 기원, 주체의 관계를 가짐을 나타내는 조사.
  ui (no equivalent expression)
  A postpositional particle used to indicate that the referent of the following word is owned by, belongs to, is related to, originates from, or is the object of what the preceding word indicates.

- **말 (noun)** : 생각이나 느낌을 표현하고 전달하는 사람의 소리.
  speech; words
  Human voice through which thoughts or feelings are expressed and conveyed.

- 에 : 앞말이 어떤 일의 원인임을 나타내는 조사.
  for; due to; because of
  A postpositional particle to indicate that the preceding statement is the cause for something.

- **다시 (adverb)** : 방법이나 목표 등을 바꿔서 새로이.
  again
  To do or begin once more by changing the method, goal, etc.

- **힘 (noun)** : 용기나 자신감.
  courage; confidence; strength
  Courage or confidence.

• 이 : 어떤 상태나 상황의 대상이나 동작의 주체를 나타내는 조사.
i (no equivalent expression)
A postpositional particle referring to a subject under a certain state or situation, or the agent of an action.

• **나다 (verb)** : 어떤 감정이나 느낌이 생기다.
feel
To feel a certain emotion or sensation.

• -는 것 같다 : 추측을 나타내는 표현.
-neun geot gatda (no equivalent expression)
An expression used to indicate that the statement is a guess.

• -아 : (두루낮춤으로) 어떤 사실을 서술하거나 물음, 명령, 권유를 나타내는 종결 어미.
-a (no equivalent expression)
(informal addressee-lowering) A sentence-final ending used to **describe** a certain fact, ask a question, give an order, or advise.

< 대화(dialogue) > - 44

쟤는 도대체 여기 언제 온 거야?
쟤는 도대체 여기 언제 온 거야?
jyaeneun dodaeche yeogi eonje on geoya?

아까 네가 잠깐 조는 사이에 왔을걸.
아까 네가 잠깐 조는 사이에 와쓸껄.
akka nega jamkkan joneun saie wasseulgeol.

< 설명(explanation) / 번역(translation) >

쟤+는 도대체 여기 언제 오+[ㄴ 것(거)]+(이)+야?
온 거야

• **쟤 (short form)** : '저 아이'가 줄어든 말.
jyae (no equivalent expression)
An abbreviated word for '저(that) 아이(third party)'.

• 는 : 문장 속에서 어떤 대상이 화제임을 나타내는 조사.
neun (no equivalent expression)
A postpositional particle used to indicate that a certain subject is the topic of a sentence.

• **도대체 (adverb)** : 아주 궁금해서 묻는 말인데.
what on earth; how on earth; why on earth
Asking just out of curiosity.

• **여기 (pronoun)** : 말하는 사람에게 가까운 곳을 가리키는 말.
here; this
A pronoun used to indicate a place close to the speaker.

• **언제 (adverb)** : 알지 못하는 어느 때에.
when; at what time
At some time one does not know.

• **오다 (verb)** : 무엇이 다른 곳에서 이곳으로 움직이다.
come
For something to move from another place to here.

• -ㄴ 것 : 명사가 아닌 것을 문장에서 명사처럼 쓰이게 하거나 '이다' 앞에 쓰일 수 있게 할 때 쓰는 표현.
-n geot (no equivalent expression)
An expression used to enable a non-noun word to be used as a noun in a sentence or to be used in front of '이다' (be).

• 이다 : 주어가 지시하는 대상의 속성이나 부류를 지정하는 뜻을 나타내는 서술격 조사.
ida (no equivalent expression)
A predicate particle indicating the meaning of the attribute or category of the thing that the subject of the sentence refers to.

• -야 : (두루낮춤으로) 어떤 사실에 대하여 서술하거나 물음을 나타내는 종결 어미.
-ya (no equivalent expression)
(informal addressee-lowering) A sentence-final ending used to describe a certain fact or **ask a question.**

아까 네+가 잠깐 졸(조)+[는 사이]+에 오+았+을걸.
조는 사이에 왔을걸

• **아까 (adverb)** : 조금 전에.
a little while ago; a moment ago
A minute ago.

• **네 (pronoun)** : '너'에 조사 '가'가 붙을 때의 형태.
you
A form of '너' (you), when the postpositional particle '가' is attached to it.

• 가 : 어떤 상태나 상황에 놓인 대상이나 동작의 주체를 나타내는 조사.
ga (no equivalent expression)
A postpositional particle referring to a subject under a certain state or situation, or the subject of an act.

• **잠깐 (adverb)** : 아주 짧은 시간 동안에.
for a moment; for an instant; for a while
For a very short time.

• **졸다 (verb)** : 완전히 잠이 들지는 않으면서 자꾸 잠이 들려는 상태가 되다.
nod; doze off
To enter a state where one has not fallen asleep but gets close to falling asleep repeatedly.

• -는 사이 : 어떤 행동이나 상황이 일어나는 중간의 어느 짧은 시간을 나타내는 표현.
-neun sai (no equivalent expression)
An expression used to indicate a certain, short time in the middle of an act or situation.

• 에 : 앞말이 시간이나 때임을 나타내는 조사.
in; at
A postpositional particle to indicate that the preceding statement refers to the time.

• **오다 (verb)** : 무엇이 다른 곳에서 이곳으로 움직이다.
come
For something to move from another place to here.

• -았- : 어떤 사건이 과거에 완료되었거나 그 사건의 결과가 현재까지 지속되는 상황을 나타내는 어미.
-at- (no equivalent expression)
An ending of a word used to indicate that an event was completed in the past or its result continues in the present.

• -을걸 : (두루낮춤으로) 미루어 짐작하거나 추측함을 나타내는 종결 어미.
-eulgeol (no equivalent expression)
(informal addressee-lowering) A sentence-final ending used to indicate a guess or assumption.

< 대화(dialogue) > - 45

오빠, 저 내일 친구들이랑 스키 타러 갈 거예요.
오빠, 저 내일 친구드리랑 스키 타러 갈 꺼예요.
oppa, jeo naeil chingudeurirang seuki tareo gal geoyeyo.

그래? 자칫하면 다칠 수 있으니까 조심해라.
그래? 자치타면 다칠 쑤 이쓰니까 조심해라.
geurae? jachitamyeon dachil su isseunikka josimhaera.

< 설명(explanation) / 번역(translation) >

오빠, 저 내일 친구+들+이랑 스키 타+러 가+[ㄹ 것(거)]+이+에요.
갈 거예요

- **오빠 (noun)** : 여자가 자기보다 나이 많은 남자를 다정하게 이르거나 부르는 말.
  elder brother
  A word used only by a girl to refer to or address endearingly another male who is older than she.

- **저 (pronoun)** : 말하는 사람이 듣는 사람에게 자신을 낮추어 가리키는 말.
  I; me
  The humble form used by the speaker to refer to himself/herself for the purpose of showing humility to the listener.

- **내일 (adverb)** : 오늘의 다음 날에.
  tomorrow
  On the day after today.

- **친구 (noun)** : 사이가 가까워 서로 친하게 지내는 사람.
  friend
  A person that one is close to and in an amicable relationship with.

- 들 : '복수'의 뜻을 더하는 접미사.
  -deul (no equivalent expression)
  A suffix used to mean plural.

• 이랑 : 어떤 일을 함께 하는 대상임을 나타내는 조사.
irang (no equivalent expression)
A postpositional particle used to indicate the subject one is doing something with.

• **스키 (noun)** : 눈 위로 미끄러져 가도록 나무나 플라스틱으로 만든 좁고 긴 기구.
ski
A long, narrow apparatus made of wood or plastic, allowing a rider to glide on snow.

• **타다 (verb)** : 바닥이 미끄러운 곳에서 기구를 이용해 미끄러지다.
slide
To slip in or on a device on a very slippery floor or ground.

• -러 : 가거나 오거나 하는 동작의 목적을 나타내는 연결 어미.
-reo (no equivalent expression)
A connective ending used to express the purpose of an action such as going and coming.

• **가다 (verb)** : 어떤 목적을 가지고 일정한 곳으로 움직이다.
go
To move to a certain place with a specific purpose.

• -ㄹ 것 : 명사가 아닌 것을 문장에서 명사처럼 쓰이게 하거나 '이다' 앞에 쓰일 수 있게 할 때 쓰는 표현.
-l geot (no equivalent expression)
An expression used to enable a non-noun word to be used as a noun in the sentence or to be used in front of '이다' (be).

• 이다 : 주어가 지시하는 대상의 속성이나 부류를 지정하는 뜻을 나타내는 서술격 조사.
ida (no equivalent expression)
A predicate particle indicating the meaning of the attribute or category of the thing that the subject of the sentence refers to.

• -에요 : (두루높임으로) 어떤 사실을 서술하거나 질문함을 나타내는 종결 어미.
-eyo (no equivalent expression)
(informal addressee-raising) A sentence-final ending used when **describing** a certain fact or asking a question.

그래?

자칫하+면 다치+[ㄹ 수 있]+으니까 조심하+여라.

다칠 수 있으니까 조심해라

• **그래 (interjection)** : 상대편의 말에 대한 감탄이나 가벼운 놀라움을 나타낼 때 쓰는 말.
really
An exclamation used to indicate that the speaker marvels at or is slightly surprised by the words of the other party.

• **자칫하다 (verb)** : 어쩌다가 조금 어긋나거나 잘못되다.
fail at the slightest slip
To go wrong or go awry accidentally.

• -면 : 뒤에 오는 말에 대한 근거나 조건이 됨을 나타내는 연결 어미.
-myeon (no equivalent expression)
A connective ending used when the preceding statement becomes the reason or condition of the following statement.

• **다치다 (verb)** : 부딪치거나 맞거나 하여 몸이나 몸의 일부에 상처가 생기다. 또는 상처가 생기게 하다.
be injured
To be hit or bumped into by something or someone, so that one's body or body part is injured; to make an injury.

• -ㄹ 수 있다 : 어떤 행동이나 상태가 가능함을 나타내는 표현.
-l su itda (no equivalent expression)
An expression used to indicate that an act or state is possible.

• -으니까 : 뒤에 오는 말에 대하여 앞에 오는 말이 원인이나 근거, 전제가 됨을 강조하여 나타내는 연결 어미.
-eunikka (no equivalent expression)
A connective ending used to emphasize that the preceding statement is the cause, reason, or premise for the following statement.

• **조심하다 (verb)** : 좋지 않은 일을 겪지 않도록 말이나 행동 등에 주의를 하다.
practice caution
To be careful in speech, behavior, etc., not to get in trouble.

• -여라 : (아주낮춤으로) 명령을 나타내는 종결 어미.
-yeora (no equivalent expression)
(formal, highly addressee-lowering) A sentence-final ending used to indicate a statement as a command.

< 대화(dialogue) > - 46

우산이 없는데 어떻게 하지?
우사니 엄는데 어떠케 하지?
usani eomneunde eotteoke haji?

그냥 비를 맞는 수밖에 없지, 뭐. 뛰어.
그냥 비를 만는 수바께 업찌, 뭐. 뛰어.
geunyang bireul manneun subakke eopji, mwo. ttwieo.

< 설명(explanation) / 번역(translation) >

우산+이 없+는데 어떻게 하+지?

• **우산 (noun)** : 긴 막대 위에 지붕 같은 막을 펼쳐서 비가 올 때 손에 들고 머리 위를 가리는 도구.
umbrella; parasol
An implement that folds out like a canopy on a rod, which one holds over one's head as a cover from rain.

• 이 : 어떤 상태나 상황의 대상이나 동작의 주체를 나타내는 조사.
i (no equivalent expression)
A postpositional particle referring to a subject under a certain state or situation, or the agent of an action.

• **없다 (adjective)** : 어떤 물건을 가지고 있지 않거나 자격이나 능력 등을 갖추지 않은 상태이다.
lacking
Not having something or not possessing a credential, ability, etc.

• -는데 : 뒤의 말을 하기 위하여 그 대상과 관련이 있는 상황을 미리 말함을 나타내는 연결 어미.
-neunde (no equivalent expression)
A connective ending used to talk in advance about a situation to follow.

• **어떻게 (adverb)** : 어떤 방법으로. 또는 어떤 방식으로.
how
In what method; in what way.

• **하다 (verb)** : 어떤 방식으로 행위를 이루다.
do
To complete an action in a certain way.

• -지 : (두루낮춤으로) 말하는 사람이 듣는 사람에게 친근함을 나타내며 물을 때 쓰는 종결 어미.
-ji (no equivalent expression)
(informal addressee-lowering) A sentence-final ending used when the speaker asks the listener in a friendly manner.

그냥 비+를 맞+[는 수밖에 없]+지, 뭐.

뛰+어.

• **그냥 (adverb)** : 그런 모양으로 그대로 계속하여.
all the time
Continuously in such a state.

• **비 (noun)** : 높은 곳에서 구름을 이루고 있던 수증기가 식어서 뭉쳐 떨어지는 물방울.
rain
Water drops generated from cloud-forming vapors high in the sky that get cold, condense, and fall.

• 를 : 동작이 직접적으로 영향을 미치는 대상을 나타내는 조사.
reul (no equivalent expression)
A postpositional particle used to indicate the subject that an act has a direct influence on.

• **맞다 (verb)** : 내리는 눈이나 비 등이 닿는 것을 그대로 받다.
be exposed to
To be touched by snow, rain, etc., as it falls.

• -는 수밖에 없다 : 그것 말고는 다른 방법이나 가능성이 없음을 나타내는 표현.
-neun subakke eopda (no equivalent expression)
An expression used to indicate that there is no other method or possibility other than that.

• -지 : (두루낮춤으로) 말하는 사람이 자신에 대한 이야기나 자신의 생각을 친근하게 말할 때 쓰는 종결 어미.
-ji (no equivalent expression)
(informal addressee-lowering) A sentence-final ending used when the speaker talks about himself/herself or his/her thoughts in a friendly manner.

• **뭐 (interjection)** : 더 이상 여러 말 할 것 없다는 뜻으로 어떤 사실을 체념하여 받아들이며 하는 말.
oh well; anyway
An exclamation used to indicate that it is useless to say anymore, when the speaker accepts a certain fact resignedly.

• **뛰다 (verb)** : 발을 재빠르게 움직여 빨리 나아가다.
run; race; dash
To move forward in quick steps.

• -어 : (두루낮춤으로) 어떤 사실을 서술하거나 물음, 명령, 권유를 나타내는 종결 어미.
-eo (no equivalent expression)
(informal addressee-lowering) A sentence-final ending used to describe a certain fact, ask a question, **give an order**, or advise.

< 대화(dialogue) > - 47

지우는 성격이 참 좋은 것 같아요.
지우는 성껴기 참 조은 걷 가타요.
jiuneun seonggyeogi cham joeun geot gatayo.

맞아요. 걔는 아무리 일이 바빠도 인상 한 번 찌푸리는 적이 없어요.
마자요. 걔는 아무리 이리 바빠도 인상 한 번 찌푸리는 저기 업써요.
majayo. gyaeneun amuri iri bappado insang han beon jjipurineun jeogi eopseoyo.

< 설명(explanation) / 번역(translation) >

지우+는 성격+이 참 좋+[은 것 같]+아요.

• **지우 (noun)** : person's name

• 는 : 문장 속에서 어떤 대상이 화제임을 나타내는 조사.
neun (no equivalent expression)
A postpositional particle used to indicate that a certain subject is the topic of a sentence.

• **성격 (noun)** : 개인이 가지고 있는 고유한 성질이나 품성.
personality; character
A person's innate quality or character.

• 이 : 어떤 상태나 상황의 대상이나 동작의 주체를 나타내는 조사.
i (no equivalent expression)
A postpositional particle referring to a subject under a certain state or situation, or the agent of an action.

• **참 (adverb)** : 사실이나 이치에 조금도 어긋남이 없이 정말로.
truly
In the manner of being not contrary to a fact or reason.

• **좋다 (adjective)** : 성격 등이 원만하고 착하다.
good; nice
Well-rounded and kind in personality.

• -은 것 같다 : 추측을 나타내는 표현.
-eun geot gatda (no equivalent expression)
An expression used to indicate that the statement is a guess.

• -아요 : (두루높임으로) 어떤 사실을 서술하거나 질문, 명령, 권유함을 나타내는 종결 어미.
-ayo (no equivalent expression)
(informal addressee-raising) A sentence-final ending used to **describe** a certain fact, ask a question, give an order, or advise.

맞+아요.

걔+는 아무리 일+이 바쁘(바ㅃ)+아도 인상 한 번 찌푸리+[는 적이 없]+어요.
바빠도

• **맞다** (verb) : 그렇거나 옳다.
be so; be right
To be so or right.

• -아요 : (두루높임으로) 어떤 사실을 서술하거나 질문, 명령, 권유함을 나타내는 종결 어미.
-ayo (no equivalent expression)
(informal addressee-raising) A sentence-final ending used to **describe** a certain fact, ask a question, give an order, or advise.

• **걔** (short form) : '그 아이'가 줄어든 말.
gyae (no equivalent expression)
An abbreviated word for '그(that) 아이(third party)'.

• 는 : 문장 속에서 어떤 대상이 화제임을 나타내는 조사.
neun (no equivalent expression)
A postpositional particle used to indicate that a certain subject is the topic of a sentence.

• **아무리** (adverb) : 정도가 매우 심하게.
no matter how
To an extremely severe degree.

• **일** (noun) : 무엇을 이루려고 몸이나 정신을 사용하는 활동. 또는 그 활동의 대상.
work; labor
An activity that uses one's body or mind in order to achieve something; the object of such an activity.

• 이 : 어떤 상태나 상황의 대상이나 동작의 주체를 나타내는 조사.
i (no equivalent expression)
A postpositional particle referring to a subject under a certain state or situation, or the agent of an action.

• **바쁘다 (adjective)** : 할 일이 많거나 시간이 없어서 다른 것을 할 여유가 없다.
busy; hectic
Having no time to do other things because one has many things to do or has little time.

• -아도 : 앞에 오는 말을 가정하거나 인정하지만 뒤에 오는 말에는 관계가 없거나 영향을 끼치지 않음을 나타내는 연결 어미.
-ado (no equivalent expression)
A connective ending used when assuming or recognizing the truth of the preceding statement, although it is not related to or does not influence the following statement.

• **인상 (noun)** : 사람 얼굴의 생김새.
impression
The appearance of a person's face.

• **한 (determiner)** : 하나의.
one
One.

• **번 (noun)** : 일의 횟수를 세는 단위.
beon (no equivalent expression)
A bound noun that serves as a unit for counting the frequency of a task.

• **찌푸리다 (verb)** : 얼굴의 근육이나 눈살 등을 몹시 찡그리다.
frown; scowl
To wrinkle the facial muscles, brow, etc.

• -는 적이 없다 : 앞의 말이 나타내는 동작이 진행되거나 그 상태가 나타나는 때가 없음을 나타내는 표현.
-neun jeogi eopda (no equivalent expression)
An expression used to indicate that the act or state mentioned in the preceding statement never existed.

• -어요 : (두루높임으로) 어떤 사실을 서술하거나 질문, 명령, 권유함을 나타내는 종결 어미.
-eoyo (no equivalent expression)
(informal addressee-raising) A sentence-final ending used to **describe** a certain fact, ask a question, give an order, or advise.

< 대화(dialogue) > - 48

명절에 한복 입어 본 적 있어요?
명저레 한복 이버 본 적 이써요?
myeongjeore hanbok ibeo bon jeok isseoyo?

그럼요. 어렸을 때 부모님하고 고향에 내려가면서 입었었죠.
그러묘. 어려쓸 때 부모님하고 고향에 내려가면서 이버썯쬬.
geureomyo. eoryeosseul ttae bumonimhago gohyange naeryeogamyeonseo ibeosseotjyo.

< 설명(explanation) / 번역(translation) >

명절+에 한복 입+[어 보]+[ㄴ 적 있]+어요?

입어 본 적 있어요

• **명절 (noun)** : 설이나 추석 등 해마다 일정하게 돌아와 전통적으로 즐기거나 기념하는 날.
national holiday
A day of commemoration or tradition which is celebrated annually such as Seollal, Lunar New Year's, and Chuseok, Korean Thanksgiving Day.

• 에 : 앞말이 시간이나 때임을 나타내는 조사.
in; at
A postpositional particle to indicate that the preceding statement refers to the time.

• **한복 (noun)** : 한국의 전통 의복.
hanbok (no equivalent expression)
Traditional Korean clothes.

• **입다 (verb)** : 옷을 몸에 걸치거나 두르다.
wear; be dressed; put on
To hang or drape clothes on or around one's body.

• -어 보다 : 앞의 말이 나타내는 행동을 이전에 경험했음을 나타내는 표현.
-eo boda (no equivalent expression)
An expression used to indicate that one experienced the act mentioned in the preceding statement earlier.

• -ㄴ 적 있다 : 앞의 말이 나타내는 동작이 일어나거나 그 상태가 나타난 때가 있음을 나타내는 표현.
-n jeog itda (no equivalent expression)
An expression used to indicate that the act or state mentioned in the preceding statement existed at some point in time.

• -어요 : (두루높임으로) 어떤 사실을 서술하거나 질문, 명령, 권유함을 나타내는 종결 어미.
-eoyo (no equivalent expression)
(informal addressee-raising) A sentence-final ending used to describe a certain fact, **ask a question**, give an order, or advise.

그럼+요.

어리+었+[을 때] 부모님+하고 고향+에 내려가+면서 입+었었+죠.
어렸을 때

• **그럼 (interjection)** : 말할 것도 없이 당연하다는 뜻으로 대답할 때 쓰는 말.
of course
An exclamation used when the speaker gives an answer meaning that something is absolutely right.

• 요 : 높임의 대상인 상대방에게 존대의 뜻을 나타내는 조사.
yo (no equivalent expression)
A postpositional particle used to indicate respect for the other person, the subject who is shown respect.

• **어리다 (adjective)** : 나이가 적다.
young
Low in age.

• -었- : 사건이 과거에 일어났음을 나타내는 어미.
-eot- (no equivalent expression)
An ending of a word used to indicate that an event happened in the past.

• -을 때 : 어떤 행동이나 상황이 일어나는 동안이나 그 시기 또는 그러한 일이 일어난 경우를 나타내는 표현.
-eul ttae (no equivalent expression)
An expression used to indicate the duration, period, or occasion of a certain act or situation.

• **부모님 (noun)** : (높이는 말로) 부모.
parents
(polite form) Someone's parents, including one's own.

• 하고 : 어떤 일을 함께 하는 대상임을 나타내는 조사.
hago (no equivalent expression)
A postpositional particle used to indicate that a person is the subject one is doing something with.

• **고향 (noun)** : 태어나서 자란 곳.
home; hometown
A place where one was born and grew up.

• 에 : 앞말이 목적지이거나 어떤 행위의 진행 방향임을 나타내는 조사.
to; at
A postpositional particle to indicate that the preceding statement refers to a destination or the course of a certain action.

• **내려가다 (verb)** : 도심이나 중심지에서 지방으로 가다.
go to a rural area
To move from a city or central area to a rural area.

• -면서 : 두 가지 이상의 동작이나 상태가 함께 일어남을 나타내는 연결 어미.
-myeonseo (no equivalent expression)
A connective ending used when more than two actions or states happen at the same time.

• **입다 (verb)** : 옷을 몸에 걸치거나 두르다.
wear; be dressed; put on
To hang or drape clothes on or around one's body.

• -었었- : 현재와 비교하여 다르거나 현재로 이어지지 않는 과거의 사건을 나타내는 어미.
-eotsseot- (no equivalent expression)
An ending of a word referring to a past event that is different from the present or does not continue to the present.

• -죠 : (두루높임으로) 말하는 사람이 자신에 대한 이야기나 자신의 생각을 친근하게 말할 때 쓰는 종결 어미.
-jyo (no equivalent expression)
(informal addressee-raising) A sentence-final ending used when the speaker talks about himself/herself or his/her thoughts in a friendly manner.

< 대화(dialogue) > - 49

왜 이렇게 늦었어? 한참 기다렸잖아.
왜 이러케 느저써? 한참 기다렫짜나.
wae ireoke neujeosseo? hancham gidaryeotjana.

미안해, 오후에도 이렇게 차가 막히는 줄 몰랐어.
미안해, 오후에도 이러케 차가 마키는 줄 몰라써.
mianhae, ohuedo ireoke chaga makineun jul mollasseo.

< 설명(explanation) / 번역(translation) >

왜 이렇+게 늦+었+어?

한참 기다리+었+잖아.
기다렸잖아

• **왜 (adverb)** : 무슨 이유로. 또는 어째서.
why
For what reason; how come.

• **이렇다 (adjective)** : 상태, 모양, 성질 등이 이와 같다.
so; like this
(for a state, appearance, nature to be) Like this.

• -게 : 앞의 말이 뒤에서 가리키는 일의 목적이나 결과, 방식, 정도 등이 됨을 나타내는 연결 어미.
-ge (no equivalent expression)
A connective ending used when the preceding statement is the purpose, result, method, amount, etc., of something mentioned in the following statement.

• **늦다 (verb)** : 정해진 때보다 지나다.
be late
To be later than the set time.

• -었- : 어떤 사건이 과거에 완료되었거나 그 사건의 결과가 현재까지 지속되는 상황을 나타내는 어미.
-eot- (no equivalent expression)
An ending of a word used to indicate that an event was completed in the past or its result continues in the present.

• -어 : (두루낮춤으로) 어떤 사실을 서술하거나 물음, 명령, 권유를 나타내는 종결 어미.
-eo (no equivalent expression)
(informal addressee-lowering) A sentence-final ending used to describe a certain fact, **ask a question**, give an order, or advise.

• **한참 (noun)** : 시간이 꽤 지나는 동안.
long time; being a while
A lapse of a fairly long time.

• **기다리다 (verb)** : 사람, 때가 오거나 어떤 일이 이루어질 때까지 시간을 보내다.
wait
To spend time until a person or time comes or a certain event is realized.

• -었- : 어떤 사건이 과거에 완료되었거나 그 사건의 결과가 현재까지 지속되는 상황을 나타내는 어미.
-eot- (no equivalent expression)
An ending of a word used to indicate that an event was completed in the past or its result continues in the present.

• -잖아 : (두루낮춤으로) 어떤 상황에 대해 말하는 사람이 상대방에게 확인하거나 정정해 주듯이 말함을 나타내는 표현.
-jana (no equivalent expression)
(informal addressee-lowering) An expression used to check with or correct the listener on something about a certain situation.

미안하+여.
미안해

오후+에+도 이렇+게 차+가 막히+[는 줄] 모르(몰ㄹ)+았+어.
몰랐어

• **미안하다 (adjective)** : 남에게 잘못을 하여 마음이 편치 못하고 부끄럽다.
regrettable; sorry
Feeling rather uncomfortable and ashamed because one did something bad to someone.

• -여 : (두루낮춤으로) 어떤 사실을 서술하거나 물음, 명령, 권유를 나타내는 종결 어미.

-yeo (no equivalent expression)
(informal addressee-lowering) A sentence-final ending used to **describe** a certain fact, ask a question, give an order, or advise.

• **오후 (noun)** : 정오부터 해가 질 때까지의 동안.
afternoon
The duration from noon to the time when the sun goes down.

• 에 : 앞말이 시간이나 때임을 나타내는 조사.
in; at
A postpositional particle to indicate that the preceding statement refers to the time.

• 도 : 일반적이지 않은 경우나 의외의 경우를 강조함을 나타내는 조사.
do (no equivalent expression)
A postpositional particle used to emphasize an unusual case or unexpected case.

• **이렇다 (adjective)** : 상태, 모양, 성질 등이 이와 같다.
so; like this
(for a state, appearance, nature to be) Like this.

• -게 : 앞의 말이 뒤에서 가리키는 일의 목적이나 결과, 방식, 정도 등이 됨을 나타내는 연결 어미.
-ge (no equivalent expression)
A connective ending used when the preceding statement is the purpose, result, method, amount, etc., of something mentioned in the following statement.

• **차 (noun)** : 바퀴가 달려 있어 사람이나 짐을 실어 나르는 기관.
car; automobile; vehicle
An apparatus with wheels that is designed to carry people or cargo.

• 가 : 어떤 상태나 상황에 놓인 대상이나 동작의 주체를 나타내는 조사.
ga (no equivalent expression)
A postpositional particle referring to a subject under a certain state or situation, or the subject of an act.

• **막히다 (verb)** : 길에 차가 많아 차가 제대로 가지 못하게 되다.
be jammed
For cars to not run easily because there are many cars on the road.

• -는 줄 : 어떤 사실이나 상태에 대해 알고 있거나 모르고 있음을 나타내는 표현.
-neun jul (no equivalent expression)
An expression used to indicate that one either knows or does not know a certain fact or state.

• **모르다 (verb)** : 사람이나 사물, 사실 등을 알지 못하거나 이해하지 못하다.
not know
To have no knowledge or understanding of a person, object or fact.

• -았- : 어떤 사건이 과거에 완료되었거나 그 사건의 결과가 현재까지 지속되는 상황을 나타내는 어미.
-at- (no equivalent expression)
An ending of a word used to indicate that an event was completed in the past or its result continues in the present.

• -어 : (두루낮춤으로) 어떤 사실을 서술하거나 물음, 명령, 권유를 나타내는 종결 어미.
-eo (no equivalent expression)
(informal addressee-lowering) A sentence-final ending used to **describe** a certain fact, ask a question, give an order, or advise.

< 대화(dialogue) > - 50

지아 씨, 하던 일은 다 됐어요?
지아 씨, 하던 이른 다 돼써요?
jia ssi, hadeon ireun da dwaesseoyo?

네, 잠깐만요. 지금 마무리하는 중이에요.
네, 잠깐마뇨. 지금 마무리하는 중이에요.
ne, jamkkanmanyo. jigeum mamurihaneun jungieyo.

< 설명(explanation) / 번역(translation) >

지아 씨, 하+던 일+은 다 되+었+어요?
됐어요

• **지아 (noun)** : person's name

• **씨 (noun)** : 그 사람을 높여 부르거나 이르는 말.
Mr.; Ms.; Mrs.
A bound noun used to address or call out to a certain person deferentially.

• **하다 (verb)** : 어떤 행동이나 동작, 활동 등을 행하다.
do; perform
To perform a certain move, action, activity, etc.

• -던 : 앞의 말이 관형어의 기능을 하게 만들고 사건이나 동작이 과거에 완료되지 않고 중단되었음을 나타내는 어미.
-deon (no equivalent expression)
An ending of a word that makes the preceding statement function as an adnominal phrase and implies that an event or action has not been completed in the past but has been stopped.

• **일 (noun)** : 무엇을 이루려고 몸이나 정신을 사용하는 활동. 또는 그 활동의 대상.
work; labor
An activity that uses one's body or mind in order to achieve something; the object of such an activity.

• 은 : 문장 속에서 어떤 대상이 화제임을 나타내는 조사.
eun (no equivalent expression)
A postpositional particle used to indicate that a certain subject is the topic of a sentence.

• **다 (adverb)** : 남거나 빠진 것이 없이 모두.
all; everything
With nothing left over or missing.

• **되다 (verb)** : 어떤 사물이나 현상이 생겨나거나 만들어지다.
be completed; be finished
For a certain object or phenomenon to be created or made.

• -었- : 어떤 사건이 과거에 완료되었거나 그 사건의 결과가 현재까지 지속되는 상황을 나타내는 어미.
-eot- (no equivalent expression)
An ending of a word used to indicate that an event was completed in the past or its result continues in the present.

• -어요 : (두루높임으로) 어떤 사실을 서술하거나 질문, 명령, 권유함을 나타내는 종결 어미.
-eoyo (no equivalent expression)
(informal addressee-raising) A sentence-final ending used to describe a certain fact, **ask a question**, give an order, or advise.

네, 잠깐+만+요.

지금 마무리하+[는 중이]+에요.

• **네 (interjection)** : 윗사람의 물음이나 명령 등에 긍정하여 대답할 때 쓰는 말.
yes; yes sir; yes ma'am
An exclamation uttered when the speaker affirmatively answers the call or order of his/her superior.

• **잠깐 (noun)** : 아주 짧은 시간 동안.
while; moment
A very short time.

• 만 : 무엇을 강조하는 뜻을 나타내는 조사.
man (no equivalent expression)
A postpositional particle that indicates an emphasis on something.

- 요 : 높임의 대상인 상대방에게 존대의 뜻을 나타내는 조사.
  yo (no equivalent expression)
  A postpositional particle used to indicate respect for the other person, the subject who is shown respect.

- **지금 (adverb)** : 말을 하고 있는 바로 이때에. 또는 그 즉시에.
  now; immediately
  At the present moment as one speaks, or that instant.

- **마무리하다 (verb)** : 일을 끝내다.
  end; finish
  To finish a task.

- -는 중이다 : 어떤 일이 진행되고 있음을 나타내는 표현.
  -neun jungida (no equivalent expression)
  An expression used to indicate that a certain thing is in progress.

- -에요 : (두루높임으로) 어떤 사실을 서술하거나 질문함을 나타내는 종결 어미.
  -eyo (no equivalent expression)
  (informal addressee-raising) A sentence-final ending used when **describing** a certain fact or asking a question.

< 대화(dialogue) > - 51

추워? 내 옷 벗어 줄까?
추워? 내 옫 버서 줄까?
chuwo? nae ot beoseo julkka?

괜찮아. 너도 추위를 많이 타는데 괜히 멋있는 척하지 않아도 돼.
괜차나. 너도 추위를 마니 타는데 괜히 머신는 처카지 아나도 돼.
gwaenchana. neodo chuwireul mani taneunde gwaenhi meosinneun cheokaji anado dwae.

< 설명(explanation) / 번역(translation) >

춥(추우)+어?
추워

나+의 옷 벗+[어 주]+ㄹ까?
내 벗어 줄까

• **춥다 (adjective)** : 몸으로 느끼기에 기온이 낮다.
cold; chilly
For one's body to feel that the air is cold and the temperature low.

• -어 : (두루낮춤으로) 어떤 사실을 서술하거나 물음, 명령, 권유를 나타내는 종결 어미.
-eo (no equivalent expression)
(informal addressee-lowering) A sentence-final ending used to describe a certain fact, **ask a question**, give an order, or advise.

• **나 (pronoun)** : 말하는 사람이 친구나 아랫사람에게 자기를 가리키는 말.
I
A pronoun used to indicate oneself to a friend or a younger person.

• 의 : 앞의 말이 뒤의 말에 대하여 소유, 소속, 소재, 관계, 기원, 주체의 관계를 가짐을 나타내는 조사.
ui (no equivalent expression)
A postpositional particle used to indicate that the referent of the following word is owned by, belongs to, is related to, originates from, or is the object of what the preceding word indicates.

• **옷 (noun)** : 사람의 몸을 가리고 더위나 추위 등으로부터 보호하며 멋을 내기 위하여 입는 것.
clothes; garment
An item that one wears to cover his/her body, protect himself/herself from cold, heat, etc., and look fashionable.

• **벗다 (verb)** : 사람이 몸에 지닌 물건이나 옷 등을 몸에서 떼어 내다.
take off
To have an object, clothes, etc., taken off one's body.

• -어 주다 : 남을 위해 앞의 말이 나타내는 행동을 함을 나타내는 표현.
-eo juda (no equivalent expression)
An expression used to indicate that one does the act mentioned in the preceding statement for someone.

• -ㄹ까 : (두루낮춤으로) 듣는 사람의 의사를 물을 때 쓰는 종결 어미.
-lkka (no equivalent expression)
(informal addressee-lowering) A sentence-final ending used to ask for the listener's opinion.

괜찮+아.

너+도 추위+를 많이 타+는데 괜히 멋있+[는 척하]+[지 않]+[아도 되]+어.

멋있는 척하지 않아도 돼

• **괜찮다 (adjective)** : 별 문제가 없다.
all right; fine
Having no particular problems.

• -아 : (두루낮춤으로) 어떤 사실을 서술하거나 물음, 명령, 권유를 나타내는 종결 어미.
-a (no equivalent expression)
(informal addressee-lowering) A sentence-final ending used to **describe** a certain fact, ask a question, give an order, or advise.

• **너 (pronoun)** : 듣는 사람이 친구나 아랫사람일 때, 그 사람을 가리키는 말.
no equivalent expression
A pronoun used to indicate the listener when he/she is the same age or younger.

• 도 : 이미 있는 어떤 것에 다른 것을 더하거나 포함함을 나타내는 조사.
do (no equivalent expression)
A postpositional particle used to indicate an addition or inclusion of another thing to something that already exists.

- **추위 (noun)** : 주로 겨울철의 추운 기운이나 추운 날씨.
  cold; chill
  Cold air or cold weather, mostly in winter.

- **를** : 동작이 직접적으로 영향을 미치는 대상을 나타내는 조사.
  reul (no equivalent expression)
  A postpositional particle used to indicate the subject that an act has a direct influence on.

- **많이 (adverb)** : 수나 양, 정도 등이 일정한 기준보다 넘게.
  much; in large numbers; in large amounts
  In a state in which a number, amount, degree, etc., are larger than a certain standard.

- **타다 (verb)** : 날씨나 계절의 영향을 쉽게 받다.
  be influenced easily
  To be easily influenced by the weather or season.

- **-는데** : 뒤의 말을 하기 위하여 그 대상과 관련이 있는 상황을 미리 말함을 나타내는 연결 어미.
  -neunde (no equivalent expression)
  A connective ending used to talk in advance about a situation to follow.

- **괜히 (adverb)** : 특별한 이유나 실속이 없게.
  vainly; in vain; to no avail
  Without substance or particular reason.

- **멋있다 (adjective)** : 매우 좋거나 훌륭하다.
  nice; stylish; elegant
  Very good or great.

- **-는 척하다** : 실제로 그렇지 않은데도 어떤 행동이나 상태를 거짓으로 꾸밈을 나타내는 표현.
  -neun cheokada (no equivalent expression)
  An expression used to indicate that one is pretending to do something or to be something, which is not true.

- **-지 않다** : 앞의 말이 나타내는 행위나 상태를 부정하는 뜻을 나타내는 표현.
  -ji anta (no equivalent expression)
  An expression used to deny the act or state indicated in the preceding statement.

- **-아도 되다** : 어떤 행동에 대한 허락이나 허용을 나타낼 때 쓰는 표현.
  -ado deoda (no equivalent expression)
  An expression used to indicate that a certain act is allowed or accepted.

- **-어** : (두루낮춤으로) 어떤 사실을 서술하거나 물음, 명령, 권유를 나타내는 종결 어미.
  -eo (no equivalent expression)
  (informal addressee-lowering) A sentence-final ending used to describe a certain fact, ask a question, give an order, or advise.

< 대화(dialogue) > - 52

어제 친구들이 너 몰래 생일 파티를 준비해서 깜짝 놀랐다면서?
어제 친구드리 너 몰래 생일 파티를 준비해서 깜짝 놀랃따면서?
eoje chingudeuri neo mollae saengil patireul junbihaeseo kkamjjak nollatdamyeonseo?

사실은 미리 눈치를 챘었는데 그래도 놀라는 체했지.
사시른 미리 눈치를 채썬는데 그래도 놀라는 체핻찌.
sasireun miri nunchireul chaesseonneunde geuraedo nollaneun chehaetji.

< 설명(explanation) / 번역(translation) >

어제 친구+들+이 너 몰래 생일 파티+를 준비하+여서 깜짝 놀라+았+다면서?
준비해서 놀랐다면서

• **어제 (adverb)** : 오늘의 하루 전날에.
yesterday
On the day before today.

• **친구 (noun)** : 사이가 가까워 서로 친하게 지내는 사람.
friend
A person that one is close to and in an amicable relationship with.

• 들 : '복수'의 뜻을 더하는 접미사.
-deul (no equivalent expression)
A suffix used to mean plural.

• 이 : 어떤 상태나 상황의 대상이나 동작의 주체를 나타내는 조사.
i (no equivalent expression)
A postpositional particle referring to a subject under a certain state or situation, or the agent of an action.

• **너 (pronoun)** : 듣는 사람이 친구나 아랫사람일 때, 그 사람을 가리키는 말.
no equivalent expression
A pronoun used to indicate the listener when he/she is the same age or younger.

• **몰래 (adverb)** : 남이 알지 못하게.
secretly; in secret; stealthily
In such a manner that others would not notice.

• **생일 (noun)** : 사람이 세상에 태어난 날.
birthday
The day a person was born.

• **파티 (noun)** : 친목을 도모하거나 무엇을 기념하기 위한 잔치나 모임.
party
A feast or gathering to make friends or to celebrate an occasion.

• 를 : 동작이 직접적으로 영향을 미치는 대상을 나타내는 조사.
reul (no equivalent expression)
A postpositional particle used to indicate the subject that an act has a direct influence on.

• **준비하다 (verb)** : 미리 마련하여 갖추다.
prepare
To have something in place with advance preparations.

• -여서 : 이유나 근거를 나타내는 연결 어미.
-yeoseo (no equivalent expression)
A connective ending used to indicate a reason or cause.

• **깜짝 (adverb)** : 갑자기 놀라는 모양.
with a startle
In the manner of being surprised suddenly.

• **놀라다 (verb)** : 뜻밖의 일을 당하거나 무서워서 순간적으로 긴장하거나 가슴이 뛰다.
be surprised; be astonished; be shocked; be scared
To become tense or feel one's heart pounding as one faces an unexpected incident or is scared.

• -았- : 사건이 과거에 일어났음을 나타내는 어미.
-at- (no equivalent expression)
An ending of a word used to indicate that an event happened in the past.

• -다면서 : (두루낮춤으로) 말하는 사람이 들어서 아는 사실을 확인하여 물음을 나타내는 종결 어미.
-damyeonseo (no equivalent expression)
(informal addressee-lowering) A sentence-final ending used when the speaker confirms and asks questions about a fact that he/she heard.

사실+은 미리 눈치+를 채+었었+는데 그러+어도 놀라+[는 체하]+였+지.

챘었는데 그래도 놀라는 체했지

- **사실 (noun)** : 겉으로 드러나지 않은 일을 솔직하게 말할 때 쓰는 말.
  truth is
  An expression used to frankly tell someone something that is not seen nor known.

- 은 : 문장 속에서 어떤 대상이 화제임을 나타내는 조사.
  eun (no equivalent expression)
  A postpositional particle used to indicate that a certain subject is the topic of a sentence.

- **미리 (adverb)** : 어떤 일이 있기 전에 먼저.
  in advance; ahead of time
  Before something happens.

- **눈치 (noun)** : 상대가 말하지 않아도 그 사람의 마음이나 일의 상황을 이해하고 아는 능력.
  tact; sense; wits
  An ability to understand and know someone's mind or situation even though they have said nothing.

- 를 : 동작이 직접적으로 영향을 미치는 대상을 나타내는 조사.
  reul (no equivalent expression)
  A postpositional particle used to indicate the subject that an act has a direct influence on.

- **채다 (verb)** : 사정이나 형편을 재빨리 미루어 헤아리거나 깨닫다.
  figure out; wise up to
  To guess or realize the situation or state of something right away.

- -었었- : 현재와 비교하여 다르거나 현재로 이어지지 않는 과거의 사건을 나타내는 어미.
  -eotsseot- (no equivalent expression)
  An ending of a word referring to a past event that is different from the present or does not continue to the present.

- -는데 : 뒤의 말을 하기 위하여 그 대상과 관련이 있는 상황을 미리 말함을 나타내는 연결 어미.
  -neunde (no equivalent expression)
  A connective ending used to talk in advance about a situation to follow.

- **그러다 (verb)** : 앞에서 일어난 일이나 말한 것과 같이 그렇게 하다.
  do so
  To do what occurred or was stated previously.

- -어도 : 앞에 오는 말을 가정하거나 인정하지만 뒤에 오는 말에는 관계가 없거나 영향을 끼치지 않음을 나타내는 연결 어미.
  -eodo (no equivalent expression)
  A connective ending used when assuming or recognizing the truth of the preceding statement, although it is not related to or does not influence the following statement.

• **놀라다 (verb)** : 뜻밖의 일을 당하거나 무서워서 순간적으로 긴장하거나 가슴이 뛰다.
be surprised; be astonished; be shocked; be scared
To become tense or feel one's heart pounding as one faces an unexpected incident or is scared.

• -는 체하다 : 실제로 그렇지 않은데도 어떤 행동이나 상태를 거짓으로 꾸밈을 나타내는 표현.
-neun chehada (no equivalent expression)
An expression used to indicate that one is pretending to do something or to be something, which is not true.

• -였- : 사건이 과거에 일어났음을 나타내는 어미.
-yeot- (no equivalent expression)
An ending of a word used to indicate that an event happened in the past.

• -지 : (두루낮춤으로) 말하는 사람이 자신에 대한 이야기나 자신의 생각을 친근하게 말할 때 쓰는 종결 어미.
-ji (no equivalent expression)
(informal addressee-lowering) A sentence-final ending used when the speaker talks about himself/herself or his/her thoughts in a friendly manner.

< 대화(dialogue) > - 53

영화를 보는 것이 취미라고 하셨는데 영화를 자주 보세요?
영화를 보는 거시 취미라고 하션는데 영화를 자주 보세요?
yeonghwareul boneun geosi chwimirago hasyeonneunde yeonghwareul jaju boseyo?

일주일에 한 편 이상 보니까 자주 보는 편이죠.
일쭈이레 한 편 이상 보니까 자주 보는 펴니죠.
iljuire han pyeon isang bonikka jaju boneun pyeonijyo.

< 설명(explanation) / 번역(translation) >

영화+를 보+[는 것]+이 취미+(이)+라고 하+시+었+는데 영화+를 자주 보+세요?
취미라고 하셨는데

• **영화** (noun) : 일정한 의미를 갖고 움직이는 대상을 촬영하여 영사기로 영사막에 비추어서 보게 하는 종합 예술.
film; movie
A composite art which captures moving objects on film with a certain message and then shows it on a screen by using a projector.

• 를 : 동작이 직접적으로 영향을 미치는 대상을 나타내는 조사.
reul (no equivalent expression)
A postpositional particle used to indicate the subject that an act has a direct influence on.

• **보다** (verb) : 눈으로 대상을 즐기거나 감상하다.
watch; see; enjoy
To enjoy or appreciate an object with eyes.

• -는 것 : 명사가 아닌 것을 문장에서 명사처럼 쓰이게 하거나 '이다' 앞에 쓰일 수 있게 할 때 쓰는 표현.
-neun geot (no equivalent expression)
An expression used to enable a non-noun word to be used as a noun in a sentence or to be used in front of '이다' (be).

• 이 : 어떤 상태나 상황의 대상이나 동작의 주체를 나타내는 조사.
i (no equivalent expression)
A postpositional particle referring to a subject under a certain state or situation, or the agent of an action.

- **취미 (noun)** : 좋아하여 재미로 즐겨서 하는 일.
  hobby
  Something one likes and enjoys doing for fun.

- 이다 : 주어가 지시하는 대상의 속성이나 부류를 지정하는 뜻을 나타내는 서술격 조사.
  ida (no equivalent expression)
  A predicate particle indicating the meaning of the attribute or category of the thing that the subject of the sentence refers to.

- -라고 : 다른 사람에게서 들은 내용을 간접적으로 전달하거나 주어의 생각, 의견 등을 나타내는 표현.
  -rago (no equivalent expression)
  An expression used to pass along what the speaker heard from another person, or to present the subject's thoughts, opinions, etc.

- **하다 (verb)** : 무엇에 대해 말하다.
  say
  To talk about something.

- -시- : 어떤 동작이나 상태의 주체를 높이는 뜻을 나타내는 어미.
  -si- (no equivalent expression)
  An ending of a word used for the subject honorifics of an action or state.

- -었- : 사건이 과거에 일어났음을 나타내는 어미.
  -eot- (no equivalent expression)
  An ending of a word used to indicate that an event happened in the past.

- -는데 : 뒤의 말을 하기 위하여 그 대상과 관련이 있는 상황을 미리 말함을 나타내는 연결 어미.
  -neunde (no equivalent expression)
  A connective ending used to talk in advance about a situation to follow.

- **영화 (noun)** : 일정한 의미를 갖고 움직이는 대상을 촬영하여 영사기로 영사막에 비추어서 보게 하는 종합 예술.
  film; movie
  A composite art which captures moving objects on film with a certain message and then shows it on a screen by using a projector.

- 를 : 동작이 직접적으로 영향을 미치는 대상을 나타내는 조사.
  reul (no equivalent expression)
  A postpositional particle used to indicate the subject that an act has a direct influence on.

- **자주 (adverb)** : 같은 일이 되풀이되는 간격이 짧게.
  often; frequently
  In the state of something being repeated at short intervals.

• **보다 (verb)** : 눈으로 대상을 즐기거나 감상하다.
watch; see; enjoy
To enjoy or appreciate an object with eyes.

• -세요 : (두루높임으로) 설명, 의문, 명령, 요청의 뜻을 나타내는 종결 어미.
-seyo (no equivalent expression)
(informal addressee-raising) A sentence-final ending used to describe, **ask a question**, order, and request.

일주일+에 한 편 이상 보+니까 자주 보+[는 편이]+죠.

• **일주일 (noun)** : 월요일부터 일요일까지 칠 일. 또는 한 주일.
one week; a week
Seven days from Monday to Sunday, or one week.

• 에 : 앞말이 기준이 되는 대상이나 단위임을 나타내는 조사.
per; for; against
A postpositional particle to indicate that the preceding statement is a unit or subject that is the standard for something.

• **한 (determiner)** : 하나의.
one
One.

• **편 (noun)** : 책이나 문학 작품, 또는 영화나 연극 등을 세는 단위.
pyeon (no equivalent expression)
A bound noun that serves as a unit to count books or literary works, or movies, plays, etc.

• **이상 (noun)** : 수량이나 정도가 일정한 기준을 포함하여 그보다 많거나 나은 것.
or more; and over
A state in which something equals to or is larger or better than a certain point of reference in quantity or degree.

• **보다 (verb)** : 눈으로 대상을 즐기거나 감상하다.
watch; see; enjoy
To enjoy or appreciate an object with eyes.

• -니까 : 뒤에 오는 말에 대하여 앞에 오는 말이 원인이나 근거, 전제가 됨을 강조하여 나타내는 연결 어미.
-nikka (no equivalent expression)
A connective ending used to emphasize that the preceding statement is the cause, reason, or premise for the following statement.

• **자주 (adverb)** : 같은 일이 되풀이되는 간격이 짧게.
often; frequently
In the state of something being repeated at short intervals.

• **보다 (verb)** : 눈으로 대상을 즐기거나 감상하다.
watch; see; enjoy
To enjoy or appreciate an object with eyes.

• -는 편이다 : 어떤 사실을 단정적으로 말하기보다는 대체로 어떤 쪽에 가깝다거나 속한다고 말할 때 쓰는 표현.
-neun pyeonida (no equivalent expression)
An expression used to indicate that something has a certain tendency or is classified as such, instead of being sure of it.

• -죠 : (두루높임으로) 말하는 사람이 자신에 대한 이야기나 자신의 생각을 친근하게 말할 때 쓰는 종결어미.
-jyo (no equivalent expression)
(informal addressee-raising) A sentence-final ending used when the speaker talks about himself/herself or his/her thoughts in a friendly manner.

< 대화(dialogue) > - 54

지아 씨, 이번 대회 우승을 축하합니다.
지아 씨, 이번 대회 우승을 추카함니다.
jia ssi, ibeon daehoe useungeul chukahamnida.

고맙습니다. 제가 음악을 계속하는 한 이 우승의 감격은 잊지 못할 것입니다.
고맙씀니다. 제가 으마글 계소카는 한 이 우승의(우승에) 감겨근 읻찌 모탈 꺼심니다.
gomapseumnida. jega eumageul gyesokaneun han i useungui(useunge) gamgyeogeun itji motal geosimnida.

< 설명(explanation) / 번역(translation) >

지아 씨, 이번 대회 우승+을 축하하+ㅂ니다.

축하합니다

• **지아 (noun)** : person's name

• **씨 (noun)** : 그 사람을 높여 부르거나 이르는 말.
Mr.; Ms.; Mrs.
A bound noun used to address or call out to a certain person deferentially.

• **이번 (noun)** : 곧 돌아올 차례. 또는 막 지나간 차례.
this time
A turn soon to come, or one that just passed.

• **대회 (noun)** : 여러 사람이 실력이나 기술을 겨루는 행사.
competition; contest
An event where many people compete with each other over their abilities or skills.

• **우승 (noun)** : 경기나 시합에서 상대를 모두 이겨 일 위를 차지함.
victory; championship
The act of defeating all opponents and taking the first place in a contest or competition.

• 을 : 동작이 직접적으로 영향을 미치는 대상을 나타내는 조사.
eul (no equivalent expression)
A postpositional particle used to indicate the subject that an action has a direct influence on.

• **축하하다 (verb)** : 남의 좋은 일에 대하여 기쁜 마음으로 인사하다.
congratulate; celebrate
To greet someone with pleasure, commenting on his/her happy occasion, achievement, etc.

• -ㅂ니다 : (아주높임으로) 현재의 동작이나 상태, 사실을 정중하게 설명함을 나타내는 종결 어미.
-pnida (no equivalent expression)
(formal, highly addressee-raising) A sentence-final ending used to explain the present action, state, or fact politely.

고맙+습니다.

제+가 음악+을 계속하+[는 한]

이 우승+의 감격+은 잊+[지 못하]+[ㄹ 것]+이+ㅂ니다.
잊지 못할 것입니다

• **고맙다 (adjective)** : 남이 자신을 위해 무엇을 해주어서 마음이 흐뭇하고 보답하고 싶다.
thankful; grateful
Pleased and wanting to return a favor to someone.

• -습니다 : (아주높임으로) 현재의 동작이나 상태, 사실을 정중하게 설명함을 나타내는 종결 어미.
-seupnida (no equivalent expression)
(formal, highly addressee-raising) A sentence-final ending used to explain the present action, state, or fact politely.

• **제 (pronoun)** : 말하는 사람이 자신을 낮추어 가리키는 말인 '저'에 조사 '가'가 붙을 때의 형태.
I
A form of '저' (I), the humble form used by the speaker to show humility, when the postpositional particle '가' is attached to it.

• 가 : 어떤 상태나 상황에 놓인 대상이나 동작의 주체를 나타내는 조사.
ga (no equivalent expression)
A postpositional particle referring to a subject under a certain state or situation, or the subject of an act.

• **음악 (noun)** : 목소리나 악기로 박자와 가락이 있게 소리 내어 생각이나 감정을 표현하는 예술.
music
A field of art, in which one expresses one's thoughts or emotions by using one's voice or a musical instrument to make sounds with beats and melody.

• 을 : 동작이 직접적으로 영향을 미치는 대상을 나타내는 조사.
eul (no equivalent expression)
A postpositional particle used to indicate the subject that an action has a direct influence on.

• **계속하다 (verb)** : 끊지 않고 이어 나가다.
continue
To keep doing something without interruption.

• -는 한 : 앞에 오는 말이 뒤의 행위나 상태에 대해 전제나 조건이 됨을 나타내는 표현.
-neun han (no equivalent expression)
An expression used to indicate that the preceding statement becomes the premise or condition for the act or state in the following statement.

• **이 (determiner)** : 말하는 사람에게 가까이 있거나 말하는 사람이 생각하고 있는 대상을 가리킬 때 쓰는 말.
this
The word that is used to refer to a person who is close to the speaker or something that the speaker is thinking of.

• **우승 (noun)** : 경기나 시합에서 상대를 모두 이겨 일 위를 차지함.
victory; championship
The act of defeating all opponents and taking the first place in a contest or competition.

• 의 : 앞의 말이 뒤의 말에 대하여 속성이나 수량을 한정하거나 같은 자격임을 나타내는 조사.
ui (no equivalent expression)
A postpositional particle used to indicate that the referent of the preceding word limits the properties or amount of the referent of the following word or that two words are on an equal footing.

• **감격 (noun)** : 마음에 깊이 느끼어 매우 감동함. 또는 그 감동.
strong feelings; strong impression; deep emotion
The state of feeling of being touched by something very deeply, or such an emotional state.

• 은 : 강조의 뜻을 나타내는 조사.
eun (no equivalent expression)
A postpositional particle used to indicate an emphasis.

• **잊다 (verb)** : 한번 알았던 것을 기억하지 못하거나 기억해 내지 못하다.
forget; be forgetful of
To not remember or fail to remember something that one knew once.

• -지 못하다 : 앞의 말이 나타내는 행동을 할 능력이 없거나 주어의 의지대로 되지 않음을 나타내는 표현.

-ji motada (no equivalent expression)

An expression used to indicate that the speaker cannot do the act mentioned in the preceding statement, or that things did not work out as the subject intended.

• -ㄹ 것 : 명사가 아닌 것을 문장에서 명사처럼 쓰이게 하거나 '이다' 앞에 쓰일 수 있게 할 때 쓰는 표현.

-l geot (no equivalent expression)

An expression used to enable a non-noun word to be used as a noun in the sentence or to be used in front of '이다' (be).

• 이다 : 주어가 지시하는 대상의 속성이나 부류를 지정하는 뜻을 나타내는 서술격 조사.

ida (no equivalent expression)

A predicate particle indicating the meaning of the attribute or category of the thing that the subject of the sentence refers to.

• -ㅂ니다 : (아주높임으로) 현재의 동작이나 상태, 사실을 정중하게 설명함을 나타내는 종결 어미.

-pnida (no equivalent expression)

(formal, highly addressee-raising) A sentence-final ending used to explain the present action, state, or fact politely.

< 대화(dialogue) > - 55

지아 씨, 영화 홍보는 어떻게 되고 있어요?
지아 씨, 영화 홍보는 어떠케 되고 이써요?
jia ssi, yeonghwa hongboneun eotteoke doego isseoyo?

길거리 홍보 활동을 벌이는 한편 관객을 초대해서 무료 시사회를 하기로 했어요.
길꺼리 홍보 활동을 버리는 한편 관개글 초대해서 무료 시사회를 하기로 해써요.
gilgeori hongbo hwaldongeul beorineun hanpyeon gwangaegeul chodaehaeseo muryo sisahoereul hagiro haesseoyo.

< 설명(explanation) / 번역(translation) >

지아 씨, 영화 홍보+는 어떻게 되+[고 있]+어요?

• **지아 (noun)** : person's name

• **씨 (noun)** : 그 사람을 높여 부르거나 이르는 말.
Mr.; Ms.; Mrs.
A bound noun used to address or call out to a certain person deferentially.

• **영화 (noun)** : 일정한 의미를 갖고 움직이는 대상을 촬영하여 영사기로 영사막에 비추어서 보게 하는 종합 예술.
film; movie
A composite art which captures moving objects on film with a certain message and then shows it on a screen by using a projector.

• **홍보 (noun)** : 널리 알림. 또는 그 소식.
promotion; publicity; advertisement
An act of promoting a product, service, program, etc., widely to a certain target; or such a promotion.

• 는 : 문장 속에서 어떤 대상이 화제임을 나타내는 조사.
neun (no equivalent expression)
A postpositional particle used to indicate that a certain subject is the topic of a sentence.

• **어떻게 (adverb)** : 어떤 방법으로. 또는 어떤 방식으로.
how
In what method; in what way.

• **되다 (verb)** : 일이 잘 이루어지다.
work; go well
For something to work out well.

• -고 있다 : 앞의 말이 나타내는 행동이 계속 진행됨을 나타내는 표현.
-go itda (no equivalent expression)
An expression used to state that the act mentioned in the preceding statement is continued.

• -어요 : (두루높임으로) 어떤 사실을 서술하거나 질문, 명령, 권유함을 나타내는 종결 어미.
-eoyo (no equivalent expression)
(informal addressee-raising) A sentence-final ending used to describe a certain fact, **ask a question**, give an order, or advise.

길거리 홍보 활동+을 벌이+[는 한편] 관객+을 초대하+여서
초대해서

무료 시사회+를 하+[기로 하]+였+어요.
하기로 했어요

• **길거리 (noun)** : 사람이나 차가 다니는 길.
road; street
A street or road for people or cars to travel on.

• **홍보 (noun)** : 널리 알림. 또는 그 소식.
promotion; publicity; advertisement
An act of promoting a product, service, program, etc., widely to a certain target; or such a promotion.

• **활동 (noun)** : 어떤 일에서 좋은 결과를 거두기 위해 힘씀.
activity; effort; campaign
An act of striving to achieve a good result in a certain task.

• 을 : 동작이 직접적으로 영향을 미치는 대상을 나타내는 조사.
eul (no equivalent expression)
A postpositional particle used to indicate the subject that an action has a direct influence on.

• **벌이다 (verb)** : 일을 계획하여 시작하거나 펼치다.
kick off; start
To plan a certain project and kick off or proceed with it.

• -는 한편 : 앞의 말이 나타내는 일을 하는 동시에 다른 쪽에서 또 다른 일을 함을 나타내는 표현.
-neun hanpyeon (no equivalent expression)
An expression used to indicate that one does a certain thing mentioned in the preceding statement, while doing another thing, simultaneously.

• **관객 (noun)** : 운동 경기, 영화, 연극, 음악회, 무용 공연 등을 구경하는 사람.
audience; concertgoer; theatergoer; moviegoer
A person who watches sports games, movies, plays, concerts, dance performances, etc.

• 을 : 동작이 직접적으로 영향을 미치는 대상을 나타내는 조사.
eul (no equivalent expression)
A postpositional particle used to indicate the subject that an action has a direct influence on.

• **초대하다 (verb)** : 다른 사람에게 어떤 자리, 모임, 행사 등에 와 달라고 요청하다.
invite
To ask someone to come to a certain place, gathering, event, etc.

• -여서 : 앞의 말과 뒤의 말이 순차적으로 일어남을 나타내는 연결 어미.
-yeoseo (no equivalent expression)
A connective ending used to indicate that the preceding event and the following one happened sequentially.

• **무료 (noun)** : 요금이 없음.
free; no charge; complimentary
A state of charging nothing.

• **시사회 (noun)** : 영화나 광고 등을 일반에게 보이기 전에 몇몇 사람들에게 먼저 보이고 평가를 받기 위한 모임.
preview
A gathering where a movie, advertisement, etc., is shown to a few people to be evaluated before being shown to the general public.

• 를 : 동작이 직접적으로 영향을 미치는 대상을 나타내는 조사.
reul (no equivalent expression)
A postpositional particle used to indicate the subject that an act has a direct influence on.

• **하다 (verb)** : 어떤 행동이나 동작, 활동 등을 행하다.
do; perform
To perform a certain move, action, activity, etc.

• -기로 하다 : 앞의 말이 나타내는 행동을 할 것을 결심하거나 약속함을 나타내는 표현.
-giro hada (no equivalent expression)
An expression used to decide or promise the performance of the act mentioned in the preceding statement.

• -였- : 어떤 사건이 과거에 완료되었거나 그 사건의 결과가 현재까지 지속되는 상황을 나타내는 어미.
-yeot- (no equivalent expression)
An ending of a word used to indicate that an event was completed in the past or its result continues in the present.

• -어요 : (두루높임으로) 어떤 사실을 서술하거나 질문, 명령, 권유함을 나타내는 종결 어미.
-eoyo (no equivalent expression)
(informal addressee-raising) A sentence-final ending used to **describe** a certain fact, ask a question, give an order, or advise.

< 대화(dialogue) > - 56

왜 절뚝거리면서 걸어요?
왜 절뚝꺼리면서 거러요?
wae jeolttukgeorimyeonseo georeoyo?

예전에 교통사고로 다리를 다쳤는데 평소에 괜찮다가도 비만 오면 다시 아파요.
예저네 교통사고로 다리를 다천는데 평소에 괜찬다가도 비만 오면 다시 아파요.
yejeone gyotongsagoro darireul dacheonneunde pyeongsoe gwaenchantagado biman omyeon dasi apayo.

< 설명(explanation) / 번역(translation) >

왜 절뚝거리+면서 걷(걸)+어요?
걸어요

• **왜 (adverb)** : 무슨 이유로. 또는 어째서.
why
For what reason; how come.

• **절뚝거리다 (verb)** : 한쪽 다리가 짧거나 다쳐서 자꾸 중심을 잃고 절다.
limp
To keep losing balance and walk lamely because one of one's legs is shorter or injured.

• -면서 : 두 가지 이상의 동작이나 상태가 함께 일어남을 나타내는 연결 어미.
-myeonseo (no equivalent expression)
A connective ending used when more than two actions or states happen at the same time.

• **걷다 (verb)** : 바닥에서 발을 번갈아 떼어 옮기면서 움직여 위치를 옮기다.
walk
To lift one's feet, one foot at a time, from the ground and change their positions.

• -어요 : (두루높임으로) 어떤 사실을 서술하거나 질문, 명령, 권유함을 나타내는 종결 어미.
-eoyo (no equivalent expression)
(informal addressee-raising) A sentence-final ending used to describe a certain fact, **ask a question**, give an order, or advise.

예전+에 교통사고+로 다리+를 다치+었+는데 평소+에 괜찮+다가도
다쳤는데

비+만 오+면 다시 아프(아ㅍ)+아요.
아파요

• **예전 (noun)** : 꽤 시간이 흐른 지난날.
past; old days
Past days after which quite a long time has passed.

• 에 : 앞말이 시간이나 때임을 나타내는 조사.
in; at
A postpositional particle to indicate that the preceding statement refers to the time.

• **교통사고 (noun)** : 자동차나 기차 등이 다른 교통 기관과 부딪치거나 사람을 치는 사고.
traffic accident; car crash
An accident between a car or train crashing into another vehicle or with a pedestrian.

• 로 : 어떤 일의 원인이나 이유를 나타내는 조사.
ro (no equivalent expression)
A postpositional particle that indicates the cause or reason for something.

• **다리 (noun)** : 사람이나 동물의 몸통 아래에 붙어, 서고 걷고 뛰는 일을 하는 신체 부위.
leg
A body part attached to the bottom of the torso of a person or animal that is used to walk or run.

• 를 : 동작이 직접적으로 영향을 미치는 대상을 나타내는 조사.
reul (no equivalent expression)
A postpositional particle used to indicate the subject that an act has a direct influence on.

• **다치다 (verb)** : 부딪치거나 맞거나 하여 몸이나 몸의 일부에 상처가 생기다. 또는 상처가 생기게 하다.
be injured
To be hit or bumped into by something or someone, so that one's body or body part is injured; to make an injury.

• -었- : 사건이 과거에 일어났음을 나타내는 어미.
-eot- (no equivalent expression)
An ending of a word used to indicate that an event happened in the past.

• -는데 : 뒤의 말을 하기 위하여 그 대상과 관련이 있는 상황을 미리 말함을 나타내는 연결 어미.
-neunde (no equivalent expression)
A connective ending used to talk in advance about a situation to follow.

• **평소 (noun)** : 특별한 일이 없는 보통 때.
ordinary times
Ordinary times in which nothing special is happening.

• 에 : 앞말이 시간이나 때임을 나타내는 조사.
in; at
A postpositional particle to indicate that the preceding statement refers to the time.

• **괜찮다 (adjective)** : 별 문제가 없다.
all right; fine
Having no particular problems.

• -다가도 : 앞의 말이 나타내는 행위나 상태가 다른 행위나 상태로 쉽게 바뀜을 나타내는 표현.
-dagado (no equivalent expression)
An expression used to indicate that a certain act or state is easily changed to another act or state.

• **비 (noun)** : 높은 곳에서 구름을 이루고 있던 수증기가 식어서 뭉쳐 떨어지는 물방울.
rain
Water drops generated from cloud-forming vapors high in the sky that get cold, condense, and fall.

• 만 : 앞의 말이 어떤 것에 대한 조건임을 나타내는 조사.
man (no equivalent expression)
A postpositional particle used when the preceding statement is a precondition for something.

• **오다 (verb)** : 비, 눈 등이 내리거나 추위 등이 닥치다.
come; arrive
For the rain, snow, etc., to fall, or for a cold spell to arrive.

• -면 : 뒤에 오는 말에 대한 근거나 조건이 됨을 나타내는 연결 어미.
-myeon (no equivalent expression)
A connective ending used when the preceding statement becomes the reason or condition of the following statement.

• **다시 (adverb)** : 같은 말이나 행동을 반복해서 또.
again
Repeatedly with the same words or behavior.

• **아프다 (adjective)** : 다치거나 병이 생겨 통증이나 괴로움을 느끼다.
hurting; aching
Feeling pain or suffering due to an injury or illness.

• -아요 : (두루높임으로) 어떤 사실을 서술하거나 질문, 명령, 권유함을 나타내는 종결 어미.
-ayo (no equivalent expression)
(informal addressee-raising) A sentence-final ending used to **describe** a certain fact, ask a question, give an order, or advise.

< 대화(dialogue) > - 57

한국어를 잘하게 된 방법이 뭐니?
한구거를 잘하게 된 방버비 뭐니?
hangugeoreul jalhage doen bangbeobi mwoni?

한국 음악을 좋아해서 많이 듣다 보니까 한국어를 잘하게 됐어.
한국 으마글 조아해서 마니 듣따 보니까 한구거를 잘하게 돼써.
hanguk eumageul joahaeseo mani deutda bonikka hangugeoreul jalhage dwaesseo.

< 설명(explanation) / 번역(translation) >

한국어+를 잘하+[게 되]+ㄴ 방법+이 뭐+(이)+니?

잘하게 된 **뭐니**

• **한국어 (noun)** : 한국에서 사용하는 말.
Korean; Korean language
The language used by the Korean people.

• 를 : 동작이 직접적으로 영향을 미치는 대상을 나타내는 조사.
reul (no equivalent expression)
A postpositional particle used to indicate the subject that an act has a direct influence on.

• **잘하다 (verb)** : 익숙하고 솜씨가 있게 하다.
be skillful; be expert; be good
To do something in a skilled and experienced manner.

• -게 되다 : 앞의 말이 나타내는 상태나 상황이 됨을 나타내는 표현.
-ge doeda (no equivalent expression)
An expression used to indicate that something will become the state or situation mentioned in the preceding statement.

• -ㄴ : 앞의 말이 관형어의 기능을 하게 만들고 사건이나 동작이 완료되어 그 상태가 유지되고 있음을 나타내는 어미.
-n (no equivalent expression)
An ending of a word that makes the preceding statement function as an adnominal phrase and indicates that an event or action has been completed and its state continues.

• **방법 (noun)** : 어떤 일을 해 나가기 위한 수단이나 방식.
way; means; manner
A method or way of doing something.

• 이 : 어떤 상태나 상황의 대상이나 동작의 주체를 나타내는 조사.
i (no equivalent expression)
A postpositional particle referring to a subject under a certain state or situation, or the agent of an action.

• **뭐 (pronoun)** : 모르는 사실이나 사물을 가리키는 말.
what
A pronoun used to refer to a fact or object that one does not know of.

• 이다 : 주어가 지시하는 대상의 속성이나 부류를 지정하는 뜻을 나타내는 서술격 조사.
ida (no equivalent expression)
A predicate particle indicating the meaning of the attribute or category of the thing that the subject of the sentence refers to.

• -니 : (아주낮춤으로) 물음을 나타내는 종결 어미.
-ni (no equivalent expression)
(formal, highly addressee-lowering) A sentence-final ending referring to a question.

한국 음악+을 좋아하+여서 많이 듣+[다(가) 보]+니까

좋아해서 듣다 보니까

한국어+를 잘하+[게 되]+었+어.

잘하게 됐어

• **한국 (noun)** : 아시아 대륙의 동쪽에 있는 나라. 한반도와 그 부속 섬들로 이루어져 있으며, 대한민국이라고도 부른다. 1950년에 일어난 육이오 전쟁 이후 휴전선을 사이에 두고 국토가 둘로 나뉘었다. 언어는 한국어이고, 수도는 서울이다.
Korea
A country located in East Asia; it consists of the Korean Peninsula and affiliated islands; divided into South Korea and North Korea since the 1953 ceasefire agreement, it is called either the Republic of Korea or South Korea; the official language is Korean and the capital is Seoul.

• **음악 (noun)** : 목소리나 악기로 박자와 가락이 있게 소리 내어 생각이나 감정을 표현하는 예술.
music
A field of art, in which one expresses one's thoughts or emotions by using one's voice or a musical instrument to make sounds with beats and melody.

• 을 : 동작이 직접적으로 영향을 미치는 대상을 나타내는 조사.
eul (no equivalent expression)
A postpositional particle used to indicate the subject that an action has a direct influence on.

• **좋아하다 (verb)** : 무엇에 대하여 좋은 느낌을 가지다.
like
To have good feelings toward something.

• -여서 : 이유나 근거를 나타내는 연결 어미.
-yeoseo (no equivalent expression)
A connective ending used to indicate a reason or cause.

• **많이 (adverb)** : 수나 양, 정도 등이 일정한 기준보다 넘게.
much; in large numbers; in large amounts
In a state in which a number, amount, degree, etc., are larger than a certain standard.

• **듣다 (verb)** : 귀로 소리를 알아차리다.
hear
To sense a sound with ears.

• -다가 보다 : 앞에 오는 말이 나타내는 행동을 하는 과정에서 뒤에 오는 말이 나타내는 사실을 새로 깨닫게 됨을 나타내는 표현.
-daga boda (no equivalent expression)
An expression used when one newly realizes a fact mentioned in the following statement, while doing an action mentioned in the preceding statement.

• -니까 : 뒤에 오는 말에 대하여 앞에 오는 말이 원인이나 근거, 전제가 됨을 강조하여 나타내는 연결 어미.
-nikka (no equivalent expression)
A connective ending used to emphasize that the preceding statement is the cause, reason, or premise for the following statement.

• **한국어 (noun)** : 한국에서 사용하는 말.
Korean; Korean language
The language used by the Korean people.

• 를 : 동작이 직접적으로 영향을 미치는 대상을 나타내는 조사.
reul (no equivalent expression)
A postpositional particle used to indicate the subject that an act has a direct influence on.

• **잘하다 (verb)** : 익숙하고 솜씨가 있게 하다.
be skillful; be expert; be good
To do something in a skilled and experienced manner.

• -게 되다 : 앞의 말이 나타내는 상태나 상황이 됨을 나타내는 표현.
-ge doeda (no equivalent expression)
An expression used to indicate that something will become the state or situation mentioned in the preceding statement.

• -었- : 어떤 사건이 과거에 완료되었거나 그 사건의 결과가 현재까지 지속되는 상황을 나타내는 어미.
-eot- (no equivalent expression)
An ending of a word used to indicate that an event was completed in the past or its result continues in the present.

• -어 : (두루낮춤으로) 어떤 사실을 서술하거나 물음, 명령, 권유를 나타내는 종결 어미.
-eo (no equivalent expression)
(informal addressee-lowering) A sentence-final ending used to **describe** a certain fact, ask a question, give an order, or advise.

< 대화(dialogue) > - 58

너 이 영화 봤어?
너 이 영화 봐써?
neo i yeonghwa bwasseo?

나는 못 보고 우리 형이 봤는데 내용이 엄청 슬프다고 그러더라.
나는 몯 보고 우리 형이 봔는데 내용이 엄청 슬프다고 그러더라.
naneun mot bogo uri hyeongi bwanneunde naeyongi eomcheong seulpeudago geureodeora.

< 설명(explanation) / 번역(translation) >

너 이 영화 보+았+어?
봤어

• **너 (pronoun)** : 듣는 사람이 친구나 아랫사람일 때, 그 사람을 가리키는 말.
no equivalent expression
A pronoun used to indicate the listener when he/she is the same age or younger.

• **이 (determiner)** : 말하는 사람에게 가까이 있거나 말하는 사람이 생각하고 있는 대상을 가리킬 때 쓰는 말.
this
The word that is used to refer to a person who is close to the speaker or something that the speaker is thinking of.

• **영화 (noun)** : 일정한 의미를 갖고 움직이는 대상을 촬영하여 영사기로 영사막에 비추어서 보게 하는 종합 예술.
film; movie
A composite art which captures moving objects on film with a certain message and then shows it on a screen by using a projector.

• **보다 (verb)** : 눈으로 대상을 즐기거나 감상하다.
watch; see; enjoy
To enjoy or appreciate an object with eyes.

• -았- : 어떤 사건이 과거에 완료되었거나 그 사건의 결과가 현재까지 지속되는 상황을 나타내는 어미.
-at- (no equivalent expression)
An ending of a word used to indicate that an event was completed in the past or its result continues in the present.

• -어 : (두루낮춤으로) 어떤 사실을 서술하거나 물음, 명령, 권유를 나타내는 종결 어미.
-eo (no equivalent expression)
(informal addressee-lowering) A sentence-final ending used to describe a certain fact, **ask a question**, give an order, or advise.

나+는 못 보+고 우리 형+이 보+았+는데 내용+이 엄청 슬프+다고 그러+더라.
봤는데

• **나 (pronoun)** : 말하는 사람이 친구나 아랫사람에게 자기를 가리키는 말.
I
A pronoun used to indicate oneself to a friend or a younger person.

• 는 : 어떤 대상이 다른 것과 대조됨을 나타내는 조사.
neun (no equivalent expression)
A postpositional particle used to indicate that a certain subject contrasts with something else.

• **못 (adverb)** : 동사가 나타내는 동작을 할 수 없게.
not
The word that negates the action represented by the verb.

• **보다 (verb)** : 눈으로 대상을 즐기거나 감상하다.
watch; see; enjoy
To enjoy or appreciate an object with eyes.

• -고 : 두 가지 이상의 대등한 사실을 나열할 때 쓰는 연결 어미.
-go (no equivalent expression)
A connective ending used when listing more than two equal facts.

• **우리 (pronoun)** : 말하는 사람이 자기보다 높지 않은 사람에게 자기와 관련된 것을 친근하게 나타낼 때 쓰는 말.
uri (no equivalent expression)
we: A pronoun used when the speaker intimately refers to something related to him/her while speaking to the person junior to himself/herself.

• **형 (noun)** : 남자가 형제나 친척 형제들 중에서 자기보다 나이가 많은 남자를 이르거나 부르는 말.
older brother
A word used only by a male to refer to or address his male siblings or cousins older than himself.

• 이 : 어떤 상태나 상황의 대상이나 동작의 주체를 나타내는 조사.
i (no equivalent expression)
A postpositional particle referring to a subject under a certain state or situation, or the agent of an action.

• **보다 (verb)** : 눈으로 대상을 즐기거나 감상하다.
watch; see; enjoy
To enjoy or appreciate an object with eyes.

• -았- : 어떤 사건이 과거에 완료되었거나 그 사건의 결과가 현재까지 지속되는 상황을 나타내는 어미.
-at- (no equivalent expression)
An ending of a word used to indicate that an event was completed in the past or its result continues in the present.

• -는데 : 뒤의 말을 하기 위하여 그 대상과 관련이 있는 상황을 미리 말함을 나타내는 연결 어미.
-neunde (no equivalent expression)
A connective ending used to talk in advance about a situation to follow.

• **내용 (noun)** : 말, 글, 그림, 영화 등의 줄거리. 또는 그것들로 전하고자 하는 것.
story; message
The story of speech, writing, picture, movie, etc., or what such things try to convey.

• 이 : 어떤 상태나 상황의 대상이나 동작의 주체를 나타내는 조사.
i (no equivalent expression)
A postpositional particle referring to a subject under a certain state or situation, or the agent of an action.

• **엄청 (adverb)** : 양이나 정도가 아주 지나치게.
very; extremely
In an unusually large manner in size or degree.

• **슬프다 (adjective)** : 눈물이 날 만큼 마음이 아프고 괴롭다.
sad
Sad and sorrowful enough to make one cry.

• -다고 : 다른 사람에게서 들은 내용을 간접적으로 전달하거나 주어의 생각, 의견 등을 나타내는 표현.
-dago (no equivalent expression)
An expression used to pass along what the speaker heard from another person, or to present the subject's thoughts, opinions, etc.

• **그러다 (verb)** : 그렇게 말하다.
say so
To say so.

• -더라 : (아주낮춤으로) 말하는 이가 직접 경험하여 새롭게 알게 된 사실을 지금 전달함을 나타내는 종결 어미.

-deora (no equivalent expression)

(formal, highly addressee-lowering) A sentence-final ending used to convey in the present a fact the speaker realized anew from the speaker's personal experience.

< 대화(dialogue) > - 59

뭘 만들기에 이렇게 냄새가 좋아요?
뭘 만들기에 이러케 냄새가 조아요?
mwol mandeulgie ireoke naemsaega joayo?

지우가 입맛이 없다길래 이것저것 만드는 중이에요.
지우가 임마시 업따길래 이걷쩌걷 만드는 중이에요.
jiuga immasi eopdagillae igeotjeogeot mandeuneun jungieyo.

< 설명(explanation) / 번역(translation) >

뭐+를 만들+기에 이렇+게 냄새+가 좋+아요?
뭘

• **뭐 (pronoun)** : 모르는 사실이나 사물을 가리키는 말.
what
A pronoun used to refer to a fact or object that one does not know of.

• 를 : 동작이 직접적으로 영향을 미치는 대상을 나타내는 조사.
reul (no equivalent expression)
A postpositional particle used to indicate the subject that an act has a direct influence on.

• **만들다 (verb)** : 힘과 기술을 써서 없던 것을 생기게 하다.
make; create; produce; manufacture
To create something that did not exist, using one's power or skill.

• -기에 : 뒤에 오는 말의 원인이나 근거를 나타내는 연결 어미.
-gie (no equivalent expression)
A connective ending referring to the cause or reason of the following statement.

• **이렇다 (adjective)** : 상태, 모양, 성질 등이 이와 같다.
so; like this
(for a state, appearance, nature to be) Like this.

• -게 : 앞의 말이 뒤에서 가리키는 일의 목적이나 결과, 방식, 정도 등이 됨을 나타내는 연결 어미.
-ge (no equivalent expression)
A connective ending used when the preceding statement is the purpose, result, method, amount, etc., of something mentioned in the following statement.

• **냄새 (noun)** : 코로 맡을 수 있는 기운.
smell; scent; odor
The trait of something the nose can sense.

• 가 : 어떤 상태나 상황에 놓인 대상이나 동작의 주체를 나타내는 조사.
ga (no equivalent expression)
A postpositional particle referring to a subject under a certain state or situation, or the subject of an act.

• **좋다 (adjective)** : 어떤 일이나 대상이 마음에 들고 만족스럽다.
fond of; in love with
Happy about and satisfied with a thing or object.

• -아요 : (두루높임으로) 어떤 사실을 서술하거나 질문, 명령, 권유함을 나타내는 종결 어미.
-ayo (no equivalent expression)
(informal addressee-raising) A sentence-final ending used to describe a certain fact, **ask a question**, give an order, or advise.

지우+가 입맛+이 없+다길래 이것저것 만들(만드)+[는 중이]+에요.

만드는 중이에요

• **지우 (noun)** : person's name

• 가 : 어떤 상태나 상황에 놓인 대상이나 동작의 주체를 나타내는 조사.
ga (no equivalent expression)
A postpositional particle referring to a subject under a certain state or situation, or the subject of an act.

• **입맛 (noun)** : 음식을 먹을 때 입에서 느끼는 맛. 또는 음식을 먹고 싶은 욕구.
taste bud; appetite
The taste that one feels when eating, or the desire to eat.

• 이 : 어떤 상태나 상황의 대상이나 동작의 주체를 나타내는 조사.
i (no equivalent expression)
A postpositional particle referring to a subject under a certain state or situation, or the agent of an action.

• **없다 (adjective)** : 어떤 사실이나 현상이 현실로 존재하지 않는 상태이다.
lacking
(for a fact or phenomenon to be) Not existent in reality.

• -다길래 : 뒤 내용의 이유나 근거로 다른 사람에게 들은 사실을 말할 때 쓰는 표현.
-dagillae (no equivalent expression)
An expression used to say something the speaker heard as the reason or basis for the following statement.

• **이것저것 (noun)** : 분명하게 정해지지 않은 여러 가지 사물이나 일.
this and that; everything
Various things or matters that are not certainly defined.

• **만들다 (verb)** : 힘과 기술을 써서 없던 것을 생기게 하다.
make; create; produce; manufacture
To create something that did not exist, using one's power or skill.

• -는 중이다 : 어떤 일이 진행되고 있음을 나타내는 표현.
-neun jungida (no equivalent expression)
An expression used to indicate that a certain thing is in progress.

• -에요 : (두루높임으로) 어떤 사실을 서술하거나 질문함을 나타내는 종결 어미.
-eyo (no equivalent expression)
(informal addressee-raising) A sentence-final ending used when **describing** a certain fact or asking a question.

< 대화(dialogue) > - 60

설명서를 아무리 봐도 무슨 말인지 잘 모르겠죠?
설명서를 아무리 봐도 무슨 마린지 잘 모르겐쬬?
seolmyeongseoreul amuri bwado museun marinji jal moreugetjyo?

그래도 자꾸 읽다 보니 조금씩 이해가 되던걸요.
그래도 자꾸 익따 보니 조금씩 이해가 되던거료.
geuraedo jakku ikda boni jogeumssik ihaega doedeongeoryo.

< 설명(explanation) / 번역(translation) >

설명서+를 아무리 보+아도 무슨 말+이+ㄴ지 잘 모르+겠+죠?

봐도 말인지

• **설명서 (noun)** : 일이나 사물의 내용, 이유, 사용법 등을 설명한 글.
directions; instructions; manual
An explanatory writing that describes the content, reasons, directions, etc., of a task or object.

• 를 : 동작이 직접적으로 영향을 미치는 대상을 나타내는 조사.
reul (no equivalent expression)
A postpositional particle used to indicate the subject that an act has a direct influence on.

• **아무리 (adverb)** : 비록 그렇다 하더라도.
no matter how; however; whatever
Even so.

• **보다 (verb)** : 책이나 신문, 지도 등의 글자나 그림, 기호 등을 읽고 내용을 이해하다.
read; look at; take a look at
To read and understand the words, pictures and symbols in a book, newspaper, map, etc.

• -아도 : 앞에 오는 말을 가정하거나 인정하지만 뒤에 오는 말에는 관계가 없거나 영향을 끼치지 않음을 나타내는 연결 어미.
-ado (no equivalent expression)
A connective ending used when assuming or recognizing the truth of the preceding statement, although it is not related to or does not influence the following statement.

• **무슨 (determiner)** : 확실하지 않거나 잘 모르는 일, 대상, 물건 등을 물을 때 쓰는 말.
what
An expression used to ask about a business, subject or object that one is not sure of or does not exactly know.

• **말 (noun)** : 단어나 구나 문장.
word; maxim
A word, phrase or sentence.

• 이다 : 주어가 지시하는 대상의 속성이나 부류를 지정하는 뜻을 나타내는 서술격 조사.
ida (no equivalent expression)
A predicate particle indicating the meaning of the attribute or category of the thing that the subject of the sentence refers to.

• -ㄴ지 : 뒤에 오는 말의 내용에 대한 막연한 이유나 판단을 나타내는 연결 어미.
-nji (no equivalent expression)
A connective ending used to indicate an ambiguous reason or judgment about the following statement.

• **잘 (adverb)** : 분명하고 정확하게.
well
Clearly and precisely.

• **모르다 (verb)** : 사람이나 사물, 사실 등을 알지 못하거나 이해하지 못하다.
not know
To have no knowledge or understanding of a person, object or fact.

• -겠- : 미래의 일이나 추측을 나타내는 어미.
-get- (no equivalent expression)
An ending of a word referring to a future event or assumption.

• -죠 : (두루높임으로) 말하는 사람이 듣는 사람에게 친근함을 나타내며 물을 때 쓰는 종결 어미.
-jyo (no equivalent expression)
(informal addressee-raising) A sentence-final ending used when the speaker asks the listener something in a friendly manner.

그렇+어도 자꾸 읽+[다(가) 보]+니 조금씩 이해+가 되+던걸요.
그래도 읽다 보니

• **그렇다 (adjective)** : 상태, 모양, 성질 등이 그와 같다.
so; as such; like that
A state, appearance, characteristic, etc. being as such.

• -어도 : 앞에 오는 말을 가정하거나 인정하지만 뒤에 오는 말에는 관계가 없거나 영향을 끼치지 않음을 나타내는 연결 어미.
-eodo (no equivalent expression)
A connective ending used when assuming or recognizing the truth of the preceding statement, although it is not related to or does not influence the following statement.

• **자꾸 (adverb)** : 여러 번 계속하여.
frequently; repeatedly; again and again
Several times.

• **읽다 (verb)** : 글을 보고 뜻을 알다.
read
To read written words and know their meaning.

• -다가 보다 : 앞에 오는 말이 나타내는 행동을 하는 과정에서 뒤에 오는 말이 나타내는 사실을 새로 깨닫게 됨을 나타내는 표현.
-daga boda (no equivalent expression)
An expression used when one newly realizes a fact mentioned in the following statement, while doing an action mentioned in the preceding statement.

• -니 : 뒤에 오는 말에 대하여 앞에 오는 말이 원인이나 근거, 전제가 됨을 나타내는 연결 어미.
-ni (no equivalent expression)
A connective ending used when the preceding statement is the cause, reason, or premise for the following statement.

• **조금씩 (adverb)** : 적은 정도로 계속해서.
little by little
Continuously in a small quantity.

• **이해 (noun)** : 무엇이 어떤 것인지를 앎. 또는 무엇이 어떤 것이라고 받아들임.
understanding; comprehension
The state of knowing what something is; the process of accepting something as something else.

• 가 : 어떤 상태나 상황에 놓인 대상이나 동작의 주체를 나타내는 조사.
ga (no equivalent expression)
A postpositional particle referring to a subject under a certain state or situation, or the subject of an act.

• **되다 (verb)** : 어떠한 심리적인 상태에 있다.
feel; become
To be in a certain mental state.

• -던걸요 : (두루높임으로) 과거의 사실에 대한 자기 생각이나 주장을 설명하듯 말하거나 그 근거를 댈 때 쓰는 표현.

-deongeolyo (no equivalent expression)

(informal addressee-raising) An expression used when explaining one's thought or argument about a fact of the past, or giving a reason for it.

< 대화(dialogue) > - 61

저는 이번에 개봉한 영화가 재미있던데요.
저는 이버네 개봉한 영화가 재미읻떤데요.
jeoneun ibeone gaebonghan yeonghwaga jaemiitdeondeyo.

그래도 원작이 더 재미있지 않나요?
그래도 원자기 더 재미읻찌 안나요?
geuraedo wonjagi deo jaemiitji annayo?

< 설명(explanation) / 번역(translation) >

저+는 이번+에 개봉하+ㄴ 영화+가 재미있+던데요.
개봉한

• **저 (pronoun)** : 말하는 사람이 듣는 사람에게 자신을 낮추어 가리키는 말.
I; me
The humble form used by the speaker to refer to himself/herself for the purpose of showing humility to the listener.

• 는 : 문장 속에서 어떤 대상이 화제임을 나타내는 조사.
neun (no equivalent expression)
A postpositional particle used to indicate that a certain subject is the topic of a sentence.

• **이번 (noun)** : 곧 돌아올 차례. 또는 막 지나간 차례.
this time
A turn soon to come, or one that just passed.

• 에 : 앞말이 시간이나 때임을 나타내는 조사.
in; at
A postpositional particle to indicate that the preceding statement refers to the time.

• **개봉하다 (verb)** : 새 영화를 처음으로 상영하다.
release; be coming soon
To show a new movie, for the first time.

• -ㄴ : 앞의 말이 관형어의 기능을 하게 만들고 사건이나 동작이 완료되어 그 상태가 유지되고 있음을 나타내는 어미.

-n (no equivalent expression)

An ending of a word that makes the preceding statement function as an adnominal phrase and indicates that an event or action has been completed and its state continues.

• **영화 (noun)** : 일정한 의미를 갖고 움직이는 대상을 촬영하여 영사기로 영사막에 비추어서 보게 하는 종합 예술.

film; movie

A composite art which captures moving objects on film with a certain message and then shows it on a screen by using a projector.

• 가 : 어떤 상태나 상황에 놓인 대상이나 동작의 주체를 나타내는 조사.

ga (no equivalent expression)

A postpositional particle referring to a subject under a certain state or situation, or the subject of an act.

• **재미있다 (adjective)** : 즐겁고 유쾌한 느낌이 있다.

interesting

Feelings of joy and pleasantness being present.

• -던데요 : (두루높임으로) 과거에 직접 경험한 사실을 전달하여 듣는 사람의 반응을 기대함을 나타내는 표현.

-deondeyo (no equivalent expression)

(informal addressee-raising) An expression used to convey the speaker's past personal experience, expecting a response from the listener.

그렇+어도 원작+이 더 재미있+[지 않]+나요?
그래도

• **그렇다 (adjective)** : 상태, 모양, 성질 등이 그와 같다.

so; as such; like that

A state, appearance, characteristic, etc. being as such.

• -어도 : 앞에 오는 말을 가정하거나 인정하지만 뒤에 오는 말에는 관계가 없거나 영향을 끼치지 않음을 나타내는 연결 어미.

-eodo (no equivalent expression)

A connective ending used when assuming or recognizing the truth of the preceding statement, although it is not related to or does not influence the following statement.

• **원작 (noun)** : 연극이나 영화의 대본으로 만들거나 다른 나라 말로 고치기 전의 원래 작품.
original work; original
The original work before being turned into the script of a play or movie, or translated into a foreign language.

• 이 : 어떤 상태나 상황의 대상이나 동작의 주체를 나타내는 조사.
i (no equivalent expression)
A postpositional particle referring to a subject under a certain state or situation, or the agent of an action.

• **더 (adverb)** : 비교의 대상이나 어떤 기준보다 정도가 크게. 그 이상으로.
more
More or higher than something being compared or a certain threshold.

• **재미있다 (adjective)** : 즐겁고 유쾌한 느낌이 있다.
interesting
Feelings of joy and pleasantness being present.

• -지 않다 : 앞의 말이 나타내는 행위나 상태를 부정하는 뜻을 나타내는 표현.
-ji anta (no equivalent expression)
An expression used to deny the act or state indicated in the preceding statement.

• -나요 : (두루높임으로) 앞의 내용에 대해 상대방에게 물어볼 때 쓰는 표현.
-nayo (no equivalent expression)
(informal addressee-raising) An expression used to ask the listener about the preceding content.

< 대화(dialogue) > - 62

이 집 강아지가 밤마다 너무 짖어서 저희가 잠을 잘 못 자요.
이 집 강아지가 밤마다 너무 지저서 저히가 자믈 잘 몯 자요.
i jip gangajiga bammada neomu jijeoseo jeohiga jameul jal mot jayo.

정말 죄송합니다. 못 짖도록 하는데도 그게 쉽지가 않네요.
정말 죄송함니다. 몯 짇또록 하는데도 그게 쉽찌가 안네요.
jeongmal joesonghamnida. mot jitdorok haneundedo geuge swipjiga anneyo.

< 설명(explanation) / 번역(translation) >

이 집 강아지+가 밤+마다 너무 짖+어서 저희+가 잠+을 잘 못 자+(아)요.
자요

• **이 (determiner)** : 말하는 사람에게 가까이 있거나 말하는 사람이 생각하고 있는 대상을 가리킬 때 쓰는 말.
this
The word that is used to refer to a person who is close to the speaker or something that the speaker is thinking of.

• **집 (noun)** : 사람이나 동물이 추위나 더위 등을 막고 그 속에 들어 살기 위해 지은 건물.
house
A structure built by a human or animal to serve as protection from cold, heat, etc., and as a place to live in.

• **강아지 (noun)** : 개의 새끼.
puppy
The pup of a dog.

• 가 : 어떤 상태나 상황에 놓인 대상이나 동작의 주체를 나타내는 조사.
ga (no equivalent expression)
A postpositional particle referring to a subject under a certain state or situation, or the subject of an act.

• **밤 (noun)** : 해가 진 후부터 다음 날 해가 뜨기 전까지의 어두운 동안.
night; evening
The period of dark hours from sunset to sunrise the next day.

• 마다 : 하나하나 빠짐없이 모두의 뜻을 나타내는 조사.
mada (no equivalent expression)
A postpositional particle that means "everything without exception."

• **너무 (adverb)** : 일정한 정도나 한계를 훨씬 넘어선 상태로.
too
To an excessive degree.

• **짖다 (verb)** : 개가 크게 소리를 내다.
bark
For a dog to make a loud sound.

• -어서 : 이유나 근거를 나타내는 연결 어미.
-eoseo (no equivalent expression)
A connective ending used for a reason or cause.

• **저희 (pronoun)** : 말하는 사람이 자기보다 높은 사람에게 자기를 포함한 여러 사람들을 가리키는 말.
our
A word used by the speaker to refer to a group of people including himself/herself when speaking to another person who is superior to him/her.

• 가 : 어떤 상태나 상황에 놓인 대상이나 동작의 주체를 나타내는 조사.
ga (no equivalent expression)
A postpositional particle referring to a subject under a certain state or situation, or the subject of an act.

• **잠 (noun)** : 눈을 감고 몸과 정신의 활동을 멈추고 한동안 쉬는 상태.
sleep
The state of taking a rest for a period of time with one's eyes closed and mental activities suspended.

• 을 : 서술어의 명사형 목적어임을 나타내는 조사.
no equivalent expression
A postpositional particle that indicates the noun object of the predicate.

• **잘 (adverb)** : 충분히 만족스럽게.
well
In a sufficiently satisfactory manner.

• **못 (adverb)** : 동사가 나타내는 동작을 할 수 없게.
not
The word that negates the action represented by the verb.

• **자다 (verb)** : 눈을 감고 몸과 정신의 활동을 멈추고 한동안 쉬는 상태가 되다.
sleep
To be in the state of taking a rest for a period of time with one's eyes closed and mental activities suspended.

• -아요 : (두루높임으로) 어떤 사실을 서술하거나 질문, 명령, 권유함을 나타내는 종결 어미.
-ayo (no equivalent expression)
(informal addressee-raising) A sentence-final ending used to **describe** a certain fact, ask a question, give an order, or advise.

정말 죄송하+ㅂ니다.
죄송합니다

못 짖+[도록 하]+는데도 그것(그거)+이 쉽+[지+가 않]+네요.
그게

• **정말 (adverb)** : 거짓이 없이 진짜로.
really
In actual truth without falsehood.

• **죄송하다 (adjective)** : 죄를 지은 것처럼 몹시 미안하다.
sorry
Very sorry as if one committed a wrongdoing.

• -ㅂ니다 : (아주높임으로) 현재의 동작이나 상태, 사실을 정중하게 설명함을 나타내는 종결 어미.
-pnida (no equivalent expression)
(formal, highly addressee-raising) A sentence-final ending used to explain the present action, state, or fact politely.

• **못 (adverb)** : 동사가 나타내는 동작을 할 수 없게.
not
The word that negates the action represented by the verb.

• **짖다 (verb)** : 개가 크게 소리를 내다.
bark
For a dog to make a loud sound.

• -도록 하다 : 남에게 어떤 행동을 하도록 시키거나 물건이 어떤 작동을 하게 만듦을 나타내는 표현.
-dorok hada (no equivalent expression)
An expression used to order someone to do a certain thing or to make something work.

• -는데도 : 앞에 오는 말이 나타내는 상황에 상관없이 뒤에 오는 말이 나타내는 상황이 일어남을 나타내는 표현.
-neundedo (no equivalent expression)
An expression used to indicate that the following situation will occur, regardless of the preceding situation.

• **그것 (pronoun)** : 앞에서 이미 이야기한 대상을 가리키는 말.
no equivalent expression
A pronoun used to indicate the previously-mentioned object.

• 이 : 어떤 상태나 상황의 대상이나 동작의 주체를 나타내는 조사.
i (no equivalent expression)
A postpositional particle referring to a subject under a certain state or situation, or the agent of an action.

• **쉽다 (adjective)** : 하기에 힘들거나 어렵지 않다.
easy
Not hard or difficult to do.

• -지 않다 : 앞의 말이 나타내는 행위나 상태를 부정하는 뜻을 나타내는 표현.
-ji anta (no equivalent expression)
An expression used to deny the act or state indicated in the preceding statement.

• 가 : 앞의 말을 강조하는 뜻을 나타내는 조사.
ga (no equivalent expression)
A postpositional particle used to emphasize the preceding statement.

• -네요 : (두루높임으로) 말하는 사람이 직접 경험하여 새롭게 알게 된 사실에 대해 감탄함을 나타낼 때 쓰는 표현.
-neyo (no equivalent expression)
(informal addressee-raising) An expression used to indicate that the speaker is impressed by a fact he/she learned anew from a past personal experience.

< 대화(dialogue) > - 63

메일 보냈습니다. 확인 좀 부탁 드립니다.
메일 보낻씀니다. 화긴 좀 부탁 드림니다.
meil bonaetseumnida. hwagin jom butak deurimnida.

네. 보내 주신 자료를 검토하고 다시 연락 드리도록 하겠습니다.
네. 보내 주신 자료를 검토하고 다시 열락 드리도록 하겓씀니다.
ne. bonae jusin jaryoreul geomtohago dasi yeollak deuridorok hagetseumnida.

< 설명(explanation) / 번역(translation) >

메일 보내+었+습니다.
보냈습니다

확인 좀 부탁 드리+ㅂ니다.
드립니다

• **메일 (noun)** : 인터넷이나 통신망으로 주고받는 편지.
e-mail; electronic mail
A letter sent and received through the Internet or other forms of computer networks.

• **보내다 (verb)** : 내용이 전달되게 하다.
deliver; convey
To have content conveyed.

• -었- : 어떤 사건이 과거에 완료되었거나 그 사건의 결과가 현재까지 지속되는 상황을 나타내는 어미.
-eot- (no equivalent expression)
An ending of a word used to indicate that an event was completed in the past or its result continues in the present.

• -습니다 : (아주높임으로) 현재의 동작이나 상태, 사실을 정중하게 설명함을 나타내는 종결 어미.
-seupnida (no equivalent expression)
(formal, highly addressee-raising) A sentence-final ending used to explain the present action, state, or fact politely.

• **확인 (noun)** : 틀림없이 그러한지를 알아보거나 인정함.
check; affirmation; confirmation; verification
An act of finding out if something is true or admitting that it is true.

• **좀 (adverb)** : 주로 부탁이나 동의를 구할 때 부드러운 느낌을 주기 위해 넣는 말.
please
A word chiefly used to soften a request for a favor or agreement.

• **부탁 (noun)** : 어떤 일을 해 달라고 하거나 맡김.
request
The act of asking someone to do something or entrusting someone with something.

• **드리다 (verb)** : 윗사람에게 어떤 말을 하거나 인사를 하다.
say; say hello
To say something or to greet an elder.

• -ㅂ니다 : (아주높임으로) 현재의 동작이나 상태, 사실을 정중하게 설명함을 나타내는 종결 어미.
-pnida (no equivalent expression)
(formal, highly addressee-raising) A sentence-final ending used to explain the present action, state, or fact politely.

네.

보내+[(어) 주]+시+ㄴ 자료+를 검토하+고 다시 연락 드리+[도록 하]+겠+습니다.
보내 주신

• **네 (interjection)** : 윗사람의 물음이나 명령 등에 긍정하여 대답할 때 쓰는 말.
yes; yes sir; yes ma'am
An exclamation uttered when the speaker affirmatively answers the call or order of his/her superior.

• **보내다 (verb)** : 내용이 전달되게 하다.
deliver; convey
To have content conveyed.

• -어 주다 : 남을 위해 앞의 말이 나타내는 행동을 함을 나타내는 표현.
-eo juda (no equivalent expression)
An expression used to indicate that one does the act mentioned in the preceding statement for someone.

• -시- : 어떤 동작이나 상태의 주체를 높이는 뜻을 나타내는 어미.
-si- (no equivalent expression)

An ending of a word used for the subject honorifics of an action or state.

• -ㄴ : 앞의 말이 관형어의 기능을 하게 만들고 사건이나 동작이 완료되어 그 상태가 유지되고 있음을 나타내는 어미.
-n (no equivalent expression)
An ending of a word that makes the preceding statement function as an adnominal phrase and indicates that an event or action has been completed and its state continues.

• **자료 (noun)** : 연구나 조사를 하는 데 기본이 되는 재료.
material; data; reference
Material which is the basis for conducting study or research.

• 를 : 동작이 직접적으로 영향을 미치는 대상을 나타내는 조사.
reul (no equivalent expression)
A postpositional particle used to indicate the subject that an act has a direct influence on.

• **검토하다 (verb)** : 어떤 사실이나 내용을 자세히 따져서 조사하고 분석하다.
review; examine
To review and analyze certain facts or information in depth.

• -고 : 앞의 말과 뒤의 말이 차례대로 일어남을 나타내는 연결 어미.
-go (no equivalent expression)
A connective ending used when the preceding statement and the following statement happen in order.

• **다시 (adverb)** : 다음에 또.
again
Once more in the future.

• **연락 (noun)** : 어떤 사실을 전하여 알림.
communication
The act of delivering a fact.

• **드리다 (verb)** : 윗사람에게 어떤 말을 하거나 인사를 하다.
say; say hello
To say something or to greet an elder.

• -도록 하다 : 말하는 사람이 어떤 행위를 할 것이라는 의지나 다짐을 나타내는 표현.
-dorok hada (no equivalent expression)
An expression used to indicate the speaker's will or determination to do a certain act.

• -겠- : 완곡하게 말하는 태도를 나타내는 어미.
-get- (no equivalent expression)
An ending of a word referring to an attitude of speaking indirectly.

- -습니다 : (아주높임으로) 현재의 동작이나 상태, 사실을 정중하게 설명함을 나타내는 종결 어미.
  -seupnida (no equivalent expression)
  (formal, highly addressee-raising) A sentence-final ending used to explain the present action, state, or fact politely.

< 대화(dialogue) > - 64

이제 아홉 신데 벌써 자려고?
이제 아홉 신데 벌써 자려고?
ije ahop sinde beolsseo jaryeogo?

시험 기간에 도서관 자리 잡기가 어려워서 내일 일찍 일어나려고요.
시험 기가네 도서관 자리 잡끼가 어려워서 내일 일찍 이러나려고요.
siheom gigane doseogwan jari japgiga eoryeowoseo naeil iljjik ireonaryeogoyo.

< 설명(explanation) / 번역(translation) >

이제 아홉 시+(이)+ㄴ데 벌써 자+려고?
신데

• **이제** (adverb) : 말하고 있는 바로 이때에.
now
At this moment of speaking.

• **아홉** (determiner) : 여덟에 하나를 더한 수의.
nine
Related to the number equal to eight plus one.

• **시** (noun) : 하루를 스물넷으로 나누었을 때 그 하나를 나타내는 시간의 단위.
o'clock
A bound noun indicating one of 24 hours of a day.

• 이다 : 주어가 지시하는 대상의 속성이나 부류를 지정하는 뜻을 나타내는 서술격 조사.
ida (no equivalent expression)
A predicate particle indicating the meaning of the attribute or category of the thing that the subject of the sentence refers to.

• -ㄴ데 : 뒤의 말을 하기 위하여 그 대상과 관련이 있는 상황을 미리 말함을 나타내는 연결 어미.
-nde (no equivalent expression)
A connective ending used to talk in advance about a situation to follow.

• **벌써** (adverb) : 생각보다 빠르게.
so soon
More quickly than one thought.

• **자다 (verb)** : 눈을 감고 몸과 정신의 활동을 멈추고 한동안 쉬는 상태가 되다.
sleep
To be in the state of taking a rest for a period of time with one's eyes closed and mental activities suspended.

• -려고 : (두루낮춤으로) 어떤 주어진 상황에 대하여 의심이나 반문을 나타내는 종결 어미.
-ryeogo (no equivalent expression)
(informal addressee-lowering) A sentence-final ending used to doubt a given situation and ask again about it.

시험 기간+에 도서관 자리 잡+기+가 어렵(어려우)+어서
어려워서

내일 일찍 일어나+려고요.

• **시험 (noun)** : 문제, 질문, 실제의 행동 등의 일정한 절차에 따라 지식이나 능력을 검사하고 평가하는 일.
test; exam
The act of testing and evaluating knowledge or capabilities through a particular process involving problems, questions, actual performance, etc.

• **기간 (noun)** : 어느 일정한 때부터 다른 일정한 때까지의 동안.
period; term
The gap from a certain time to another time.

• 에 : 앞말이 시간이나 때임을 나타내는 조사.
in; at
A postpositional particle to indicate that the preceding statement refers to the time.

• **도서관 (noun)** : 책과 자료 등을 많이 모아 두고 사람들이 빌려 읽거나 공부를 할 수 있게 마련한 시설.
library
A facility with lots of books and materials for people to borrow and read or study.

• **자리 (noun)** : 사람이 앉을 수 있도록 만들어 놓은 곳.
seat
A place where a person can sit.

• **잡다 (verb)** : 자리, 방향, 시기 등을 정하다.
fix; determine
To decide on a location, direction, time, etc.

• -기 : 앞의 말이 명사의 기능을 하게 하는 어미.
-gi (no equivalent expression)
An ending of a word used to make the preceding word function as a noun.

• 가 : 어떤 상태나 상황에 놓인 대상이나 동작의 주체를 나타내는 조사.
ga (no equivalent expression)
A postpositional particle referring to a subject under a certain state or situation, or the subject of an act.

• **어렵다 (adjective)** : 하기가 복잡하거나 힘이 들다.
difficult; challenging
Very complicated or hard to do.

• -어서 : 이유나 근거를 나타내는 연결 어미.
-eoseo (no equivalent expression)
A connective ending used for a reason or cause.

• **내일 (adverb)** : 오늘의 다음 날에.
tomorrow
On the day after today.

• **일찍 (adverb)** : 정해진 시간보다 빠르게.
early
Before the specified time.

• **일어나다 (verb)** : 잠에서 깨어나다.
get up
To wake up.

• -려고요 : (두루높임으로) 어떤 행동을 할 의도나 욕망을 가지고 있음을 나타내는 표현.
-ryeogoyo (no equivalent expression)
(informal addressee-raising) An expression used to indicate that the speaker has the intention or desire to do a certain act.

< 대화(dialogue) > - 65

나 지금 마트에 가려고 하는데 혹시 필요한 거 있니?
나 지금 마트에 가려고 하는데 혹씨 피료한 거 인니?
na jigeum mateue garyeogo haneunde hoksi piryohan geo inni?

그럼 오는 길에 휴지 좀 사다 줄래?
그럼 오는 기레 휴지 좀 사다 줄래?
geureom oneun gire hyuji jom sada jullae?

< 설명(explanation) / 번역(translation) >

나 지금 마트+에 가+[려고 하]+는데 혹시 필요하+[ㄴ 것(거)] 있+니?

필요한 거

• **나 (pronoun)** : 말하는 사람이 친구나 아랫사람에게 자기를 가리키는 말.
I
A pronoun used to indicate oneself to a friend or a younger person.

• **지금 (adverb)** : 말을 하고 있는 바로 이때에. 또는 그 즉시에.
now; immediately
At the present moment as one speaks, or that instant.

• **마트 (noun)** : 각종 생활용품을 판매하는 대형 매장.
mart
A big store that sells all kinds of household items.

• 에 : 앞말이 목적지이거나 어떤 행위의 진행 방향임을 나타내는 조사.
to; at
A postpositional particle to indicate that the preceding statement refers to a destination or the course of a certain action.

• **가다 (verb)** : 한 곳에서 다른 곳으로 장소를 이동하다.
go; travel
To move from one place to another place.

• -려고 하다 : 앞의 말이 나타내는 행동을 할 의도나 의향이 있음을 나타내는 표현.
-ryeogo hada (no equivalent expression)
An expression used to indicate that one has the intention or wish to do the act mentioned in the preceding statement.

• -는데 : 뒤의 말을 하기 위하여 그 대상과 관련이 있는 상황을 미리 말함을 나타내는 연결 어미.
-neunde (no equivalent expression)
A connective ending used to talk in advance about a situation to follow.

• **혹시 (adverb)** : 그러리라 생각하지만 분명하지 않아 말하기를 망설일 때 쓰는 말.
by any chance
The word that is used when one is hesitant to say something he/she thinks is possible but he/she is uncertain about.

• **필요하다 (adjective)** : 꼭 있어야 하다.
necessary; needed
Being necessary.

• -ㄴ 것 : 명사가 아닌 것을 문장에서 명사처럼 쓰이게 하거나 '이다' 앞에 쓰일 수 있게 할 때 쓰는 표현.
-n geot (no equivalent expression)
An expression used to enable a non-noun word to be used as a noun in a sentence or to be used in front of '이다' (be).

• **있다 (adjective)** : 사람, 동물, 물체 등이 존재하는 상태이다.
existent; existing
A person, an animal, an object, etc., being in existence.

• -니 : (아주낮춤으로) 물음을 나타내는 종결 어미.
-ni (no equivalent expression)
(formal, highly addressee-lowering) A sentence-final ending referring to a question.

그럼 오+[는 길에] 휴지 좀 사+(아)다 주+ㄹ래?
사다 줄래

• **그럼 (adverb)** : 앞의 내용을 받아들이거나 그 내용을 바탕으로 하여 새로운 주장을 할 때 쓰는 말.
then
A word used when accepting the preceding statement or making a new suggestion based on it.

• **오다 (verb)** : 무엇이 다른 곳에서 이곳으로 움직이다.
come
For something to move from another place to here.

• -는 길에 : 어떤 일을 하는 도중이나 기회임을 나타내는 표현.
-neun gire (no equivalent expression)
An expression used to indicate the process of or opportunity for a certain thing.

• **휴지 (noun)** : 더러운 것을 닦는 데 쓰는 얇은 종이.
toilet paper; toilet tissue
A thin sheet of paper used for wiping off something dirty.

• **좀 (adverb)** : 주로 부탁이나 동의를 구할 때 부드러운 느낌을 주기 위해 넣는 말.
please
A word chiefly used to soften a request for a favor or agreement.

• **사다 (verb)** : 돈을 주고 어떤 물건이나 권리 등을 자기 것으로 만들다.
buy; purchase; get
To get ownership of an item, right, etc., by paying for it.

• -아다 : 어떤 행동을 한 뒤 그 행동의 결과를 가지고 뒤의 말이 나타내는 행동을 이어 함을 나타내는 연결 어미.
-ada (no equivalent expression)
A connective ending used when one does a certain act and does the following act based on the result of the preceding one.

• **주다 (verb)** : 물건 등을 남에게 건네어 가지거나 쓰게 하다.
give
To give an item to someone else so he/she can have or use it.

• -ㄹ래 : (두루낮춤으로) 앞으로 어떤 일을 하려고 하는 자신의 의사를 나타내거나 그 일에 대하여 듣는 사람의 의사를 물어봄을 나타내는 종결 어미.
-llae (no equivalent expression)
(informal addressee-lowering) A sentence-final ending used to indicate the speaker's intention to do something in the future, or to ask for the listener's thoughts about that.

< 대화(dialogue) > - 66

오늘 회의 몇 시부터 시작하지?
오늘 회이 멷 시부터 시자카지?
oneul hoei myeot sibuteo sijakaji?

지금 시작하려고 하니까 빨리 준비하고 와.
지금 시자카려고 하니까 빨리 준비하고 와.
jigeum sijakaryeogo hanikka ppalli junbihago wa.

< 설명(explanation) / 번역(translation) >

오늘 회의 몇 시+부터 시작하+지?

• **오늘** (noun) : 지금 지나가고 있는 이날.
today
The day that is passing at the present time.

• **회의** (noun) : 여럿이 모여 의논함. 또는 그런 모임.
meeting; conference
A state in which people gather and discuss a topic, issue, etc.; or such a meeting.

• **몇** (determiner) : 잘 모르는 수를 물을 때 쓰는 말.
how many
A phrase used when the speaker asks about the number of things or people.

• **시** (noun) : 하루를 스물넷으로 나누었을 때 그 하나를 나타내는 시간의 단위.
o'clock
A bound noun indicating one of 24 hours of a day.

• 부터 : 어떤 일의 시작이나 처음을 나타내는 조사.
buteo (no equivalent expression)
A postpositional particle that indicates the start or beginning of something.

• **시작하다** (verb) : 어떤 일이나 행동의 처음 단계를 이루거나 이루게 하다.
start; begin; initiate
To constitute or cause to constitute the initial phase of an affair or action.

• -지 : (두루낮춤으로) 말하는 사람이 듣는 사람에게 친근함을 나타내며 물을 때 쓰는 종결 어미.
-ji (no equivalent expression)
(informal addressee-lowering) A sentence-final ending used when the speaker asks the listener in a friendly manner.

지금 시작하+[려고 하]+니까 빨리 준비하+고 오+아.
와

• **지금 (adverb)** : 말을 하고 있는 바로 이때에. 또는 그 즉시에.
now; immediately
At the present moment as one speaks, or that instant.

• **시작하다 (verb)** : 어떤 일이나 행동의 처음 단계를 이루거나 이루게 하다.
start; begin; initiate
To constitute or cause to constitute the initial phase of an affair or action.

• -려고 하다 : 앞의 말이 나타내는 일이 곧 일어날 것 같거나 시작될 것임을 나타내는 표현.
-ryeogo hada (no equivalent expression)
An expression used to indicate that the incident mentioned in the preceding statement is likely to happen or begin soon.

• -니까 : 뒤에 오는 말에 대하여 앞에 오는 말이 원인이나 근거, 전제가 됨을 강조하여 나타내는 연결 어미.
-nikka (no equivalent expression)
A connective ending used to emphasize that the preceding statement is the cause, reason, or premise for the following statement.

• **빨리 (adverb)** : 걸리는 시간이 짧게.
quickly
In a short duration of time.

• **준비하다 (verb)** : 미리 마련하여 갖추다.
prepare
To have something in place with advance preparations.

• -고 : 앞의 말과 뒤의 말이 차례대로 일어남을 나타내는 연결 어미.
-go (no equivalent expression)
A connective ending used when the preceding statement and the following statement happen in order.

• **오다 (verb)** : 무엇이 다른 곳에서 이곳으로 움직이다.
come
For something to move from another place to here.

• -아 : (두루낮춤으로) 어떤 사실을 서술하거나 물음, 명령, 권유를 나타내는 종결 어미.

-a (no equivalent expression)

(informal addressee-lowering) A sentence-final ending used to describe a certain fact, ask a question, **give an order**, or advise.

< 대화(dialogue) > - 67

장마도 끝났으니 이제 정말 더워지려나 봐.
장마도 끈나쓰니 이제 정말 더워지려나 봐.
jangmado kkeunnasseuni ije jeongmal deowojiryeona bwa.

맞아. 오늘 아침에 걸어오는데 땀이 줄줄 나더라.
마자. 오늘 아치메 거러오는데 따미 줄줄 나더라.
maja. oneul achime georeooneunde ttami juljul nadeora.

< 설명(explanation) / 번역(translation) >

장마+도 끝나+았+으니 이제 정말 더워지+[려나 보]+아.
끝났으니 더워지려나 봐

• **장마 (noun)** : 여름철에 여러 날 계속해서 비가 오는 현상이나 날씨. 또는 그 비.
monsoon; monsoon season
A phenomenon or weather where it keeps raining for consecutive days in summer, or such rainfall.

• 도 : 이미 있는 어떤 것에 다른 것을 더하거나 포함함을 나타내는 조사.
do (no equivalent expression)
A postpositional particle used to indicate an addition or inclusion of another thing to something that already exists.

• **끝나다 (verb)** : 정해진 기간이 모두 지나가다.
expire; run out
For a certain period to be over.

• -았- : 어떤 사건이 과거에 완료되었거나 그 사건의 결과가 현재까지 지속되는 상황을 나타내는 어미.
-at- (no equivalent expression)
An ending of a word used to indicate that an event was completed in the past or its result continues in the present.

• -으니 : 뒤에 오는 말에 대하여 앞에 오는 말이 원인이나 근거, 전제가 됨을 나타내는 연결 어미.
-euni (no equivalent expression)
A connective ending used when the preceding statement is the cause, reason, or premise for the following statement.

• **이제 (adverb)** : 지금부터 앞으로.
henceforth; henceforward
From now on.

• **정말 (adverb)** : 거짓이 없이 진짜로.
really
In actual truth without falsehood.

• **더워지다 (verb)** : 온도가 올라가다. 또는 그로 인해 더위나 뜨거움을 느끼다.
become hot
For the temperature to go up; to feel the heat or hotness from it.

• -려나 보다 : 앞의 말이 나타내는 일이 일어날 것이라고 추측함을 나타내는 표현.
-ryeona boda (no equivalent expression)
An expression used to guess that the something mentioned in the preceding statement is likely to happen.

• -아 : (두루낮춤으로) 어떤 사실을 서술하거나 물음, 명령, 권유를 나타내는 종결 어미.
-a (no equivalent expression)
(informal addressee-lowering) A sentence-final ending used to **describe** a certain fact, ask a question, give an order, or advise.

맞+아.

오늘 아침+에 걸어오+는데 땀+이 줄줄 나+더라.

• **맞다 (verb)** : 그렇거나 옳다.
be so; be right
To be so or right.

• -아 : (두루낮춤으로) 어떤 사실을 서술하거나 물음, 명령, 권유를 나타내는 종결 어미.
-a (no equivalent expression)
(informal addressee-lowering) A sentence-final ending used to **describe** a certain fact, ask a question, give an order, or advise.

• **오늘 (noun)** : 지금 지나가고 있는 이날.
today
The day that is passing at the present time.

• **아침 (noun)** : 날이 밝아올 때부터 해가 떠올라 하루의 일이 시작될 때쯤까지의 시간.
morning
The hours between dawn and the time when the sun is up and daily activities start.

• 에 : 앞말이 시간이나 때임을 나타내는 조사.
in; at
A postpositional particle to indicate that the preceding statement refers to the time.

• **걸어오다 (verb)** : 목적지를 향하여 다리를 움직여서 이동하여 오다.
walk; come on foot
To take a step forward in the direction of a destination.

• -는데 : 뒤의 말을 하기 위하여 그 대상과 관련이 있는 상황을 미리 말함을 나타내는 연결 어미.
-neunde (no equivalent expression)
A connective ending used to talk in advance about a situation to follow.

• **땀 (noun)** : 덥거나 몸이 아프거나 긴장을 했을 때 피부를 통해 나오는 짭짤한 맑은 액체.
sweat
A clear salty liquid that is excreted through the skin when one is hot, sick or nervous.

• 이 : 어떤 상태나 상황의 대상이나 동작의 주체를 나타내는 조사.
i (no equivalent expression)
A postpositional particle referring to a subject under a certain state or situation, or the agent of an action.

• **줄줄 (adverb)** : 굵은 물줄기 등이 계속 흐르는 소리. 또는 그 모양.
continuously
With a sound resembling one that is produced when a thick flow of water, etc., keeps running, or such a shape.

• **나다 (verb)** : 몸에서 땀, 피, 눈물 등이 흐르다.
run; flow
For sweat, blood, tears, etc., to flow on the body.

• -더라 : (아주낮춤으로) 말하는 이가 직접 경험하여 새롭게 알게 된 사실을 지금 전달함을 나타내는 종결 어미.
-deora (no equivalent expression)
(formal, highly addressee-lowering) A sentence-final ending used to convey in the present a fact the speaker realized anew from the speaker's personal experience.

< 대화(dialogue) > - 68

나는 아내를 위해서 대신 죽을 수도 있을 것 같아.
나는 아내를 위해서 대신 주글 쑤도 이쓸 껃 가타.
naneun anaereul wihaeseo daesin jugeul sudo isseul geot gata.

네가 아내를 정말 사랑하는구나.
네가 아내를 정말 사랑하는구나.
nega anaereul jeongmal saranghaneunguna.

< 설명(explanation) / 번역(translation) >

나+는 아내+[를 위해서] 대신 죽+[을 수+도 있]+[을 것 같]+아.

• **나 (pronoun)** : 말하는 사람이 친구나 아랫사람에게 자기를 가리키는 말.
I
A pronoun used to indicate oneself to a friend or a younger person.

• 는 : 문장 속에서 어떤 대상이 화제임을 나타내는 조사.
neun (no equivalent expression)
A postpositional particle used to indicate that a certain subject is the topic of a sentence.

• **아내 (noun)** : 결혼하여 남자의 짝이 된 여자.
wife
The man's female partner in marriage.

• 를 위해서 : 어떤 대상에게 이롭게 하거나 어떤 목표나 목적을 이루려고 함을 나타내는 표현.
reul wihaeseo (no equivalent expression)
An expression used to indicate that something is for the benefit of someone or for a goal or purpose.

• **대신 (noun)** : 어떤 대상이 맡던 구실을 다른 대상이 새로 맡음. 또는 그렇게 새로 맡은 대상.
substitute
A state in which a subject is newly responsible for something that another subject was responsible for; such a subject that is newly responsible.

• **죽다 (verb)** : 생물이 생명을 잃다.
die
For a living plant, animal, or insect to lose its life.

• -을 수 있다 : 어떤 행동이나 상태가 가능함을 나타내는 표현.
-eul su itda (no equivalent expression)
An expression used to indicate that an act or state is possible.

• 도 : 극단적인 경우를 들어 다른 경우는 말할 것도 없음을 나타내는 조사.
do (no equivalent expression)
A postpositional particle used when giving an extreme case in order to show that it is obvious in another case.

• -을 것 같다 : 추측을 나타내는 표현.
-eul geot gatda (no equivalent expression)
An expression used to indicate that the statement is a guess.

• -아 : (두루낮춤으로) 어떤 사실을 서술하거나 물음, 명령, 권유를 나타내는 종결 어미.
-a (no equivalent expression)
(informal addressee-lowering) A sentence-final ending used to **describe** a certain fact, ask a question, give an order, or advise.

네+가 아내+를 정말 사랑하+는구나.

• **네 (pronoun)** : '너'에 조사 '가'가 붙을 때의 형태.
you
A form of '너' (you), when the postpositional particle '가' is attached to it.

• 가 : 어떤 상태나 상황에 놓인 대상이나 동작의 주체를 나타내는 조사.
ga (no equivalent expression)
A postpositional particle referring to a subject under a certain state or situation, or the subject of an act.

• **아내 (noun)** : 결혼하여 남자의 짝이 된 여자.
wife
The man's female partner in marriage.

• 를 : 동작이 직접적으로 영향을 미치는 대상을 나타내는 조사.
reul (no equivalent expression)
A postpositional particle used to indicate the subject that an act has a direct influence on.

• **정말 (adverb)** : 거짓이 없이 진짜로.
really
In actual truth without falsehood.

- **사랑하다 (verb)** : 상대에게 성적으로 매력을 느껴 열렬히 좋아하다.
  love
  To be sexually attracted to someone and like him/her very much.

- -는구나 : (아주낮춤으로) 새롭게 알게 된 사실에 어떤 느낌을 실어 말함을 나타내는 종결 어미.
  -neunguna (no equivalent expression)
  (formal, highly addressee-lowering) A sentence-final ending used to imply a certain feeling in a newly learned fact.

< 대화(dialogue) > - 69

이 약은 하루에 몇 번이나 먹어야 하나요?
이 야근 하루에 멷 버니나 머거야 하나요?
i yageun harue myeot beonina meogeoya hanayo?

아침저녁으로 두 번만 드시면 됩니다.
아침저녀그로 두 번만 드시면 됨니다.
achimjeonyeogeuro du beonman deusimyeon doemnida.

< 설명(explanation) / 번역(translation) >

이 약+은 하루+에 몇 번+이나 먹+[어야 하]+나요?

• **이 (determiner)** : 말하는 사람에게 가까이 있거나 말하는 사람이 생각하고 있는 대상을 가리킬 때 쓰는 말.
this
The word that is used to refer to a person who is close to the speaker or something that the speaker is thinking of.

• **약 (noun)** : 병이나 상처 등을 낫게 하거나 예방하기 위하여 먹거나 바르거나 주사하는 물질.
medicine; medication; pill; drug
A substance orally administered, applied or injected to treat or prevent an illness, wound, etc.

• 은 : 문장 속에서 어떤 대상이 화제임을 나타내는 조사.
eun (no equivalent expression)
A postpositional particle used to indicate that a certain subject is the topic of a sentence.

• **하루 (noun)** : 밤 열두 시부터 다음 날 밤 열두 시까지의 스물네 시간.
day
The 24 hours from midnight to the following midnight.

• 에 : 앞말이 기준이 되는 대상이나 단위임을 나타내는 조사.
per; for; against
A postpositional particle to indicate that the preceding statement is a unit or subject that is the standard for something.

• **몇 (determiner)** : 잘 모르는 수를 물을 때 쓰는 말.
how many
A phrase used when the speaker asks about the number of things or people.

• **번 (noun)** : 일의 횟수를 세는 단위.
beon (no equivalent expression)
A bound noun that serves as a unit for counting the frequency of a task.

• 이나 : 수량이나 정도를 대강 짐작할 때 쓰는 조사.
ina (no equivalent expression)
A postpositional particle used to make a rough guess at the amount or extent.

• **먹다 (verb)** : 약을 입에 넣어 삼키다.
take; dose up with
To put medicine into one's mouth and swallow it.

• -어야 하다 : 앞에 오는 말이 어떤 일을 하거나 어떤 상황에 이르기 위한 의무적인 행동이거나 필수적인 조건임을 나타내는 표현.
-eoya hada (no equivalent expression)
An expression used to indicate that the preceding statement is the required act or condition to realize a certain incident or situation.

• -나요 : (두루높임으로) 앞의 내용에 대해 상대방에게 물어볼 때 쓰는 표현.
-nayo (no equivalent expression)
(informal addressee-raising) An expression used to ask the listener about the preceding content.

아침저녁+으로 두 번+만 들(드)+시+[면 되]+ㅂ니다.
드시면 됩니다

• **아침저녁 (noun)** : 아침과 저녁.
morning and evening; all day
The morning and the evening.

• 으로 : 시간을 나타내는 조사.
euro (no equivalent expression)
A postpositional particle that indicates time.

• **두 (determiner)** : 둘의.
two
Two

• **번 (noun)** : 일의 횟수를 세는 단위.
beon (no equivalent expression)
A bound noun that serves as a unit for counting the frequency of a task.

• 만 : 다른 것은 제외하고 어느 것을 한정함을 나타내는 조사.
man (no equivalent expression)
A postpositional particle used when limiting the field to one thing, excluding all the others.

• **들다 (verb)** : (높임말로) 먹다.
have; eat
(honorific) To eat.

• -시- : 어떤 동작이나 상태의 주체를 높이는 뜻을 나타내는 어미.
-si- (no equivalent expression)
An ending of a word used for the subject honorifics of an action or state.

• -면 되다 : 조건이 되는 어떤 행동을 하거나 어떤 상태만 갖추어지면 문제가 없거나 충분함을 나타내는 표현.
-myeon doeda (no equivalent expression)
An expression used to indicate that, as long as one does or reaches a certain act or state, there is no problem or it is enough.

• -ㅂ니다 : (아주높임으로) 현재의 동작이나 상태, 사실을 정중하게 설명함을 나타내는 종결 어미.
-pnida (no equivalent expression)
(formal, highly addressee-raising) A sentence-final ending used to explain the present action, state, or fact politely.

< 대화(dialogue) > - 70

다음부터는 수업 시간에 떠들면 안 돼.
다음부터는 수업 시가네 떠들면 안 돼.
daeumbuteoneun sueop sigane tteodeulmyeon an dwae.

네, 선생님. 다음부터는 절대 떠들지 않을게요.
네, 선생님. 다음부터는 절대 떠들지 아늘께요.
ne, seonsaengnim. daeumbuteoneun jeoldae tteodeulji aneulgeyo.

< 설명(explanation) / 번역(translation) >

다음+부터+는 수업 시간+에 떠들+[면 안 되]+어.
떠들면 안 돼

• **다음 (noun)** : 이번 차례의 바로 뒤.
next; following
The thing that comes right after this time or turn in sequence.

• 부터 : 어떤 일의 시작이나 처음을 나타내는 조사.
buteo (no equivalent expression)
A postpositional particle that indicates the start or beginning of something.

• 는 : 어떤 대상이 다른 것과 대조됨을 나타내는 조사.
neun (no equivalent expression)
A postpositional particle used to indicate that a certain subject contrasts with something else.

• **수업 (noun)** : 교사가 학생에게 지식이나 기술을 가르쳐 줌.
class; lesson; course
A teacher teaching a student certain studies or skills.

• **시간 (noun)** : 어떤 일이 시작되어 끝날 때까지의 동안.
time; hours
An interval from the time something starts to the time it ends.

• 에 : 앞말이 시간이나 때임을 나타내는 조사.
in; at
A postpositional particle to indicate that the preceding statement refers to the time.

• **떠들다 (verb)** : 큰 소리로 시끄럽게 말하다.
clamor; make a noise
To speak noisily in a loud voice.

• -면 안 되다 : 어떤 행동이나 상태를 금지하거나 제한함을 나타내는 표현.
-myeon an doeda (no equivalent expression)
An expression used to indicate that a certain act or state is banned or limited.

• -어 : (두루낮춤으로) 어떤 사실을 서술하거나 물음, 명령, 권유를 나타내는 종결 어미.
-eo (no equivalent expression)
(informal addressee-lowering) A sentence-final ending used to describe a certain fact, ask a question, **give an order**, or advise.

네, 선생님.

다음+부터+는 절대 떠들+[지 않]+을게요.

• **네 (interjection)** : 윗사람의 물음이나 명령 등에 긍정하여 대답할 때 쓰는 말.
yes; yes sir; yes ma'am
An exclamation uttered when the speaker affirmatively answers the call or order of his/her superior.

• **선생님 (noun)** : (높이는 말로) 학생을 가르치는 사람.
teacher; master
(polite form) A person who teaches students.

• **다음 (noun)** : 이번 차례의 바로 뒤.
next; following
The thing that comes right after this time or turn in sequence.

• 부터 : 어떤 일의 시작이나 처음을 나타내는 조사.
buteo (no equivalent expression)
A postpositional particle that indicates the start or beginning of something.

• 는 : 어떤 대상이 다른 것과 대조됨을 나타내는 조사.
neun (no equivalent expression)
A postpositional particle used to indicate that a certain subject contrasts with something else.

• **절대 (adverb)** : 어떤 경우라도 반드시.
absolutely; never
Surely and in any case.

• **떠들다 (verb)** : 큰 소리로 시끄럽게 말하다.
clamor; make a noise
To speak noisily in a loud voice.

• -지 않다 : 앞의 말이 나타내는 행위나 상태를 부정하는 뜻을 나타내는 표현.
-ji anta (no equivalent expression)
An expression used to deny the act or state indicated in the preceding statement.

• -을게요 : (두루높임으로) 말하는 사람이 어떤 행동을 할 것을 듣는 사람에게 약속하거나 의지를 나타내는 표현.
-eulgeyo (no equivalent expression)
(informal addressee-raising) An expression used used when the speaker promises or notifies the listener that he/she will do something.

< 대화(dialogue) > - 71

엄마, 할머니 댁은 아직 멀었어요?
엄마, 할머니 대근 아직 머러써요?
eomma, halmeoni daegeun ajik meoreosseoyo?

아냐. 다 와 가. 삼십 분만 더 가면 되니까 조금만 참아.
아냐. 다 와 가. 삼십 분만 더 가면 되니까 조금만 차마.
anya. da wa ga. samsip bunman deo gamyeon doenikka jogeumman chama.

< 설명(explanation) / 번역(translation) >

엄마, 할머니 댁+은 아직 멀+었+어요?

• **엄마 (noun)** : 격식을 갖추지 않아도 되는 상황에서 어머니를 이르거나 부르는 말.
mom
A word used to refer to or address one's mother in an informal situation.

• **할머니 (noun)** : 아버지의 어머니, 또는 어머니의 어머니를 이르거나 부르는 말.
grandmother; granny
A word used to refer to or address the mother of one's father or mother.

• **댁 (noun)** : (높이는 말로) 남의 집이나 가정.
one's family
(polite form) Another person's home or family.

• 은 : 문장 속에서 어떤 대상이 화제임을 나타내는 조사.
eun (no equivalent expression)
A postpositional particle used to indicate that a certain subject is the topic of a sentence.

• **아직 (adverb)** : 어떤 일이나 상태 또는 어떻게 되기까지 시간이 더 지나야 함을 나타내거나, 어떤 일이나 상태가 끝나지 않고 계속 이어지고 있음을 나타내는 말.
yet; still
An adverb used to indicate that more time is needed to reach a certain state, or that something or a certain state has not ended, but is going on.

• **멀다 (adjective)** : 지금으로부터 시간이 많이 남아 있다. 오랜 시간이 필요하다.
long time until something occurs
A lot of time being left from now on; a long time being needed.

• -었- : 어떤 사건이 과거에 완료되었거나 그 사건의 결과가 현재까지 지속되는 상황을 나타내는 어미.
-eot- (no equivalent expression)
An ending of a word used to indicate that an event was completed in the past or its result continues in the present.

• -어요 : (두루높임으로) 어떤 사실을 서술하거나 질문, 명령, 권유함을 나타내는 종결 어미.
-eoyo (no equivalent expression)
(informal addressee-raising) A sentence-final ending used to describe a certain fact, **ask a question**, give an order, or advise.

아냐.

다 오+[아 가]+(아).

와 가

삼십 분+만 더 가+[면 되]+니까 조금+만 참+아.

• **아냐 (interjection)** : 묻는 말에 대하여 강조하며, 또는 단호하게 부정하며 대답할 때 쓰는 말.
no; nope; no way
An exclamation uttered when answering negatively in an emphatic and resolute manner.

• **다 (adverb)** : 행동이나 상태의 정도가 한정된 정도에 거의 가깝게.
almost
Nearly close to the limit in terms of the degree of behavior or state.

• **오다 (verb)** : 가고자 하는 곳에 이르다.
arrive; reach; come
To reach a place that one wants to go to.

• -아 가다 : 앞의 말이 나타내는 행동이나 상태가 계속 진행됨을 나타내는 표현.
-a gada (no equivalent expression)
An expression used to indicate that the act or state mentioned in the preceding statement is continued.

• -아 : (두루낮춤으로) 어떤 사실을 서술하거나 물음, 명령, 권유를 나타내는 종결 어미.
-a (no equivalent expression)
(informal addressee-lowering) A sentence-final ending used to **describe** a certain fact, ask a question, give an order, or advise.

• **삼십 (determiner)** : 서른의.
thirty
Being the number thirty.

• **분 (noun)** : 한 시간의 60분의 1을 나타내는 시간의 단위.
minute
A bound noun indicating a unit of time, which is one-sixtieth of an hour.

• 만 : 앞의 말이 어떤 것에 대한 조건임을 나타내는 조사.
man (no equivalent expression)
A postpositional particle used when the preceding statement is a precondition for something.

• **더 (adverb)** : 보태어 계속해서.
more
In a continuous addition.

• **가다 (verb)** : 한 곳에서 다른 곳으로 장소를 이동하다.
go; travel
To move from one place to another place.

• -면 되다 : 조건이 되는 어떤 행동을 하거나 어떤 상태만 갖추어지면 문제가 없거나 충분함을 나타내는 표현.
-myeon doeda (no equivalent expression)
An expression used to indicate that, as long as one does or reaches a certain act or state, there is no problem or it is enough.

• -니까 : 뒤에 오는 말에 대하여 앞에 오는 말이 원인이나 근거, 전제가 됨을 강조하여 나타내는 연결 어미.
-nikka (no equivalent expression)
A connective ending used to emphasize that the preceding statement is the cause, reason, or premise for the following statement.

• **조금 (noun)** : 짧은 시간 동안.
a while
A duration of short time.

• 만 : 말하는 사람이 기대하는 최소의 선을 나타내는 조사.
man (no equivalent expression)
A postpositional particle that indicates the speaker's least expectation.

• **참다 (verb)** : 어떤 시간 동안을 견디고 기다리다.
wait
To endure and wait for a certain time.

• -아 : (두루낮춤으로) 어떤 사실을 서술하거나 물음, 명령, 권유를 나타내는 종결 어미.
-a (no equivalent expression)
(informal addressee-lowering) A sentence-final ending used to describe a certain fact, ask a question, **give an order**, or advise.

< 대화(dialogue) > - 72

부산까지는 시간이 꽤 오래 걸리니까 번갈아 가면서 운전하는 게 어때?
부산까지는 시가니 꽤 오래 걸리니까 번가라 가면서 운전하는 게 어때?
busankkajineun sigani kkwae orae geollinikka beongara gamyeonseo unjeonhaneun ge eottae?

그래. 그게 좋겠다.
그래. 그게 조켇따.
geurae. geuge joketda.

< 설명(explanation) / 번역(translation) >

부산+까지+는 시간+이 꽤 오래 걸리+니까 번갈+[아 가]+면서

운전하+[는 것(거)]+이 어떻+어?
운전하는 게 어때

• **부산 (noun)** : 경상남도 동남부에 있는 광역시. 서울에 다음가는 대도시이며 한국 최대의 무역항이 있다.
Busan
A metropolitan city in the southeastern region of Gyeongsangnam-do, or South Gyeongsang Province; the biggest city second to Seoul, it has the largest trade port in Korea.

• 까지 : 어떤 범위의 끝임을 나타내는 조사.
kkaji (no equivalent expression)
A postpositional particle referring to the end of a certain range.

• 는 : 문장 속에서 어떤 대상이 화제임을 나타내는 조사.
neun (no equivalent expression)
A postpositional particle used to indicate that a certain subject is the topic of a sentence.

• **시간 (noun)** : 어떤 때에서 다른 때까지의 동안.
time
The amount of time from one point to another.

• 이 : 어떤 상태나 상황의 대상이나 동작의 주체를 나타내는 조사.
i (no equivalent expression)
A postpositional particle referring to a subject under a certain state or situation, or the agent of an action.

• **꽤 (adverb)** : 예상이나 기대 이상으로 상당히.
quite; fairly
Considerably more than expected.

• **오래 (adverb)** : 긴 시간 동안.
long
For a long time.

• **걸리다 (verb)** : 시간이 들다.
take
To take time.

• -니까 : 뒤에 오는 말에 대하여 앞에 오는 말이 원인이나 근거, 전제가 됨을 강조하여 나타내는 연결 어미.
-nikka (no equivalent expression)
A connective ending used to emphasize that the preceding statement is the cause, reason, or premise for the following statement.

• **번갈다 (verb)** : 여럿이 어떤 일을 할 때, 일정한 시간 동안 한 사람씩 차례를 바꾸다.
take turns
To change people one by one after a fixed period of time, when many people do a certain thing together.

• -아 가다 : 앞의 말이 나타내는 행동을 이따금 반복함과 동시에 또 다른 행동을 이어 함을 나타내는 표현.
-a gada (no equivalent expression)
An expression used to indicate that one occasionally repeats a certain act mentioned in the preceding statement, while continuing another act.

• -면서 : 두 가지 이상의 동작이나 상태가 함께 일어남을 나타내는 연결 어미.
-myeonseo (no equivalent expression)
A connective ending used when more than two actions or states happen at the same time.

• **운전하다 (verb)** : 기계나 자동차를 움직이고 조종하다.
drive; operate
To move and handle a machine or car.

• -는 것 : 명사가 아닌 것을 문장에서 명사처럼 쓰이게 하거나 '이다' 앞에 쓰일 수 있게 할 때 쓰는 표현.
-neun geot (no equivalent expression)
An expression used to enable a non-noun word to be used as a noun in a sentence or to be used in front of '이다' (be).

• 이 : 어떤 상태나 상황의 대상이나 동작의 주체를 나타내는 조사.
i (no equivalent expression)
A postpositional particle referring to a subject under a certain state or situation, or the agent of an action.

• **어떻다 (adjective)** : 생각, 느낌, 상태, 형편 등이 어찌 되어 있다.
such
Being such in one's thoughts, feelings, state, situation, etc.

• -어 : (두루낮춤으로) 어떤 사실을 서술하거나 물음, 명령, 권유를 나타내는 종결 어미.
-eo (no equivalent expression)
(informal addressee-lowering) A sentence-final ending used to describe a certain fact, **ask a question**, give an order, or advise.

그래.

그것(그거)+이 좋+겠+다.
그게

• **그래 (interjection)** : '그렇게 하겠다, 그렇다, 알았다' 등 긍정하는 뜻으로, 대답할 때 쓰는 말.
okay; sure
An exclamation used when giving a positive answer that means 'I'll do so', 'Yes, it is', or 'I see.'

• **그것 (pronoun)** : 앞에서 이미 이야기한 대상을 가리키는 말.
no equivalent expression
A pronoun used to indicate the previously-mentioned object.

• 이 : 어떤 상태나 상황의 대상이나 동작의 주체를 나타내는 조사.
i (no equivalent expression)
A postpositional particle referring to a subject under a certain state or situation, or the agent of an action.

• **좋다 (adjective)** : 어떤 일이나 대상이 마음에 들고 만족스럽다.
fond of; in love with
Happy about and satisfied with a thing or object.

• -겠- : 미래의 일이나 추측을 나타내는 어미.
-get- (no equivalent expression)
An ending of a word referring to a future event or assumption.

• -다 : (아주낮춤으로) 어떤 사건이나 사실, 상태를 서술함을 나타내는 종결 어미.
-da (no equivalent expression)
(formal, highly addressee-lowering) A sentence-final ending used when describing a certain event, fact, state, etc.

< 대화(diálogo) > - 73

처음 해 보는 일에 새롭게 도전하는 것이 두렵지 않으세요?
처음 해 보는 이레 새롭께 도전하는 거시 두렵찌 아느세요?
cheoeum hae boneun ire saeropge dojeonhaneun geosi duryeopji aneuseyo?

아니요. 더디지만 하나씩 알아 나가는 재미가 있어요.
아니요. 더디지만 하나씩 아라 나가는 재미가 이써요.
aniyo. deodijiman hanassik ara naganeun jaemiga isseoyo.

< 설명(explicación) / 번역(traducción) >

처음 하+[여 보]+는 일+에 새롭+게 도전하+[는 것]+이 두렵+[지 않]+으세요?
해 보는

• **처음 (sustantivo)** : 차례나 시간상으로 맨 앞.
principio, inicio
Delante de todo en orden o en tiempo.

• **하다 (verbo)** : 어떤 행동이나 동작, 활동 등을 행하다.
hacer, realizar
Llevar a cabo un acto o una acción.

• -여 보다 : 앞의 말이 나타내는 행동을 시험 삼아 함을 나타내는 표현.
No hay expresión equivalente
Expresión que indica la realización de la acción que indica el comentario anterior a modo de prueba.

• -는 : 앞의 말이 관형어의 기능을 하게 만들고 사건이나 동작이 현재 일어남을 나타내는 어미.
No hay expresión equivalente
Desinencia que hace que la palabra antecedente ejerza la función de un componente determinante, e indica que un suceso o una acción se produce en el presente.

• **일 (sustantivo)** : 무엇을 이루려고 몸이나 정신을 사용하는 활동. 또는 그 활동의 대상.
tarea, trabajo
Actividad psíquica y física que se hace para realizar algo. U objeto de esa actvidad.

• 에 : 앞말이 어떤 행위나 감정 등의 대상임을 나타내는 조사.
No hay expresión equivalente
Posposición que se usa cuando la palabra anterior es objeto de cierta acción, sentimiento, etc.

• **새롭다 (adjetivo)** : 지금까지의 것과 다르거나 있은 적이 없다.
nuevo
Diferido de algo que había antes o algo que no había antes.

• -게 : 앞의 말이 뒤에서 가리키는 일의 목적이나 결과, 방식, 정도 등이 됨을 나타내는 연결 어미.
No hay expresión equivalente
Desinencia conectora que se usa cuando la palabra anterior es el objetivo, resultado, método, grado, etc. que indica al posterior. **<método>**

• **도전하다 (verbo)** : (비유적으로) 가치 있는 것이나 목표한 것을 얻기 위해 어려움에 맞서다.
desafiar
(FIGURADO) Afrontar o enfrentarse a una dificultad para el logro de algún fin.

• -는 것 : 명사가 아닌 것을 문장에서 명사처럼 쓰이게 하거나 '이다' 앞에 쓰일 수 있게 할 때 쓰는 표현.
No hay expresión equivalente
Expresión que se usa para hacer que una palabra que no es sustantivo sea utilizada como tal en una oración, o para hacer que se use delante de '이다' .

• 이 : 어떤 상태나 상황의 대상이나 동작의 주체를 나타내는 조사.
No hay expresión equivalente
Posposición que se usa para indicar el objeto de cierto estado o situación o el agente de un movimiento.

• **두렵다 (adjetivo)** : 걱정되고 불안하다.
preocupado, inquieto, intranquilo
Que está preocupado e inquieto.

• -지 않다 : 앞의 말이 나타내는 행위나 상태를 부정하는 뜻을 나타내는 표현.
No hay expresión equivalente
Expresión para negar la acción o la situación de lo que se mencionó anteriormente.

• -으세요 : (두루높임으로) 설명, 의문, 명령, 요청의 뜻을 나타내는 종결 어미.
No hay expresión equivalente
(TRATAMIENTO HONORÍFICO GENERAL) Desinencia de terminación que se usa cuando se manifiesta el sentido de explicación, duda, orden, reclamación, etc. **<pregunta>**

아니요.

더디+지만 하나+씩 알+[아 나가]+는 재미+가 있+어요.

• **아니요 (interjección)** : 윗사람이 묻는 말에 대하여 부정하며 대답할 때 쓰는 말.
¡no!
Interjección que se usa para dar una respuesta negativa a una pregunta hecha por alguien de edad o rango mayor que el hablante.

• **더디다 (adjetivo)** : 속도가 느려 무엇을 하는 데 걸리는 시간이 길다.
lento, tardo
Pausado en el movimiento o la acción, por lo que tarda mucho tiempo en hacer algo.

• -지만 : 앞에 오는 말을 인정하면서 그와 반대되거나 다른 사실을 덧붙일 때 쓰는 연결 어미.
No hay expresión equivalente
Desinencia conectora que se usa cuando alguien acepta el contenido anterior pero agrega otro hecho o un hecho contario a él.

• **하나 (pronombre numeral)** : 숫자를 셀 때 맨 처음의 수.
uno
El primero en orden numérico.

• 씩 : '그 수량이나 크기로 나뉨'의 뜻을 더하는 접미사.
No hay expresión equivalente
Sufijo que añade el significado de 'que se divide por tal número o tamaño'.

• **알다 (verbo)** : 교육이나 경험, 생각 등을 통해 사물이나 상황에 대한 정보 또는 지식을 갖추다.
saber, conocer, aprender
Adquirir un conocimiento o una información sobre la situación de un objeto mediante la educación, experiencia o pensamiento.

• -아 나가다 : 앞의 말이 나타내는 행동을 계속 진행함을 나타내는 표현.
No hay expresión equivalente
Expresión que indica que la acción que representa el comentario previo continúa.

• -는 : 앞의 말이 관형어의 기능을 하게 만들고 사건이나 동작이 현재 일어남을 나타내는 어미.
No hay expresión equivalente
Desinencia que hace que la palabra antecedente ejerza la función de un componente determinante, e indica que un suceso o una acción se produce en el presente.

• **재미 (sustantivo)** : 어떤 것이 주는 즐거운 기분이나 느낌.
diversión, placer, entretenimiento
Sentimiento o humor alegre que proporciona algo.

- 가 : 어떤 상태나 상황에 놓인 대상이나 동작의 주체를 나타내는 조사.
  No hay expresión equivalente
  Posposición que se usa para indicar el objeto de cierto estado o situación o el agente de un movimiento.

- **있다 (adjetivo)** : 사실이나 현상이 존재하다.
  existente
  Que existe un hecho o un fenómeno.

- -어요 : (두루높임으로) 어떤 사실을 서술하거나 질문, 명령, 권유함을 나타내는 종결 어미.
  No hay expresión equivalente
  (TRATAMIENTO HONORÍFICO GENERAL) Desinencia de terminación que se usa cuando se describe cierto hecho; o pregunta, ordena o reclama algo. **<narración>**

< 대화(dialogue) > - 74

너 지우랑 화해했니?
너 지우랑 화해핸니?
neo jiurang hwahaehaenni?

아니. 난 지우한테 먼저 사과를 받아 낼 거야.
아니. 난 지우한테 먼저 사과를 바다 낼 꺼야.
ani. nan jiuhante meonjeo sagwareul bada nael geoya.

< 설명(explanation) / 번역(translation) >

너 지우+랑 화해하+였+니?
화해했니

• **너 (pronoun)** : 듣는 사람이 친구나 아랫사람일 때, 그 사람을 가리키는 말.
no equivalent expression
A pronoun used to indicate the listener when he/she is the same age or younger.

• **지우 (noun)** : person's name

• 랑 : 누군가를 상대로 하여 어떤 일을 할 때 그 상대임을 나타내는 조사.
rang (no equivalent expression)
A postpositional particle that indicates the person who one is doing something with.

• **화해하다 (verb)** : 싸움을 멈추고 서로 가지고 있던 안 좋은 감정을 풀어 없애다.
reconcile; settle; compromise
To stop fighting and let go of negative feelings toward another.

• -였- : 어떤 사건이 과거에 완료되었거나 그 사건의 결과가 현재까지 지속되는 상황을 나타내는 어미.
-yeot- (no equivalent expression)
An ending of a word used to indicate that an event was completed in the past or its result continues in the present.

• -니 : (아주낮춤으로) 물음을 나타내는 종결 어미.
-ni (no equivalent expression)
(formal, highly addressee-lowering) A sentence-final ending referring to a question.

아니.

나+는 지우+한테 먼저 사과+를 받+[아 내]+[ㄹ 것(거)]+(이)+야.
난 받아 낼 거야

• **아니 (interjection)** : 아랫사람이나 나이나 지위 등이 비슷한 사람이 물어보는 말에 대해 부정하여 대답할 때 쓰는 말.
no; nope; no way
An exclamation uttered when the speaker gives a negative answer to the question asked by his/her junior or someone of a similar age or position.

• **나 (pronoun)** : 말하는 사람이 친구나 아랫사람에게 자기를 가리키는 말.
I
A pronoun used to indicate oneself to a friend or a younger person.

• 는 : 문장 속에서 어떤 대상이 화제임을 나타내는 조사.
neun (no equivalent expression)
A postpositional particle used to indicate that a certain subject is the topic of a sentence.

• **지우 (noun)** : person's name

• 한테 : 어떤 행동의 주체이거나 비롯되는 대상임을 나타내는 조사.
hante (no equivalent expression)
A postpositional particle used to refer to the entity is the subject of an act, or source or cause of such an act.

• **먼저 (adverb)** : 시간이나 순서에서 앞서.
earlier; first
Being or happening before something else in time or order.

• **사과 (noun)** : 자신의 잘못을 인정하며 용서해 달라고 빎.
apology
An act of admitting one's own mistakes and begging for forgiveness.

• 를 : 동작이 직접적으로 영향을 미치는 대상을 나타내는 조사.
reul (no equivalent expression)
A postpositional particle used to indicate the subject that an act has a direct influence on.

• **받다 (verb)** : 요구나 신청, 질문, 공격, 신호 등과 같은 작용을 당하거나 그에 응하다.
receive; get
To receive or respond to an action such as a request, application, inquiry, attack, signal, etc.

• -아 내다 : 앞의 말이 나타내는 행동을 스스로의 힘으로 끝내 이룸을 나타내는 표현.
-a naeda (no equivalent expression)
An expression used to indicate that one has finally accomplished the act mentioned in the preceding statement by oneself.

• -ㄹ 것 : 명사가 아닌 것을 문장에서 명사처럼 쓰이게 하거나 '이다' 앞에 쓰일 수 있게 할 때 쓰는 표현.
-l geot (no equivalent expression)
An expression used to enable a non-noun word to be used as a noun in the sentence or to be used in front of '이다' (be).

• 이다 : 주어가 지시하는 대상의 속성이나 부류를 지정하는 뜻을 나타내는 서술격 조사.
ida (no equivalent expression)
A predicate particle indicating the meaning of the attribute or category of the thing that the subject of the sentence refers to.

• -야 : (두루낮춤으로) 어떤 사실에 대하여 서술하거나 물음을 나타내는 종결 어미.
-ya (no equivalent expression)
(informal addressee-lowering) A sentence-final ending used to **describe** a certain fact or ask a question.

< 대화(dialogue) > - 75

왜 교실에 안 들어가고 밖에 서 있어?
왜 교시레 안 드러가고 바께 서 이써?
wae gyosire an deureogago bakke seo isseo?

누가 문을 잠가 놓았는지 문이 안 열려요.
누가 무늘 잠가 노안는지 무니 안 열려요.
nuga muneul jamga noanneunji muni an yeollyeoyo.

< 설명(explanation) / 번역(translation) >

왜 교실+에 안 들어가+고 밖+에 서+[(어) 있]+어?
서 있어

• **왜 (adverb)** : 무슨 이유로. 또는 어째서.
why
For what reason; how come.

• **교실 (noun)** : 유치원, 초등학교, 중학교, 고등학교에서 교사가 학생들을 가르치는 방.
classroom
In a kindergarten, elementary school, and secondary school, a room where a teacher teaches students.

• 에 : 앞말이 목적지이거나 어떤 행위의 진행 방향임을 나타내는 조사.
to; at
A postpositional particle to indicate that the preceding statement refers to a destination or the course of a certain action.

• **안 (adverb)** : 부정이나 반대의 뜻을 나타내는 말.
not
An adverb that has the meaning of negation or opposite.

• **들어가다 (verb)** : 밖에서 안으로 향하여 가다.
enter; go into
To go inside from outside.

• -고 : 앞의 말이 나타내는 행동이나 그 결과가 뒤에 오는 행동이 일어나는 동안에 그대로 지속됨을 나타내는 연결 어미.
-go (no equivalent expression)
A connective ending used when an action or result of the preceding statement remains the same while the following action happens.

• **밖 (noun)** : 선이나 경계를 넘어선 쪽.
outside
The side beyond a line or boundary.

• 에 : 앞말이 어떤 장소나 자리임을 나타내는 조사.
on; in; at
A postpositional particle to indicate that the preceding statement refers to a certain place or space.

• **서다 (verb)** : 사람이나 동물이 바닥에 발을 대고 몸을 곧게 하다.
stand
For a human or animal to place his/her feet on the ground and assume an upright position.

• -어 있다 : 앞의 말이 나타내는 상태가 계속됨을 나타내는 표현.
-eo itda (no equivalent expression)
An expression used to indicate that the state mentioned in the preceding statement is continued.

• -어 : (두루낮춤으로) 어떤 사실을 서술하거나 물음, 명령, 권유를 나타내는 종결 어미.
-eo (no equivalent expression)
(informal addressee-lowering) A sentence-final ending used to describe a certain fact, **ask a question**, give an order, or advise.

누(구)+가 문+을 잠그(잠ㄱ)+[아 놓]+았+는지 문+이 안 열리+어요.

누가 잠가 놓았는지 열려요

• **누구 (pronoun)** : 모르는 사람을 가리키는 말.
no equivalent expression
A pronoun used to indicate a person that one does not know.

• 가 : 어떤 상태나 상황에 놓인 대상이나 동작의 주체를 나타내는 조사.
ga (no equivalent expression)
A postpositional particle referring to a subject under a certain state or situation, or the subject of an act.

• **문 (noun)** : 사람이 안과 밖을 드나들거나 물건을 넣고 꺼낼 수 있게 하기 위해 열고 닫을 수 있도록 만든 시설.

door

An openable structure through which people go in and come out of a place; or put in or take out things.

• 을 : 동작이 직접적으로 영향을 미치는 대상을 나타내는 조사.

eul (no equivalent expression)

A postpositional particle used to indicate the subject that an action has a direct influence on.

• **잠그다 (verb)** : 문 등을 자물쇠나 고리로 남이 열 수 없게 채우다.

lock; fasten

To lock or latch a door, etc., so that others cannot open it.

• -아 놓다 : 앞의 말이 나타내는 행동을 끝내고 그 결과를 유지함을 나타내는 표현.

-a nota (no equivalent expression)

An expression used to indicate that a certain act mentioned in the preceding statement is completed and its result remains.

• -았- : 어떤 사건이 과거에 완료되었거나 그 사건의 결과가 현재까지 지속되는 상황을 나타내는 어미.

-at- (no equivalent expression)

An ending of a word used to indicate that an event was completed in the past or its result continues in the present.

• -는지 : 뒤에 오는 말의 내용에 대한 막연한 이유나 판단을 나타내는 연결 어미.

-neunji (no equivalent expression)

A connective ending used to indicate an ambiguous reason or judgment about the following statement.

• **문 (noun)** : 사람이 안과 밖을 드나들거나 물건을 넣고 꺼낼 수 있게 하기 위해 열고 닫을 수 있도록 만든 시설.

door

An openable structure through which people go in and come out of a place; or put in or take out things.

• 이 : 어떤 상태나 상황의 대상이나 동작의 주체를 나타내는 조사.

i (no equivalent expression)

A postpositional particle referring to a subject under a certain state or situation, or the agent of an action.

• **안 (adverb)** : 부정이나 반대의 뜻을 나타내는 말.

not

An adverb that has the meaning of negation or opposite.

• **열리다 (verb)** : 닫히거나 잠겨 있던 것이 트이거나 풀리다.
open; be unlocked; unlock
For something closed or locked to be opened or unlocked.

• -어요 : (두루높임으로) 어떤 사실을 서술하거나 질문, 명령, 권유함을 나타내는 종결 어미.
-eoyo (no equivalent expression)
(informal addressee-raising) A sentence-final ending used to **describe** a certain fact, ask a question, give an order, or advise.

< 대화(dialogue) > - 76

오늘 행사는 아홉 시부터 시작인데 왜 벌써 가?
오늘 행사는 아홉 시부터 시자긴데 왜 벌써 가?
oneul haengsaneun ahop sibuteo sijaginde wae beolsseo ga?

준비할 게 많으니까 조금 일찍 와 달라는 부탁을 받았어.
준비할 께 마느니까 조금 일찍 와 달라는 부타글 바다써.
junbihal ge maneunikka jogeum iljjik wa dallaneun butageul badasseo.

< 설명(explanation) / 번역(translation) >

오늘 행사+는 아홉 시+부터 시작+이+ㄴ데 왜 벌써 가+(아)?
시작인데 가

• **오늘 (noun)** : 지금 지나가고 있는 이날.
today
The day that is passing at the present time.

• **행사 (noun)** : 목적이나 계획을 가지고 절차에 따라서 어떤 일을 시행함. 또는 그 일.
event; occasion; ceremony
An act of performing a certain task with a purpose or plan according to a procedure; or such a task.

• 는 : 문장 속에서 어떤 대상이 화제임을 나타내는 조사.
neun (no equivalent expression)
A postpositional particle used to indicate that a certain subject is the topic of a sentence.

• **아홉 (determiner)** : 여덟에 하나를 더한 수의.
nine
Related to the number equal to eight plus one.

• **시 (noun)** : 하루를 스물넷으로 나누었을 때 그 하나를 나타내는 시간의 단위.
o'clock
A bound noun indicating one of 24 hours of a day.

• 부터 : 어떤 일의 시작이나 처음을 나타내는 조사.
buteo (no equivalent expression)
A postpositional particle that indicates the start or beginning of something.

• **시작 (noun)** : 어떤 일이나 행동의 처음 단계를 이루거나 이루게 함. 또는 그런 단계.
start; beginning
The act of constituting or causing to constitute the initial phase of an affair or action, or such a phase.

• 이다 : 주어가 지시하는 대상의 속성이나 부류를 지정하는 뜻을 나타내는 서술격 조사.
ida (no equivalent expression)
A predicate particle indicating the meaning of the attribute or category of the thing that the subject of the sentence refers to.

• -ㄴ데 : 뒤의 말을 하기 위하여 그 대상과 관련이 있는 상황을 미리 말함을 나타내는 연결 어미.
-nde (no equivalent expression)
A connective ending used to talk in advance about a situation to follow.

• **왜 (adverb)** : 무슨 이유로. 또는 어째서.
why
For what reason; how come.

• **벌써 (adverb)** : 생각보다 빠르게.
so soon
More quickly than one thought.

• **가다 (verb)** : 한 곳에서 다른 곳으로 장소를 이동하다.
go; travel
To move from one place to another place.

• -아 : (두루낮춤으로) 어떤 사실을 서술하거나 물음, 명령, 권유를 나타내는 종결 어미.
-a (no equivalent expression)
(informal addressee-lowering) A sentence-final ending used to describe a certain fact, **ask a question**, give an order, or advise.

준비하+[ㄹ 것(거)]+이 많+으니까 조금 일찍 오+[아 달]+라는 부탁+을 받+았+어.
준비할 게 **와 달라는**

• **준비하다 (verb)** : 미리 마련하여 갖추다.
prepare
To have something in place with advance preparations.

• -ㄹ 것 : 명사가 아닌 것을 문장에서 명사처럼 쓰이게 하거나 '이다' 앞에 쓰일 수 있게 할 때 쓰는 표현.
-l geot (no equivalent expression)
An expression used to enable a non-noun word to be used as a noun in the sentence or to be used in front of '이다' (be).

• 이 : 어떤 상태나 상황의 대상이나 동작의 주체를 나타내는 조사.
i (no equivalent expression)
A postpositional particle referring to a subject under a certain state or situation, or the agent of an action.

• **많다 (adjective)** : 수나 양, 정도 등이 일정한 기준을 넘다.
plentiful; many; a lot of
A number, amount, etc., exceeding a certain standard.

• -으니까 : 뒤에 오는 말에 대하여 앞에 오는 말이 원인이나 근거, 전제가 됨을 강조하여 나타내는 연결 어미.
-eunikka (no equivalent expression)
A connective ending used to emphasize that the preceding statement is the cause, reason, or premise for the following statement.

• **조금 (adverb)** : 시간이 짧게.
a little
For a short while.

• **일찍 (adverb)** : 정해진 시간보다 빠르게.
early
Before the specified time.

• **오다 (verb)** : 무엇이 다른 곳에서 이곳으로 움직이다.
come
For something to move from another place to here.

• -아 달다 : 앞의 말이 나타내는 행동을 해 줄 것을 요구함을 나타내는 표현.
-a dalda (no equivalent expression)
An expression used to demand that the act mentioned in the preceding statement be carried out.

• -라는 : 명령이나 요청 등의 말을 인용하여 전달하면서 그 뒤에 오는 명사를 꾸며 줄 때 쓰는 표현.
-raneun (no equivalent expression)
An expression used to quote a remark such as an order, request, etc., while modifying the following noun.

• **부탁 (noun)** : 어떤 일을 해 달라고 하거나 맡김.
request
The act of asking someone to do something or entrusting someone with something.

• 을 : 동작이 직접적으로 영향을 미치는 대상을 나타내는 조사.
eul (no equivalent expression)
A postpositional particle used to indicate the subject that an action has a direct influence on.

• **받다 (verb)** : 요구나 신청, 질문, 공격, 신호 등과 같은 작용을 당하거나 그에 응하다.
receive; get
To receive or respond to an action such as a request, application, inquiry, attack, signal, etc.

• -았- : 어떤 사건이 과거에 완료되었거나 그 사건의 결과가 현재까지 지속되는 상황을 나타내는 어미.
-at- (no equivalent expression)
An ending of a word used to indicate that an event was completed in the past or its result continues in the present.

• -어 : (두루낮춤으로) 어떤 사실을 서술하거나 물음, 명령, 권유를 나타내는 종결 어미.
-eo (no equivalent expression)
(informal addressee-lowering) A sentence-final ending used to **describe** a certain fact, ask a question, give an order, or advise.

< 대화(dialogue) > - 77

이 옷 한번 입어 봐도 되죠?
이 옫 한번 이버 봐도 되죠?
i ot hanbeon ibeo bwado doejyo?

그럼요, 손님. 탈의실은 이쪽입니다.
그러묘, 손님. 타리시른 이쪼김니다.
geureomyo, sonnim. tarisireun ijjogimnida.

< 설명(explanation) / 번역(translation) >

이 옷 한번 입+[어 보]+[아도 되]+죠?
입어 봐도 되죠

• **이 (determiner)** : 말하는 사람에게 가까이 있거나 말하는 사람이 생각하고 있는 대상을 가리킬 때 쓰는 말.
this
The word that is used to refer to a person who is close to the speaker or something that the speaker is thinking of.

• **옷 (noun)** : 사람의 몸을 가리고 더위나 추위 등으로부터 보호하며 멋을 내기 위하여 입는 것.
clothes; garment
An item that one wears to cover his/her body, protect himself/herself from cold, heat, etc., and look fashionable.

• **한번 (adverb)** : 어떤 일을 시험 삼아 시도함을 나타내는 말.
no equivalent expression
An adverb used to indicate that the speaker tries something.

• **입다 (verb)** : 옷을 몸에 걸치거나 두르다.
wear; be dressed; put on
To hang or drape clothes on or around one's body.

• -어 보다 : 앞의 말이 나타내는 행동을 시험 삼아 함을 나타내는 표현.
-eo boda (no equivalent expression)
An expression used to indicate that one does the act mentioned in the preceding statement, as a test.

• -아도 되다 : 어떤 행동에 대한 허락이나 허용을 나타낼 때 쓰는 표현.
-ado deoda (no equivalent expression)
An expression used to indicate that a certain act is allowed or accepted.

• -죠 : (두루높임으로) 말하는 사람이 듣는 사람에게 친근함을 나타내며 물을 때 쓰는 종결 어미.
-jyo (no equivalent expression)
(informal addressee-raising) A sentence-final ending used when the speaker asks the listener something in a friendly manner.

그럼+요, 손님.

탈의실+은 이쪽+이+ㅂ니다.
이쪽입니다

• **그럼 (interjection)** : 말할 것도 없이 당연하다는 뜻으로 대답할 때 쓰는 말.
of course
An exclamation used when the speaker gives an answer meaning that something is absolutely right.

• 요 : 높임의 대상인 상대방에게 존대의 뜻을 나타내는 조사.
yo (no equivalent expression)
A postpositional particle used to indicate respect for the other person, the subject who is shown respect.

• **손님 (noun)** : (높임말로) 여관이나 음식점 등의 가게에 찾아온 사람.
guest; customer
(honorific) A person who visits an inn, restaurant, etc.

• **탈의실 (noun)** : 옷을 벗거나 갈아입는 방.
changing room; locker room
A room where one takes one's clothes off or changes clothes.

• 은 : 문장 속에서 어떤 대상이 화제임을 나타내는 조사.
eun (no equivalent expression)
A postpositional particle used to indicate that a certain subject is the topic of a sentence.

• **이쪽 (pronoun)** : 말하는 사람에게 가까운 곳이나 방향을 가리키는 말.
this side
A pronoun used to indicate a place or direction close to the speaker.

- 이다 : 주어가 지시하는 대상의 속성이나 부류를 지정하는 뜻을 나타내는 서술격 조사.
  ida (no equivalent expression)
  A predicate particle indicating the meaning of the attribute or category of the thing that the subject of the sentence refers to.

- -ㅂ니다 : (아주높임으로) 현재의 동작이나 상태, 사실을 정중하게 설명함을 나타내는 종결 어미.
  -pnida (no equivalent expression)
  (formal, highly addressee-raising) A sentence-final ending used to explain the present action, state, or fact politely.

< 대화(dialogue) > - 78

많이 취하신 거 같아요. 제가 택시 잡아 드릴게요.
마니 취하신 거 가타요. 제가 택씨 자바 드릴께요.
mani chwihasin geo gatayo. jega taeksi jaba deurilgeyo.

괜찮아요. 좀 걷다가 지하철 타고 가면 됩니다.
괜차나요. 좀 걷따가 지하철 타고 가면 됨니다.
gwaenchanayo. jom geotdaga jihacheol tago gamyeon doemnida.

< 설명(explanation) / 번역(translation) >

많이 취하+시+[ㄴ 것(거) 같]+아요.
취하신 거 같아요

제+가 택시 잡+[아 드리]+ㄹ게요.
잡아 드릴게요

- **많이 (adverb)** : 수나 양, 정도 등이 일정한 기준보다 넘게.
  much; in large numbers; in large amounts
  In a state in which a number, amount, degree, etc., are larger than a certain standard.

- **취하다 (verb)** : 술이나 약 등의 기운으로 정신이 흐려지고 몸을 제대로 움직일 수 없게 되다.
  be drunk; be intoxicated
  To be unable to think or move properly, due to the effect of alcoholic drinks, medicine, etc.

- -시- : 어떤 동작이나 상태의 주체를 높이는 뜻을 나타내는 어미.
  -si- (no equivalent expression)
  An ending of a word used for the subject honorifics of an action or state.

- -ㄴ 것 같다 : 추측을 나타내는 표현.
  -n geot gatda (no equivalent expression)
  An expression used to indicate that the statement is a guess.

• -아요 : (두루높임으로) 어떤 사실을 서술하거나 질문, 명령, 권유함을 나타내는 종결 어미.
-ayo (no equivalent expression)
(informal addressee-raising) A sentence-final ending used to **describe** a certain fact, ask a question, give an order, or advise.

• **제 (pronoun)** : 말하는 사람이 자신을 낮추어 가리키는 말인 '저'에 조사 '가'가 붙을 때의 형태.
I
A form of '저' (I), the humble form used by the speaker to show humility, when the postpositional particle '가' is attached to it.

• 가 : 어떤 상태나 상황에 놓인 대상이나 동작의 주체를 나타내는 조사.
ga (no equivalent expression)
A postpositional particle referring to a subject under a certain state or situation, or the subject of an act.

• **택시 (noun)** : 돈을 받고 손님이 원하는 곳까지 태워 주는 일을 하는 승용차.
taxi; cab
A car that takes a passenger to a requested destination for money.

• **잡다 (verb)** : 자동차 등을 타기 위하여 세우다.
pick up; take
To stop a cab, etc., to ride in it.

• -아 드리다 : (높임말로) 남을 위해 앞의 말이 나타내는 행동을 함을 나타내는 표현.
-a deurida (no equivalent expression)
(honorific) An expression used to indicate that one does the act mentioned in the preceding statement for a respected person.

• -ㄹ게요 : (두루높임으로) 말하는 사람이 어떤 행동을 할 것을 듣는 사람에게 약속하거나 의지를 나타내는 표현.
-lgeyo (no equivalent expression)
(informal addressee-raising) An expression used when the speaker promises or notifies the listener that he/she will do something.

괜찮+아요.

좀 걷+다가 지하철 타+고 가+[면 되]+ㅂ니다.
가면 됩니다

• **괜찮다 (adjective)** : 별 문제가 없다.
all right; fine
Having no particular problems.

• -아요 : (두루높임으로) 어떤 사실을 서술하거나 질문, 명령, 권유함을 나타내는 종결 어미.
-ayo (no equivalent expression)
(informal addressee-raising) A sentence-final ending used to **describe** a certain fact, ask a question, give an order, or advise.

• **좀 (adverb)** : 시간이 짧게.
a little
For a short while.

• **걷다 (verb)** : 바닥에서 발을 번갈아 떼어 옮기면서 움직여 위치를 옮기다.
walk
To lift one's feet, one foot at a time, from the ground and change their positions.

• -다가 : 어떤 행동이나 상태 등이 중단되고 다른 행동이나 상태로 바뀜을 나타내는 연결 어미.
-daga (no equivalent expression)
A connective ending used when an action or state, etc., is stopped and changed to another action or state.

• **지하철 (noun)** : 지하 철도로 다니는 전동차.
subway
An electric vehicle operating on an underground railway.

• **타다 (verb)** : 탈것이나 탈것으로 이용하는 짐승의 몸 위에 오르다.
ride; get on; board
To mount a vehicle or the body of an animal used as a vehicle.

• -고 : 앞의 말이 나타내는 행동이나 그 결과가 뒤에 오는 행동이 일어나는 동안에 그대로 지속됨을 나타내는 연결 어미.
-go (no equivalent expression)
A connective ending used when an action or result of the preceding statement remains the same while the following action happens.

• **가다 (verb)** : 한 곳에서 다른 곳으로 장소를 이동하다.
go; travel
To move from one place to another place.

• -면 되다 : 조건이 되는 어떤 행동을 하거나 어떤 상태만 갖추어지면 문제가 없거나 충분함을 나타내는 표현.
-myeon doeda (no equivalent expression)
An expression used to indicate that, as long as one does or reaches a certain act or state, there is no problem or it is enough.

• -ㅂ니다 : (아주높임으로) 현재의 동작이나 상태, 사실을 정중하게 설명함을 나타내는 종결 어미.

-pnida (no equivalent expression)

(formal, highly addressee-raising) A sentence-final ending used to explain the present action, state, or fact politely.

< 대화(dialogue) > - 79

책상 위에 있는 쓰레기 같은 것들은 좀 치워 버려라.
책쌍 위에 인는 쓰레기 가튼 걷뜨른 좀 치워 버려라.
chaeksang wie inneun sseuregi gateun geotdeureun jom chiwo beoryeora.

아냐. 다 필요한 것들이니까 버리면 안 돼.
아냐. 다 피료한 걷뜨리니까 버리면 안 돼.
anya. da piryohan geotdeurinikka beorimyeon an dwae.

< 설명(explanation) / 번역(translation) >

책상 위+에 있+는 쓰레기 같+[은 것]+들+은 좀 치우+[어 버리]+어라.
치워 버려라

- **책상 (noun)** : 책을 읽거나 글을 쓰거나 사무를 볼 때 앞에 놓고 쓰는 상.
  desk
  A table at which one reads a book, writes, or handles office work.

- **위 (noun)** : 어떤 것의 겉면이나 평평한 표면.
  surface; top
  The outside or flat surface of something.

- 에 : 앞말이 어떤 장소나 자리임을 나타내는 조사.
  on; in; at
  A postpositional particle to indicate that the preceding statement refers to a certain place or space.

- **있다 (adjective)** : 무엇이 어떤 곳에 자리나 공간을 차지하고 존재하는 상태이다.
  no equivalent expression
  Something occupying a certain place or space and existing there.

- -는 : 앞의 말이 관형어의 기능을 하게 만들고 사건이나 동작이 현재 일어남을 나타내는 어미.
  -neun (no equivalent expression)
  An ending of a word that makes the preceding statement function as an adnominal phrase and implies that an event or action is happening in the present.

• **쓰레기 (noun)** : 쓸어 낸 먼지, 또는 못 쓰게 되어 내다 버릴 물건이나 내다 버린 물건.
rubbish; trash; garbage
Dust swept away, or something that has been thrown away or to discarded.

• **같다 (adjective)** : 무엇과 비슷한 종류에 속해 있음을 나타내는 말.
such as; like
A term used to indicate that one belongs to a similar group with something.

• -은 것 : 명사가 아닌 것을 문장에서 명사처럼 쓰이게 하거나 '이다' 앞에 쓰일 수 있게 할 때 쓰는 표현.
-eun geot (no equivalent expression)
An expression used to enable a non-noun word to be used as a noun in the sentence or to be used in front of '이다' (be).

• 들 : '복수'의 뜻을 더하는 접미사.
-deul (no equivalent expression)
A suffix used to mean plural.

• 은 : 문장 속에서 어떤 대상이 화제임을 나타내는 조사.
eun (no equivalent expression)
A postpositional particle used to indicate that a certain subject is the topic of a sentence.

• **좀 (adverb)** : 주로 부탁이나 동의를 구할 때 부드러운 느낌을 주기 위해 넣는 말.
please
A word chiefly used to soften a request for a favor or agreement.

• **치우다 (verb)** : 청소하거나 정리하다.
clean; tidy up
To clean up a place or put things away.

• -어 버리다 : 앞의 말이 나타내는 행동이 완전히 끝났음을 나타내는 표현.
-eo beorida (no equivalent expression)
An expression used to indicate that the act mentioned in the preceding statement is completely done.

• -어라 : (아주낮춤으로) 명령을 나타내는 종결 어미.
-eora (no equivalent expression)
(formal, highly addressee-lowering) A sentence-final ending used to indicate a statement as a command.

아니야.
아냐

다 필요하+[ㄴ 것]+들+이+니까 버리+[면 안 되]+어.
필요한 것들이니까 **버리면 안 돼**

• **아니야 (interjection)** : 묻는 말에 대하여 강조하며, 또는 단호하게 부정하며 대답할 때 쓰는 말.
no; no way; absolutely not
An exclamation uttered when answering negatively in an emphatic and resolute manner.

• **다 (adverb)** : 남거나 빠진 것이 없이 모두.
all; everything
With nothing left over or missing.

• **필요하다 (adjective)** : 꼭 있어야 하다.
necessary; needed
Being necessary.

• -ㄴ 것 : 명사가 아닌 것을 문장에서 명사처럼 쓰이게 하거나 '이다' 앞에 쓰일 수 있게 할 때 쓰는 표현.
-n geot (no equivalent expression)
An expression used to enable a non-noun word to be used as a noun in a sentence or to be used in front of '이다' (be).

• 들 : '복수'의 뜻을 더하는 접미사.
-deul (no equivalent expression)
A suffix used to mean plural.

• 이다 : 주어가 지시하는 대상의 속성이나 부류를 지정하는 뜻을 나타내는 서술격 조사.
ida (no equivalent expression)
A predicate particle indicating the meaning of the attribute or category of the thing that the subject of the sentence refers to.

• -니까 : 뒤에 오는 말에 대하여 앞에 오는 말이 원인이나 근거, 전제가 됨을 강조하여 나타내는 연결 어미.
-nikka (no equivalent expression)
A connective ending used to emphasize that the preceding statement is the cause, reason, or premise for the following statement.

• **버리다 (verb)** : 가지고 있을 필요가 없는 물건을 내던지거나 쏟거나 하다.
throw away; dump
To throw or pour out unnecessary things that one has had.

• -면 안 되다 : 어떤 행동이나 상태를 금지하거나 제한함을 나타내는 표현.
-myeon an doeda (no equivalent expression)
An expression used to indicate that a certain act or state is banned or limited.

• -어 : (두루낮춤으로) 어떤 사실을 서술하거나 물음, 명령, 권유를 나타내는 종결 어미.
-eo (no equivalent expression)
(informal addressee-lowering) A sentence-final ending used to **describe** a certain fact, ask a question, give an order, or advise.

< 대화(dialogue) > - 80

좋은 일 있었나 봐? 기분이 좋아 보이네.
조은 일 이썬나 봐? 기부니 조아 보이네.
joeun il isseonna bwa? gibuni joa boine.

아, 어제 남자 친구한테 반지를 선물로 받았거든요.
아, 어제 남자 친구한테 반지를 선물로 바닫꺼드뇨.
a, eoje namja chinguhante banjireul seonmullo badatgeodeunyo.

< 설명(explanation) / 번역(translation) >

좋+은 일 있+었+[나 보]+아?
있었나 봐

기분+이 좋+[아 보이]+네.

• **좋다 (adjective)** : 어떤 일이나 대상이 마음에 들고 만족스럽다.
fond of; in love with
Happy about and satisfied with a thing or object.

• -은 : 앞의 말이 관형어의 기능을 하게 만들고 현재의 상태를 나타내는 어미.
-eun (no equivalent expression)
An ending of a word that makes the preceding word function as an adnominal phrase and refers to the present state.

• **일 (noun)** : 어떤 내용을 가진 상황이나 사실.
matter; affair
A certain situation or fact.

• **있다 (adjective)** : 어떤 사람에게 무슨 일이 생긴 상태이다.
no equivalent expression
Something happening to someone.

• -었- : 사건이 과거에 일어났음을 나타내는 어미.
-eot- (no equivalent expression)
An ending of a word used to indicate that an event happened in the past.

• -나 보다 : 앞의 말이 나타내는 사실을 추측함을 나타내는 표현.
-na boda (no equivalent expression)
An expression used to guess about a fact mentioned in the preceding statement.

• -아 : (두루낮춤으로) 어떤 사실을 서술하거나 물음, 명령, 권유를 나타내는 종결 어미.
-a (no equivalent expression)
(informal addressee-lowering) A sentence-final ending used to describe a certain fact, **ask a question**, give an order, or advise.

• **기분 (noun)** : 불쾌, 유쾌, 우울, 분노 등의 감정 상태.
mood; feelings
The state of one's emotion such as displeasure, pleasure, gloom, anger, etc.

• 이 : 어떤 상태나 상황의 대상이나 동작의 주체를 나타내는 조사.
i (no equivalent expression)
A postpositional particle referring to a subject under a certain state or situation, or the agent of an action.

• **좋다 (adjective)** : 감정 등이 기쁘고 흐뭇하다.
good
Having a feeling, etc., of happiness and satisfaction.

• -아 보이다 : 겉으로 볼 때 앞의 말이 나타내는 것처럼 느껴지거나 추측됨을 나타내는 표현.
-a boida (no equivalent expression)
An expression used to indicate that one feels or guesses something by the appearance of something mentioned in the preceding statement.

• -네 : (아주낮춤으로) 지금 깨달은 일에 대하여 말함을 나타내는 종결 어미.
-ne (no equivalent expression)
(formal, highly addressee-lowering) A sentence-final ending used when talking about something that one just learned.

아, 어제 남자 친구+한테 반지+를 선물+로 받+았+거든요.

• **아 (interjection)** : 기쁨이나 감동의 느낌을 나타낼 때 내는 소리.
oh; wow; ah
An exclamation uttered when the speaker expresses his/her delight or excitement.

• **어제 (adverb)** : 오늘의 하루 전날에.
yesterday
On the day before today.

• **남자 친구 (noun)** : 여자가 사랑하는 감정을 가지고 사귀는 남자.
boyfriend
A man that a woman dates with a feeling of love.

• 한테 : 어떤 행동의 주체이거나 비롯되는 대상임을 나타내는 조사.
hante (no equivalent expression)
A postpositional particle used to refer to the entity is the subject of an act, or source or cause of such an act.

• **반지 (noun)** : 손가락에 끼는 동그란 장신구.
ring
A round accessory for wearing on one's finger.

• 를 : 동작이 직접적으로 영향을 미치는 대상을 나타내는 조사.
reul (no equivalent expression)
A postpositional particle used to indicate the subject that an act has a direct influence on.

• **선물 (noun)** : 고마움을 표현하거나 어떤 일을 축하하기 위해 다른 사람에게 물건을 줌. 또는 그 물건.
gift; present
The act of giving an object to another person in order to show thanks or celebrate something, or the object itself.

• 로 : 신분이나 자격을 나타내는 조사.
ro (no equivalent expression)
A postpositional particle that indicates a status or capacity.

• **받다 (verb)** : 다른 사람이 주거나 보내온 것을 가지다.
receive; get
To take something that someone else has given or sent.

• -았- : 사건이 과거에 일어났음을 나타내는 어미.
-at- (no equivalent expression)
An ending of a word used to indicate that an event happened in the past.

• -거든요 : (두루높임으로) 앞의 내용에 대해 말하는 사람이 생각한 이유나 원인, 근거를 나타내는 표현.
-geodeunnyo (no equivalent expression)
(informal addressee-raising) An expression used to indicate the speaker's reasoning or the basis for the preceding content.

< 대화(dialogue) > - 81

저는 한국에 온 지 일 년쯤 됐어요.
저는 한구게 온 지 일 년쯤 돼써요.
jeoneun hanguge on ji il nyeonjjeum dwaesseoyo.

일 년밖에 안 됐는데도 한국어를 정말 잘하시네요.
일 년바께 안 됀는데도 한구거를 정말 잘하시네요.
il nyeonbakke an dwaenneundedo hangugeoreul jeongmal jalhasineyo.

< 설명(explanation) / 번역(translation) >

저+는 한국+에 오+[ㄴ 지] 일 년+쯤 되+었+어요.
온 지 됐어요

• **저 (pronoun)** : 말하는 사람이 듣는 사람에게 자신을 낮추어 가리키는 말.
I; me
The humble form used by the speaker to refer to himself/herself for the purpose of showing humility to the listener.

• 는 : 문장 속에서 어떤 대상이 화제임을 나타내는 조사.
neun (no equivalent expression)
A postpositional particle used to indicate that a certain subject is the topic of a sentence.

• **한국 (noun)** : 아시아 대륙의 동쪽에 있는 나라. 한반도와 그 부속 섬들로 이루어져 있으며, 대한민국이라고도 부른다. 1950년에 일어난 육이오 전쟁 이후 휴전선을 사이에 두고 국토가 둘로 나뉘었다. 언어는 한국어이고, 수도는 서울이다.
Korea
A country located in East Asia; it consists of the Korean Peninsula and affiliated islands; divided into South Korea and North Korea since the 1953 ceasefire agreement, it is called either the Republic of Korea or South Korea; the official language is Korean and the capital is Seoul.

• 에 : 앞말이 목적지이거나 어떤 행위의 진행 방향임을 나타내는 조사.
to; at
A postpositional particle to indicate that the preceding statement refers to a destination or the course of a certain action.

• **오다 (verb)** : 무엇이 다른 곳에서 이곳으로 움직이다.
come
For something to move from another place to here.

• -ㄴ 지 : 앞의 말이 나타내는 행동을 한 후 시간이 얼마나 지났는지를 나타내는 표현.
-n ji (no equivalent expression)
An expression used to indicate that a certain amount of time has passed since a certain act mentioned in the preceding statement occurred.

• **일 (determiner)** : 하나의.
one
Amounting to one.

• **년 (noun)** : 한 해를 세는 단위.
nyeon (no equivalent expression)
A bound noun that serves as a unit for counting the number of years.

• 쯤 : '정도'의 뜻을 더하는 접미사.
-jjeum (no equivalent expression)
A suffix used to mean an approximate amount.

• **되다 (verb)** : 어떤 때나 시기, 상태에 이르다.
come; fall
To reach a certain timing or state.

• -었- : 어떤 사건이 과거에 완료되었거나 그 사건의 결과가 현재까지 지속되는 상황을 나타내는 어미.
-eot- (no equivalent expression)
An ending of a word used to indicate that an event was completed in the past or its result continues in the present.

• -어요 : (두루높임으로) 어떤 사실을 서술하거나 질문, 명령, 권유함을 나타내는 종결 어미.
-eoyo (no equivalent expression)
(informal addressee-raising) A sentence-final ending used to **describe** a certain fact, ask a question, give an order, or advise.

일 년+밖에 안 되+었+는데도 한국어+를 정말 잘하+시+네요.
됐는데도

• **일 (determiner)** : 하나의.
one
Amounting to one.

• **년 (noun)** : 한 해를 세는 단위.
nyeon (no equivalent expression)
A bound noun that serves as a unit for counting the number of years.

• 밖에 : '그것을 제외하고는', '그것 말고는'의 뜻을 나타내는 조사.
bakke (no equivalent expression)
A postpositional particle that means "except for that" or "other than that."

• **안 (adverb)** : 부정이나 반대의 뜻을 나타내는 말.
not
An adverb that has the meaning of negation or opposite.

• **되다 (verb)** : 어떤 때나 시기, 상태에 이르다.
come; fall
To reach a certain timing or state.

• -었- : 어떤 사건이 과거에 완료되었거나 그 사건의 결과가 현재까지 지속되는 상황을 나타내는 어미.
-eot- (no equivalent expression)
An ending of a word used to indicate that an event was completed in the past or its result continues in the present.

• -는데도 : 앞에 오는 말이 나타내는 상황에 상관없이 뒤에 오는 말이 나타내는 상황이 일어남을 나타내는 표현.
-neundedo (no equivalent expression)
An expression used to indicate that the following situation will occur, regardless of the preceding situation.

• **한국어 (noun)** : 한국에서 사용하는 말.
Korean; Korean language
The language used by the Korean people.

• 를 : 동작이 직접적으로 영향을 미치는 대상을 나타내는 조사.
reul (no equivalent expression)
A postpositional particle used to indicate the subject that an act has a direct influence on.

• **정말 (adverb)** : 거짓이 없이 진짜로.
really
In actual truth without falsehood.

• **잘하다 (verb)** : 익숙하고 솜씨가 있게 하다.
be skillful; be expert; be good
To do something in a skilled and experienced manner.

- -시- : 어떤 동작이나 상태의 주체를 높이는 뜻을 나타내는 어미.

  -si- (no equivalent expression)

  An ending of a word used for the subject honorifics of an action or state.

- -네요 : (두루높임으로) 말하는 사람이 직접 경험하여 새롭게 알게 된 사실에 대해 감탄함을 나타낼 때 쓰는 표현.

  -neyo (no equivalent expression)

  (informal addressee-raising) An expression used to indicate that the speaker is impressed by a fact he/she learned anew from a past personal experience.

< 대화(dialogue) > - 82

지우가 결혼하더니 많이 밝아졌지?
지우가 결혼하더니 마니 발가전찌?
jiuga gyeolhonhadeoni mani balgajeotji?

맞아. 지우를 십 년 동안 봐 왔지만 요새처럼 행복해 보일 때가 없었어.
마자. 지우를 십 년 동안 봐 왇찌만 요새처럼 행보캐 보일 때가 업써써.
maja. jiureul sip nyeon dongan bwa watjiman yosaecheoreom haengbokae boil ttaega eopseosseo.

< 설명(explanation) / 번역(translation) >

지우+가 결혼하+더니 많이 밝아지+었+지?
밝아졌지

- **지우 (noun)** : person's name

- 가 : 어떤 상태나 상황에 놓인 대상이나 동작의 주체를 나타내는 조사.
  ga (no equivalent expression)
  A postpositional particle referring to a subject under a certain state or situation, or the subject of an act.

- **결혼하다 (verb)** : 남자와 여자가 법적으로 부부가 되다.
  marry
  For a man and a woman to become a legally married couple.

- -더니 : 과거의 사실이나 상황에 뒤이어 어떤 사실이나 상황이 일어남을 나타내는 연결 어미.
  -deoni (no equivalent expression)
  A connective ending used when a certain fact or situation happened after a fact or situation in the past.

- **많이 (determiner)** : 수나 양, 정도 등이 일정한 기준보다 넘게.
  much; in large numbers; in large amounts
  In a state in which a number, amount, degree, etc., are larger than a certain standard.

- **밝아지다 (verb)** : 밝게 되다.
  brighten; lighten
  To turn bright.

• -었- : 어떤 사건이 과거에 완료되었거나 그 사건의 결과가 현재까지 지속되는 상황을 나타내는 어미.
-eot- (no equivalent expression)
An ending of a word used to indicate that an event was completed in the past or its result continues in the present.

• -지 : (두루낮춤으로) 이미 알고 있는 것을 다시 확인하듯이 물을 때 쓰는 종결 어미.
-ji (no equivalent expression)
(informal addressee-lowering) A sentence-final ending used to ask something that the speaker already knows to cross-check the information.

맞+아.

지우+를 십 년 동안 보+[아 오]+았+지만
봐 왔지만

요새+처럼 행복하+[여 보이]+[ㄹ 때]+가 없+었+어.
행복해 보일 때가

• **맞다 (verb)** : 그렇거나 옳다.
be so; be right
To be so or right.

• -아 : (두루낮춤으로) 어떤 사실을 서술하거나 물음, 명령, 권유를 나타내는 종결 어미.
-a (no equivalent expression)
(informal addressee-lowering) A sentence-final ending used to **describe** a certain fact, ask a question, give an order, or advise.

• **지우 (noun)** : person's name

• 를 : 동작이 간접적인 영향을 미치는 대상이나 목적임을 나타내는 조사.
reul (no equivalent expression)
A postpositional particle used to indicate the subject or target that an action has an indirect influence on.

• **십 (determiner)** : 열의.
ten
Amounting to ten.

• **년 (noun)** : 한 해를 세는 단위.
nyeon (no equivalent expression)
A bound noun that serves as a unit for counting the number of years.

• **동안 (noun)** : 한때에서 다른 때까지의 시간의 길이.
while
The period from one time to another.

• **보다 (verb)** : 사람을 만나다.
meet; see
To meet a person.

• -아 오다 : 앞의 말이 나타내는 행동이나 상태가 어떤 기준점으로 가까워지면서 계속 진행됨을 나타내는 표현.
-a oda (no equivalent expression)
An expression used to indicate that the act or state mentioned in the preceding statement is continued as a certain set point of time is approaching.

• -았- : 어떤 사건이 과거에 완료되었거나 그 사건의 결과가 현재까지 지속되는 상황을 나타내는 어미.
-at- (no equivalent expression)
An ending of a word used to indicate that an event was completed in the past or its result continues in the present.

• -지만 : 앞에 오는 말을 인정하면서 그와 반대되거나 다른 사실을 덧붙일 때 쓰는 연결 어미.
-jiman (no equivalent expression)
A connective ending used to recognize the truth of the preceding statement and add facts that are the opposite of it or different.

• **요새 (noun)** : 얼마 전부터 이제까지의 매우 짧은 동안.
these days; nowadays; lately
An abbreviated word for these days, meaning an extremely short period from a while ago to the present.

• 처럼 : 모양이나 정도가 서로 비슷하거나 같음을 나타내는 조사.
cheoreom (no equivalent expression)
A postpositional particle used when something is similar or identical to something else in shape or level.

• **행복하다 (adjective)** : 삶에서 충분한 만족과 기쁨을 느껴 흐뭇하다.
happy; content; joyful
Being delighted as one feels enough satisfaction or enjoyment in life.

• -여 보이다 : 겉으로 볼 때 앞의 말이 나타내는 것처럼 느껴지거나 추측됨을 나타내는 표현.
-yeo boida (no equivalent expression)
An expression used to indicate that one feels or guesses something by appearance as mentioned in the preceding statement.

• -ㄹ 때 : 어떤 행동이나 상황이 일어나는 동안이나 그 시기 또는 그러한 일이 일어난 경우를 나타내는 표현.
-l ttae (no equivalent expression)
An expression used to indicate the duration, period, or occasion of a certain act or situation.

• 가 : 어떤 행동이나 상황이 일어나는 동안이나 그 시기 또는 그러한 일이 일어난 경우를 나타내는 표현.
ga (no equivalent expression)
A postpositional particle referring to a subject under a certain state or situation, or the subject of an act.

• **없다 (adjective)** : 어떤 사실이나 현상이 현실로 존재하지 않는 상태이다.
lacking
(for a fact or phenomenon to be) Not existent in reality.

• -었- : 사건이 과거에 일어났음을 나타내는 어미.
-eot- (no equivalent expression)
An ending of a word used to indicate that an event happened in the past.

• -어 : (두루낮춤으로) 어떤 사실을 서술하거나 물음, 명령, 권유를 나타내는 종결 어미.
-eo (no equivalent expression)
(informal addressee-lowering) A sentence-final ending used to **describe** a certain fact, ask a question, give an order, or advise.

< 대화(dialogue) > - 83

나는 먼저 가 있을 테니까 너도 빨리 와.
나는 먼저 가 이쓸 테니까 너도 빨리 와.
naneun meonjeo ga isseul tenikka neodo ppalli wa.

응. 알았어. 금방 따라갈게.
응. 아라써. 금방 따라갈께.
eung. arasseo. geumbang ttaragalge.

< 설명(explanation) / 번역(translation) >

나+는 먼저 가+[(아) 있]+[을 테니까] 너+도 빨리 오+아.
가 있을 테니까 와

• **나 (pronoun)** : 말하는 사람이 친구나 아랫사람에게 자기를 가리키는 말.
I
A pronoun used to indicate oneself to a friend or a younger person.

• 는 : 어떤 대상이 다른 것과 대조됨을 나타내는 조사.
neun (no equivalent expression)
A postpositional particle used to indicate that a certain subject contrasts with something else.

• **먼저 (adverb)** : 시간이나 순서에서 앞서.
earlier; first
Being or happening before something else in time or order.

• **가다 (verb)** : 한 곳에서 다른 곳으로 장소를 이동하다.
go; travel
To move from one place to another place.

• -아 있다 : 앞의 말이 나타내는 상태가 계속됨을 나타내는 표현.
-a itda (no equivalent expression)
An expression used to indicate that the state mentioned in the preceding statement is continued.

• -을 테니까 : 뒤에 오는 말에 대한 조건임을 강조하여 앞에 오는 말에 대한 말하는 사람의 의지를 나타내는 표현.
-eul tenikka (no equivalent expression)
An expression used to indicate the speaker's intention to do the act mentioned in the preceding statement, as a condition for the following statement.

• **너 (pronoun)** : 듣는 사람이 친구나 아랫사람일 때, 그 사람을 가리키는 말.
no equivalent expression
A pronoun used to indicate the listener when he/she is the same age or younger.

• 도 : 이미 있는 어떤 것에 다른 것을 더하거나 포함함을 나타내는 조사.
do (no equivalent expression)
A postpositional particle used to indicate an addition or inclusion of another thing to something that already exists.

• **빨리 (adverb)** : 걸리는 시간이 짧게.
quickly
In a short duration of time.

• **오다 (verb)** : 무엇이 다른 곳에서 이곳으로 움직이다.
come
For something to move from another place to here.

• -아 : (두루낮춤으로) 어떤 사실을 서술하거나 물음, 명령, 권유를 나타내는 종결 어미.
-a (no equivalent expression)
(informal addressee-lowering) A sentence-final ending used to describe a certain fact, ask a question, **give an order**, or advise.

응.

알+았+어.

금방 따라가+ㄹ게.
따라갈게

• **응 (interjection)** : 상대방의 물음이나 명령 등에 긍정하여 대답할 때 쓰는 말.
yes; right
An exclamation uttered when the speaker gives an affirmative answer to someone's question, order, etc.

• **알다 (verb)** : 상대방의 어떤 명령이나 요청에 대해 그대로 하겠다는 동의의 뜻을 나타내는 말.
will; say yes
To respond affirmatively to an order or request, agreeing to do as one has been told.

• -았- : 어떤 사건이 과거에 완료되었거나 그 사건의 결과가 현재까지 지속되는 상황을 나타내는 어미.
-at- (no equivalent expression)
An ending of a word used to indicate that an event was completed in the past or its result continues in the present.

• -어 : (두루낮춤으로) 어떤 사실을 서술하거나 물음, 명령, 권유를 나타내는 종결 어미.
-eo (no equivalent expression)
(informal addressee-lowering) A sentence-final ending used to **describe** a certain fact, ask a question, give an order, or advise.

• **금방 (adverb)** : 시간이 얼마 지나지 않아 곧바로.
immediately; soon
Before long; shortly

• **따라가다 (verb)** : 앞에서 가는 것을 뒤에서 그대로 쫓아가다.
follow; go after
To follow someone or something ahead on the same track.

• -ㄹ게 : (두루낮춤으로) 말하는 사람이 어떤 행동을 할 것을 듣는 사람에게 약속하거나 의지를 나타내는 종결 어미.
-lge (no equivalent expression)
(informal addressee-lowering) A sentence-final ending used when the speaker promises or notifies the listener that he/she will do something.

< 대화(dialogue) > - 84

오늘 정말 잘 먹고 갑니다. 초대해 주셔서 감사합니다.
오늘 정말 잘 먹꼬 감니다. 초대해 주셔서 감사함니다.
oneul jeongmal jal meokgo gamnida. chodaehae jusyeoseo gamsahamnida.

아니에요. 바쁜데 이렇게 먼 곳까지 와 줘서 고마워요.
아니에요. 바쁜데 이러케 먼 곧까지 와 줘서 고마워요.
anieyo. bappeunde ireoke meon gotkkaji wa jwoseo gomawoyo.

< 설명(explanation) / 번역(translation) >

오늘 정말 잘 먹+고 가+ㅂ니다.
갑니다

초대하+[여 주]+시+어서 감사하+ㅂ니다.
초대해 주셔서 감사합니다

• **오늘 (adverb)** : 지금 지나가고 있는 이날에.
today
The day that is passing at the present time.

• **정말 (adverb)** : 거짓이 없이 진짜로.
really
In actual truth without falsehood.

• **잘 (adverb)** : 충분히 만족스럽게.
well
In a sufficiently satisfactory manner.

• **먹다 (verb)** : 음식 등을 입을 통하여 배 속에 들여보내다.
eat; have; consume; take
To put food into one's mouth and take it in one's stomach.

• -고 : 앞의 말과 뒤의 말이 차례대로 일어남을 나타내는 연결 어미.
-go (no equivalent expression)
A connective ending used when the preceding statement and the following statement happen in order.

• **가다 (verb)** : 한 곳에서 다른 곳으로 장소를 이동하다.
go; travel
To move from one place to another place.

• -ㅂ니다 : (아주높임으로) 현재의 동작이나 상태, 사실을 정중하게 설명함을 나타내는 종결 어미.
-pnida (no equivalent expression)
(formal, highly addressee-raising) A sentence-final ending used to explain the present action, state, or fact politely.

• **초대하다 (verb)** : 다른 사람에게 어떤 자리, 모임, 행사 등에 와 달라고 요청하다.
invite
To ask someone to come to a certain place, gathering, event, etc.

• -여 주다 : 남을 위해 앞의 말이 나타내는 행동을 함을 나타내는 표현.
-yeo juda (no equivalent expression)
An expression used to indicate that one does the act mentioned in the preceding statement for someone.

• -시- : 어떤 동작이나 상태의 주체를 높이는 뜻을 나타내는 어미.
-si- (no equivalent expression)
An ending of a word used for the subject honorifics of an action or state.

• -어서 : 이유나 근거를 나타내는 연결 어미.
-eoseo (no equivalent expression)
A connective ending used for a reason or cause.

• **감사하다 (verb)** : 고맙게 여기다.
appreciate
To feel thankful for something.

• -ㅂ니다 : (아주높임으로) 현재의 동작이나 상태, 사실을 정중하게 설명함을 나타내는 종결 어미.
-pnida (no equivalent expression)
(formal, highly addressee-raising) A sentence-final ending used to explain the present action, state, or fact politely.

아니+에요.

바쁘+ㄴ데 이렇+게 멀+ㄴ 곳+까지 오+[아 주]+어서 고맙(고마우)+어요.
바쁜데 먼 와 줘서 고마워요

• **아니다 (adjective)** : 어떤 사실이나 내용을 부정하는 뜻을 나타내는 말.
not
Used to negate a fact or statement.

• -에요 : (두루높임으로) 어떤 사실을 서술하거나 질문함을 나타내는 종결 어미.
-eyo (no equivalent expression)
(informal addressee-raising) A sentence-final ending used when **describing** a certain fact or asking a question.

• **바쁘다 (adjective)** : 할 일이 많거나 시간이 없어서 다른 것을 할 여유가 없다.
busy; hectic
Having no time to do other things because one has many things to do or has little time.

• -ㄴ데 : 뒤의 말을 하기 위하여 그 대상과 관련이 있는 상황을 미리 말함을 나타내는 연결 어미.
-nde (no equivalent expression)
A connective ending used to talk in advance about a situation to follow.

• **이렇다 (adjective)** : 상태, 모양, 성질 등이 이와 같다.
so; like this
(for a state, appearance, nature to be) Like this.

• -게 : 앞의 말이 뒤에서 가리키는 일의 목적이나 결과, 방식, 정도 등이 됨을 나타내는 연결 어미.
-ge (no equivalent expression)
A connective ending used when the preceding statement is the purpose, result, method, amount, etc., of something mentioned in the following statement.

• **멀다 (adjective)** : 두 곳 사이의 떨어진 거리가 길다.
distant; far-off
The distance between two places being long.

• -ㄴ : 앞의 말이 관형어의 기능을 하게 만들고 현재의 상태를 나타내는 어미.
-n (no equivalent expression)
An ending of a word that makes the preceding statement function as an adnominal phrase and refers to the present state.

• **곳 (noun)** : 일정한 장소나 위치.
place; spot; location
A certain spot or location.

• 까지 : 어떤 범위의 끝임을 나타내는 조사.
kkaji (no equivalent expression)
A postpositional particle referring to the end of a certain range.

• **오다 (verb)** : 무엇이 다른 곳에서 이곳으로 움직이다.
come
For something to move from another place to here.

• -아 주다 : 남을 위해 앞의 말이 나타내는 행동을 함을 나타내는 표현.
-a juda (no equivalent expression)
An expression used to indicate that one does the act mentioned in the preceding statement for someone.

• -어서 : 이유나 근거를 나타내는 연결 어미.
-eoseo (no equivalent expression)
A connective ending used for a reason or cause.

• **고맙다 (adjective)** : 남이 자신을 위해 무엇을 해주어서 마음이 흐뭇하고 보답하고 싶다.
thankful; grateful
Pleased and wanting to return a favor to someone.

• -어요 : (두루높임으로) 어떤 사실을 서술하거나 질문, 명령, 권유함을 나타내는 종결 어미.
-eoyo (no equivalent expression)
(informal addressee-raising) A sentence-final ending used to **describe** a certain fact, ask a question, give an order, or advise.

< 대화(dialogue) > - 85

백화점에는 왜 다시 가려고?
배콰저메는 왜 다시 가려고?
baekwajeomeneun wae dasi garyeogo?

어제 산 옷이 맞는 줄 알았더니 작아서 교환해야 해.
어제 산 오시 만는 줄 아랃떠니 자가서 교환해야 해.
eoje san osi manneun jul aratdeoni jagaseo gyohwanhaeya hae.

< 설명(explanation) / 번역(translation) >

백화점+에+는 왜 다시 가+려고?

• **백화점 (noun)** : 한 건물 안에 온갖 상품을 종류에 따라 나누어 벌여 놓고 판매하는 큰 상점.
department store
A large retail store divided into departments selling a great many kinds of goods in one building.

• 에 : 앞말이 목적지이거나 어떤 행위의 진행 방향임을 나타내는 조사.
to; at
A postpositional particle to indicate that the preceding statement refers to a destination or the course of a certain action.

• 는 : 문장 속에서 어떤 대상이 화제임을 나타내는 조사.
neun (no equivalent expression)
A postpositional particle used to indicate that a certain subject is the topic of a sentence.

• **왜 (adverb)** : 무슨 이유로. 또는 어째서.
why
For what reason; how come.

• **다시 (adverb)** : 같은 말이나 행동을 반복해서 또.
again
Repeatedly with the same words or behavior.

• **가다 (verb)** : 한 곳에서 다른 곳으로 장소를 이동하다.
go; travel
To move from one place to another place.

• -려고 : (두루낮춤으로) 어떤 주어진 상황에 대하여 의심이나 반문을 나타내는 종결 어미.
-ryeogo (no equivalent expression)
(informal addressee-lowering) A sentence-final ending used to doubt a given situation and ask again about it.

어제 사+ㄴ 옷+이 맞+[는 줄] 알+았더니 작+아서 교환하+[여야 하]+여.
산 교환해야 해

• **어제 (adverb)** : 오늘의 하루 전날에.
yesterday
On the day before today.

• **사다 (verb)** : 돈을 주고 어떤 물건이나 권리 등을 자기 것으로 만들다.
buy; purchase; get
To get ownership of an item, right, etc., by paying for it.

• -ㄴ : 앞의 말이 관형어의 기능을 하게 만들고 사건이나 동작이 과거에 일어났음을 나타내는 어미.
-n (no equivalent expression)
An ending of a word that makes the preceding statement function as an adnominal phrase and indicates an event or action having occurred in the past.

• **옷 (noun)** : 사람의 몸을 가리고 더위나 추위 등으로부터 보호하며 멋을 내기 위하여 입는 것.
clothes; garment
An item that one wears to cover his/her body, protect himself/herself from cold, heat, etc., and look fashionable.

• 이 : 어떤 상태나 상황의 대상이나 동작의 주체를 나타내는 조사.
i (no equivalent expression)
A postpositional particle referring to a subject under a certain state or situation, or the agent of an action.

• **맞다 (verb)** : 크기나 규격 등이 어떤 것과 일치하다.
fit; be the same as
For a size, specification, etc., to be the same as something.

• -는 줄 : 어떤 사실이나 상태에 대해 알고 있거나 모르고 있음을 나타내는 표현.
-neun jul (no equivalent expression)
An expression used to indicate that one either knows or does not know a certain fact or state.

• **알다 (verb)** : 어떤 사실을 그러하다고 여기거나 생각하다.
know; think
To consider or assume a fact as being of a certain quality.

• -았더니 : 과거의 사실이나 상황과 다른 새로운 사실이나 상황이 있음을 나타내는 표현.
-atdeoni (no equivalent expression)
An expression used to indicate that there is a new incident or situation, different from a past one.

• **작다 (adjective)** : 정해진 크기에 모자라서 맞지 아니하다.
small
Not fitting since the size is smaller than required.

• -아서 : 이유나 근거를 나타내는 연결 어미.
-aseo (no equivalent expression)
A connective ending used for a reason or cause.

• **교환하다 (verb)** : 무엇을 다른 것으로 바꾸다.
change
To change one thing for another.

• -여야 하다 : 앞에 오는 말이 어떤 일을 하거나 어떤 상황에 이르기 위한 의무적인 행동이거나 필수적인 조건임을 나타내는 표현.
-yeoya hada (no equivalent expression)
An expression used to indicate that the preceding statement is the required act or condition to realize a certain incident or situation.

• -여 : (두루낮춤으로) 어떤 사실을 서술하거나 물음, 명령, 권유를 나타내는 종결 어미.
-yeo (no equivalent expression)
(informal addressee-lowering) A sentence-final ending used to **describe** a certain fact, ask a question, give an order, or advi

< 대화(dialogue) > - 86

물을 계속 틀어 놓은 채 설거지를 하지 마세요.
무를 계속 트러 노은 채 설거지를 하지 마세요.
mureul gesok teureo noeun chae seolgeojireul haji maseyo.

방금 잠갔어요. 앞으로는 헹굴 때만 물을 틀어 놓을게요.
방금 잠가써요. 아프로는 헹굴 때만 무를 트러 노을께요.
banggeum jamgasseoyo. apeuroneun henggul ttaeman mureul teureo noeulgeyo.

< 설명(explanation) / 번역(translation) >

물+을 계속 틀+[어 놓]+[은 채] 설거지+를 하+[지 말(마)]+세요.

하지 마세요

• **물 (noun)** : 강, 호수, 바다, 지하수 등에 있으며 순수한 것은 빛깔, 냄새, 맛이 없고 투명한 액체.
water
A liquid that constitutes rivers, lakes, oceans, underground reservoirs, etc., a pure form of which is colorless, orderless, tasteless and transparent.

• 을 : 동작이 직접적으로 영향을 미치는 대상을 나타내는 조사.
eul (no equivalent expression)
A postpositional particle used to indicate the subject that an action has a direct influence on.

• **계속 (adverb)** : 끊이지 않고 잇따라.
continuously; successively
Continually without interruption.

• **틀다 (verb)** : 수도와 같은 장치를 작동시켜 물이 나오게 하다.
turn
To operate a device such as a water tap, making water run.

• -어 놓다 : 앞의 말이 나타내는 행동을 끝내고 그 결과를 유지함을 나타내는 표현.
-eo nota (no equivalent expression)
An expression used to indicate that a certain act mentioned in the preceding statement is completed and its result remains.

• -은 채 : 앞의 말이 나타내는 어떤 행위를 한 상태 그대로 있음을 나타내는 표현.
-eun chae (no equivalent expression)
An expression used to indicate that the state remains the same as when a certain act mentioned in the preceding statement occurred.

• **설거지 (noun)** : 음식을 먹고 난 뒤에 그릇을 씻어서 정리하는 일.
dishwashing; doing the dishes
The act of washing and putting away the dishes after eating.

• 를 : 동작이 직접적으로 영향을 미치는 대상을 나타내는 조사.
reul (no equivalent expression)
A postpositional particle used to indicate the subject that an act has a direct influence on.

• **하다 (verb)** : 어떤 행동이나 동작, 활동 등을 행하다.
do; perform
To perform a certain move, action, activity, etc.

• -지 말다 : 앞의 말이 나타내는 행동을 하지 못하게 함을 나타내는 표현.
-ji malda (no equivalent expression)
An expression used to prohibit the act mentioned in the preceding statement.

• -세요 : (두루높임으로) 설명, 의문, 명령, 요청의 뜻을 나타내는 종결 어미.
-seyo (no equivalent expression)
(informal addressee-raising) A sentence-final ending used to describe, ask a question, order, and request. <order>

방금 잠그(잠ㄱ)+았+어요.
잠갔어요

앞+으로+는 헹구+[ㄹ 때]+만 물+을 틀+[어 놓]+을게요.
헹굴 때만

• **방금 (adverb)** : 말하고 있는 시점보다 바로 조금 전에.
a moment ago
Just before the time of speaking.

• **잠그다 (verb)** : 물, 가스 등이 나오지 않도록 하다.
turn off
To make water, gas, etc., stop running.

• -았- : 어떤 사건이 과거에 완료되었거나 그 사건의 결과가 현재까지 지속되는 상황을 나타내는 어미.
-at- (no equivalent expression)
An ending of a word used to indicate that an event was completed in the past or its result continues in the present.

• -어요 : (두루높임으로) 어떤 사실을 서술하거나 질문, 명령, 권유함을 나타내는 종결 어미.
-eoyo (no equivalent expression)
(informal addressee-raising) A sentence-final ending used to **describe** a certain fact, ask a question, give an order, or advise.

• **앞 (noun)** : 다가올 시간.
future
A time to come.

• 으로 : 시간을 나타내는 조사.
euro (no equivalent expression)
A postpositional particle that indicates time.

• 는 : 어떤 대상이 다른 것과 대조됨을 나타내는 조사.
neun (no equivalent expression)
A postpositional particle used to indicate that a certain subject contrasts with something else.

• **헹구다 (verb)** : 깨끗한 물에 넣어 비눗물이나 더러운 때가 빠지도록 흔들어 씻다.
rinse
To put laundry, etc., into clean water and swirl it gently to remove soap or dirt.

• -ㄹ 때 : 어떤 행동이나 상황이 일어나는 동안이나 그 시기 또는 그러한 일이 일어난 경우를 나타내는 표현.
-l ttae (no equivalent expression)
An expression used to indicate the duration, period, or occasion of a certain act or situation.

• 만 : 다른 것은 제외하고 어느 것을 한정함을 나타내는 조사.
man (no equivalent expression)
A postpositional particle used when limiting the field to one thing, excluding all the others.

• **물 (noun)** : 강, 호수, 바다, 지하수 등에 있으며 순수한 것은 빛깔, 냄새, 맛이 없고 투명한 액체.
water
A liquid that constitutes rivers, lakes, oceans, underground reservoirs, etc., a pure form of which is colorless, orderless, tasteless and transparent.

• 을 : 동작이 직접적으로 영향을 미치는 대상을 나타내는 조사.
eul (no equivalent expression)
A postpositional particle used to indicate the subject that an action has a direct influence on.

• **틀다 (verb)** : 수도와 같은 장치를 작동시켜 물이 나오게 하다.
turn
To operate a device such as a water tap, making water run.

• -어 놓다 : 앞의 말이 나타내는 행동을 끝내고 그 결과를 유지함을 나타내는 표현.
-eo nota (no equivalent expression)
An expression used to indicate that a certain act mentioned in the preceding statement is completed and its result remains.

• -을게요 : (두루높임으로) 말하는 사람이 어떤 행동을 할 것을 듣는 사람에게 약속하거나 의지를 나타내는 표현.
-eulgeyo (no equivalent expression)
(informal addressee-raising) An expression used used when the speaker promises or notifies the listener that he/she will do something.

< 대화(dialogue) > - 87

작년에 갔던 그 바닷가에 또 가고 싶다.
장녀네 갇떤 그 바닫까에 또 가고 십따.
jangnyeone gatdeon geu badatgae tto gago sipda.

나도 그래. 그때 우리 참 재밌게 놀았었지.
나도 그래. 그때 우리 참 재믿께 노라썯찌.
nado geurae. geuttae uri cham jaemitge norasseotji.

< 설명(explanation) / 번역(translation) >

작년+에 가+았던 그 바닷가+에 또 가+[고 싶]+다.
갔던

• **작년 (noun)** : 지금 지나가고 있는 해의 바로 전 해.
last year
The previous year of the current year.

• 에 : 앞말이 시간이나 때임을 나타내는 조사.
in; at
A postpositional particle to indicate that the preceding statement refers to the time.

• **가다 (verb)** : 한 곳에서 다른 곳으로 장소를 이동하다.
go; travel
To move from one place to another place.

• -았던 : 과거의 사건이나 상태를 다시 떠올리거나 그 사건이나 상태가 완료되지 않고 중단되었다는 의미를 나타내는 표현.
-atdeon (no equivalent expression)
An expression used to recall a past incident or state, and indicate that activity related to the incident or state has been suspended, and remains incomplete.

• **그 (determiner)** : 듣는 사람에게 가까이 있거나 듣는 사람이 생각하고 있는 대상을 가리킬 때 쓰는 말.
that
A term referring to something near the listener or what the listener is thinking.

• **바닷가 (noun)** : 바다와 육지가 맞닿은 곳이나 그 근처.
beach; coast; seaside; seashore
A place where sea and land meet, or an area near that place.

• 에 : 앞말이 목적지이거나 어떤 행위의 진행 방향임을 나타내는 조사.
to; at
A postpositional particle to indicate that the preceding statement refers to a destination or the course of a certain action.

• **또 (adverb)** : 어떤 일이나 행동이 다시.
once more
In the manner of happening or behaving again.

• **가다 (verb)** : 한 곳에서 다른 곳으로 장소를 이동하다.
go; travel
To move from one place to another place.

• -고 싶다 : 앞의 말이 나타내는 행동을 하기를 원함을 나타내는 표현.
-go sipda (no equivalent expression)
An expression used to state that the speaker wants to do the act mentioned in the preceding statement.

• -다 : (아주낮춤으로) 어떤 사건이나 사실, 상태를 서술함을 나타내는 종결 어미.
-da (no equivalent expression)
(formal, highly addressee-lowering) A sentence-final ending used when describing a certain event, fact, state, etc.

나+도 그렇+어.
그래

그때 우리 참 재밌+게 놀+았었+지.

• **나 (pronoun)** : 말하는 사람이 친구나 아랫사람에게 자기를 가리키는 말.
I
A pronoun used to indicate oneself to a friend or a younger person.

• 도 : 이미 있는 어떤 것에 다른 것을 더하거나 포함함을 나타내는 조사.
do (no equivalent expression)
A postpositional particle used to indicate an addition or inclusion of another thing to something that already exists.

• **그렇다 (adjective)** : 상태, 모양, 성질 등이 그와 같다.
so; as such; like that
A state, appearance, characteristic, etc. being as such.

• -어 : (두루낮춤으로) 어떤 사실을 서술하거나 물음, 명령, 권유를 나타내는 종결 어미.
-eo (no equivalent expression)
(informal addressee-lowering) A sentence-final ending used to **describe** a certain fact, ask a question, give an order, or advise.

• **그때 (noun)** : 앞에서 이야기한 어떤 때.
that time; that moment; then
The previously-mentioned time.

• **우리 (pronoun)** : 말하는 사람이 자기와 듣는 사람 또는 이를 포함한 여러 사람들을 가리키는 말.
we
A pronoun used when the speaker refers to himself/herself and the listener or listeners, or a group of people including the speaker and listener or listeners.

• **참 (adverb)** : 사실이나 이치에 조금도 어긋남이 없이 정말로.
truly
In the manner of being not contrary to a fact or reason.

• **재밌다 (adjective)** : 즐겁고 유쾌한 느낌이 있다.
interesting
Having the quality of being pleasant and joyful.

• -게 : 앞의 말이 뒤에서 가리키는 일의 목적이나 결과, 방식, 정도 등이 됨을 나타내는 연결 어미.
-ge (no equivalent expression)
A connective ending used when the preceding statement is the purpose, result, method, amount, etc., of something mentioned in the following statement.

• **놀다 (verb)** : 놀이 등을 하면서 재미있고 즐겁게 지내다.
play; have fun
To have a good time while playing.

• -았었- : 현재와 비교하여 다르거나 현재로 이어지지 않는 과거의 사건을 나타내는 어미.
-atsseot- (no equivalent expression)
An ending of a word used for a past event that is different from the present or does not continue to the present.

• -지 : (두루낮춤으로) 말하는 사람이 듣는 사람이 이미 알고 있다고 생각하는 것을 확인하며 말할 때 쓰는 종결 어미.
-ji (no equivalent expression)
(informal addressee-lowering) A sentence-final ending used when the speaker confirms and says something that the listener thought he/she already knew.

< 대화(dialogue) > - 88

계속 돌아다녔더니 배고프다. 점심은 뭘 먹을까?
계속 도라다녇떠니 배고프다. 점시믄 뭘 머글까?
gesok doradanyeotdeoni baegopeuda. jeomsimeun mwol meogeulkka?

전주에 왔으면 비빔밥을 먹어야지.
전주에 와쓰면 비빔빠블 머거야지.
jeonjue wasseumyeon bibimbabeul meogeoyaji.

< 설명(explanation) / 번역(translation) >

계속 돌아다니+었더니 배고프+다.
돌아다녔더니

점심+은 뭐+를 먹+을까?
뭘

• **계속 (adverb)** : 끊이지 않고 잇따라.
continuously; successively
Continually without interruption.

• **돌아다니다 (verb)** : 여기저기를 두루 다니다.
wander; stroll
To travel around to lots of places.

• -었더니 : 과거의 사실이나 상황이 뒤에 오는 말의 원인이나 이유가 됨을 나타내는 표현.
-eotdeoni (no equivalent expression)
An expression used to indicate that a past incident or situation becomes the cause or reason for the following statement.

• **배고프다 (adjective)** : 배 속이 빈 것을 느껴 음식이 먹고 싶다.
hungry
Feeling that one's stomach is empty and wanting to eat food.

• -다 : (아주낮춤으로) 어떤 사건이나 사실, 상태를 서술함을 나타내는 종결 어미.
-da (no equivalent expression)
(formal, highly addressee-lowering) A sentence-final ending used when describing a certain event, fact, state, etc.

• **점심 (noun)** : 아침과 저녁 식사 중간에, 낮에 하는 식사.
lunch
A meal eaten in the afternoon between breakfast and dinner.

• 은 : 문장 속에서 어떤 대상이 화제임을 나타내는 조사.
eun (no equivalent expression)
A postpositional particle used to indicate that a certain subject is the topic of a sentence.

• **뭐 (pronoun)** : 모르는 사실이나 사물을 가리키는 말.
what
A pronoun used to refer to a fact or object that one does not know of.

• 를 : 동작이 직접적으로 영향을 미치는 대상을 나타내는 조사.
reul (no equivalent expression)
A postpositional particle used to indicate the subject that an act has a direct influence on.

• **먹다 (verb)** : 음식 등을 입을 통하여 배 속에 들여보내다.
eat; have; consume; take
To put food into one's mouth and take it in one's stomach.

• -을까 : (두루낮춤으로) 듣는 사람의 의사를 물을 때 쓰는 종결 어미.
-eulkka (no equivalent expression)
(informal addressee-lowering) A sentence-final ending used to ask for the listener's opinion.

전주+에 오+았으면 비빔밥+을 먹+어야지.
왔으면

• **전주 (noun)** : 한국의 전라북도 중앙부에 있는 시. 전라북도의 도청 소재지이며, 창호지, 장판지의 생산과 전주비빔밥 등으로 유명하다.
Jeonju
The city located in the central part of Jeollabuk-do, or North Jeolla Province, South Korea; as the seat of the provincial government, it is famous for traditional Korean paper for windows and doors, laminated paper for floors, Jeonju bibimbap, etc.

• 에 : 앞말이 목적지이거나 어떤 행위의 진행 방향임을 나타내는 조사.
to; at
A postpositional particle to indicate that the preceding statement refers to a destination or the course of a certain action.

• **오다 (verb)** : 가고자 하는 곳에 이르다.
arrive; reach; come
To reach a place that one wants to go to.

• -았으면 : 앞의 말이 나타내는 과거의 상황이 뒤의 내용의 조건이 됨을 나타내는 표현.
-atsseumyeon (no equivalent expression)
An expression used to indicate that the past situation mentioned in the preceding statement becomes the condition for the following content.

• **비빔밥 (noun)** : 고기, 버섯, 계란, 나물 등에 여러 가지 양념을 넣고 비벼 먹는 밥.
bibimbap (no equivalent expression)
Rice topped with sliced meat, mushrooms, eggs, namul, seasoned vegetables, some seasonings, etc., of which all the ingredients are stirred before eating.

• 을 : 동작이 직접적으로 영향을 미치는 대상을 나타내는 조사.
eul (no equivalent expression)
A postpositional particle used to indicate the subject that an action has a direct influence on.

• **먹다 (verb)** : 음식 등을 입을 통하여 배 속에 들여보내다.
eat; have; consume; take
To put food into one's mouth and take it in one's stomach.

• -어야지 : (두루낮춤으로) 말하는 사람의 결심이나 의지를 나타내는 종결 어미.
-eoyaji (no equivalent expression)
(informal addressee-lowering) A sentence-final ending used to indicate the speaker's determination or will.

< 대화(dialogue) > - 89

내일이 소풍인데 비가 너무 많이 오네.
내이리 소풍인데 비가 너무 마니 오네.
naeiri sopunginde biga neomu mani one.

그러게. 내일은 날씨가 맑았으면 좋겠다.
그러게. 내이른 날씨가 말가쓰면 조켇따.
geureoge. naeireun nalssiga malgasseumyeon joketda.

< 설명(explanation) / 번역(translation) >

내일+이 소풍+이+ㄴ데 비+가 너무 많이 오+네.
소풍인데

• **내일** (noun) : 오늘의 다음 날.
days to come; future
The day after today.

• 이 : 어떤 상태나 상황의 대상이나 동작의 주체를 나타내는 조사.
i (no equivalent expression)
A postpositional particle referring to a subject under a certain state or situation, or the agent of an action.

• **소풍** (noun) : 경치를 즐기거나 놀이를 하기 위하여 야외에 나갔다 오는 일.
trip; picnic; outing
The act of going outside to admire the scenery or to relax, play, etc.

• 이다 : 주어가 지시하는 대상의 속성이나 부류를 지정하는 뜻을 나타내는 서술격 조사.
ida (no equivalent expression)
A predicate particle indicating the meaning of the attribute or category of the thing that the subject of the sentence refers to.

• -ㄴ데 : 뒤의 말을 하기 위하여 그 대상과 관련이 있는 상황을 미리 말함을 나타내는 연결 어미.
-nde (no equivalent expression)
A connective ending used to talk in advance about a situation to follow.

• **비 (noun)** : 높은 곳에서 구름을 이루고 있던 수증기가 식어서 뭉쳐 떨어지는 물방울.
rain
Water drops generated from cloud-forming vapors high in the sky that get cold, condense, and fall.

• 가 : 어떤 상태나 상황에 놓인 대상이나 동작의 주체를 나타내는 조사.
ga (no equivalent expression)
A postpositional particle referring to a subject under a certain state or situation, or the subject of an act.

• **너무 (adverb)** : 일정한 정도나 한계를 훨씬 넘어선 상태로.
too
To an excessive degree.

• **많이 (adverb)** : 수나 양, 정도 등이 일정한 기준보다 넘게.
much; in large numbers; in large amounts
In a state in which a number, amount, degree, etc., are larger than a certain standard.

• **오다 (verb)** : 비, 눈 등이 내리거나 추위 등이 닥치다.
come; arrive
For the rain, snow, etc., to fall, or for a cold spell to arrive.

• -네 : (아주낮춤으로) 지금 깨달은 일에 대하여 말함을 나타내는 종결 어미.
-ne (no equivalent expression)
(formal, highly addressee-lowering) A sentence-final ending used when talking about something that one just learned.

그러게.

내일+은 날씨+가 맑+[았으면 좋겠]+다.

• **그러게 (interjection)** : 상대방의 말에 찬성하거나 동의하는 뜻을 나타낼 때 쓰는 말.
right; I know; yeah
An exclamation used to indicate that the speaker supports or agrees with the words of the other party.

• **내일 (noun)** : 오늘의 다음 날.
days to come; future
The day after today.

• 은 : 어떤 대상이 다른 것과 대조됨을 나타내는 조사.
eun (no equivalent expression)
A postpositional particle used to indicate that a certain subject contrasts with something else.

• **날씨 (noun)** : 그날그날의 기온이나 공기 중에 비, 구름, 바람, 안개 등이 나타나는 상태.
weather
The daily temperature or the conditions of rain, clouds, wind, fog, etc., in the atmosphere.

• 가 : 어떤 상태나 상황에 놓인 대상이나 동작의 주체를 나타내는 조사.
ga (no equivalent expression)
A postpositional particle referring to a subject under a certain state or situation, or the subject of an act.

• **맑다 (adjective)** : 구름이나 안개가 끼지 않아 날씨가 좋다.
clear; fine
(for the weather) Fine without clouds or mist.

• -았으면 좋겠다 : 말하는 사람의 소망이나 바람을 나타내거나 현실과 다르게 되기를 바라는 것을 나타내는 표현.
-asseumyeon joketda (no equivalent expression)
An expression used to indicate the speaker's hope or wish, or the speaker's wish that the result would be different from reality.

• -다 : (아주낮춤으로) 어떤 사건이나 사실, 상태를 서술함을 나타내는 종결 어미.
-da (no equivalent expression)
(formal, highly addressee-lowering) A sentence-final ending used when describing a certain event, fact, state, etc.

< 대화(dialogue) > - 90

교수님, 오늘 수업 내용에 대한 질문이 있습니다.
교수님, 오늘 수업 내용에 대한 질무니 읻씀니다.
gyosunim, oneul sueop naeyonge daehan jilmuni itseumnida.

이해가 안 되는 부분이 있으면 편하게 얘기하세요.
이해가 안 되는 부부니 이쓰면 편하게 얘기하세요.
ihaega an doeneun bubuni isseumyeon pyeonhage yaegihaseyo.

< 설명(explanation) / 번역(translation) >

교수+님, 오늘 수업 내용+[에 대한] 질문+이 있+습니다.

• **교수 (noun)** : 대학에서 학문을 연구하고 가르치는 일을 하는 사람. 또는 그 직위.
professor
A person who researches and teaches in colleges; or such a position.

• 님 : '높임'의 뜻을 더하는 접미사.
-nim (no equivalent expression)
A suffix used to mean "honorific."

• **오늘 (noun)** : 지금 지나가고 있는 이날.
today
The day that is passing at the present time.

• **수업 (noun)** : 교사가 학생에게 지식이나 기술을 가르쳐 줌.
class; lesson; course
A teacher teaching a student certain studies or skills.

• **내용 (noun)** : 사물이나 일의 속을 이루는 사정이나 형편.
content; details; circumstances
Details or circumstances that constitute the content of an object or task.

• 에 대한 : 뒤에 오는 명사를 수식하며 앞에 오는 명사를 뒤에 오는 명사의 대상으로 함을 나타내는 표현.
e daehan (no equivalent expression)
An expression that modifies the following noun and indicates that the preceding noun is the subject of the following noun.

• **질문 (noun)** : 모르는 것이나 알고 싶은 것을 물음.
question
An act of asking something one does not know or wants to know.

• 이 : 어떤 상태나 상황의 대상이나 동작의 주체를 나타내는 조사.
i (no equivalent expression)
A postpositional particle referring to a subject under a certain state or situation, or the agent of an action.

• **있다 (adjective)** : 사실이나 현상이 존재하다.
no equivalent expression
A fact or a phenomenon being existent.

• -습니다 : (아주높임으로) 현재의 동작이나 상태, 사실을 정중하게 설명함을 나타내는 종결 어미.
-seupnida (no equivalent expression)
(formal, highly addressee-raising) A sentence-final ending used to explain the present action, state, or fact politely.

이해+가 안 되+는 부분+이 있+으면 편하+게 얘기하+세요.

• **이해 (noun)** : 무엇을 깨달아 앎. 또는 잘 알아서 받아들임.
understanding
The state of having realized and knowing something; the process of knowing and accepting something.

• 가 : 바뀌게 되는 대상이나 부정하는 대상임을 나타내는 조사.
ga (no equivalent expression)
A postpositional particle referring to the subject that is to be changed, or the subject that one denies.

• **안 (adverb)** : 부정이나 반대의 뜻을 나타내는 말.
not
An adverb that has the meaning of negation or opposite.

• **되다 (verb)** : 어떠한 심리적인 상태에 있다.
feel; become
To be in a certain mental state.

• -는 : 앞의 말이 관형어의 기능을 하게 만들고 사건이나 동작이 현재 일어남을 나타내는 어미.
-neun (no equivalent expression)
An ending of a word that makes the preceding statement function as an adnominal phrase and implies that an event or action is happening in the present.

- **부분 (noun)** : 전체를 이루고 있는 작은 범위. 또는 전체를 여러 개로 나눈 것 가운데 하나.
  part
  One of the parts that comprises the whole; one of the parts into which the whole is divided.

- 이 : 어떤 상태나 상황의 대상이나 동작의 주체를 나타내는 조사.
  i (no equivalent expression)
  A postpositional particle referring to a subject under a certain state or situation, or the agent of an action.

- **있다 (adjective)** : 사실이나 현상이 존재하다.
  no equivalent expression
  A fact or a phenomenon being existent.

- -으면 : 뒤에 오는 말에 대한 근거나 조건이 됨을 나타내는 연결 어미.
  -eumyeon (no equivalent expression)
  A connective ending used when the preceding statement becomes the condition of the following statement.

- **편하다 (adjective)** : 몸이나 마음이 괴롭지 않고 좋다.
  comfortable; easy; peaceful
  The state of one's body or mind being good, neither sick, nor troubled.

- -게 : 앞의 말이 뒤에서 가리키는 일의 목적이나 결과, 방식, 정도 등이 됨을 나타내는 연결 어미.
  -ge (no equivalent expression)
  A connective ending used when the preceding statement is the purpose, result, method, amount, etc., of something mentioned in the following statement.

- **얘기하다 (verb)** : 어떠한 사실이나 상태, 현상, 경험, 생각 등에 관해 누군가에게 말을 하다.
  tell; say; speak
  To talk to someone about a certain fact, state, phenomenon, experience, thought, etc.

- -세요 : (두루높임으로) 설명, 의문, 명령, 요청의 뜻을 나타내는 종결 어미.
  -seyo (no equivalent expression)
  (informal addressee-raising) A sentence-final ending used to describe, ask a question, order, and request.

< 대화(dialogue) > - 91

어디 아프니? 안색이 안 좋아 보여.
어디 아프니? 안새기 안 조아 보여.
어디 아프니? 안색이 안 좋아 보여.

배가 고파서 빵을 급하게 먹었더니 체한 것 같아요.
배가 고파서 빵을 그파게 머걷떠니 체한 걷 가타요.
baega gopaseo ppangeul geupage meogeotdeoni chehan geot gatayo.

< 설명(explanation) / 번역(translation) >

어디 아프+니?

안색+이 안 좋+[아 보이]+어.
좋아 보여

• 어디 (pronoun) : 모르는 곳을 가리키는 말.
where
The word that means a place which one does not know.

• 아프다 (adjective) : 다치거나 병이 생겨 통증이나 괴로움을 느끼다.
hurting; aching
Feeling pain or suffering due to an injury or illness.

• -니 : (아주낮춤으로) 물음을 나타내는 종결 어미.
-ni (no equivalent expression)
(formal, highly addressee-lowering) A sentence-final ending referring to a question.

• 안색 (noun) : 얼굴에 나타나는 표정이나 빛깔.
complexion
A facial expression or color of one's face.

• 이 : 어떤 상태나 상황의 대상이나 동작의 주체를 나타내는 조사.
i (no equivalent expression)
A postpositional particle referring to a subject under a certain state or situation, or the agent of an action.

• **안 (adverb)** : 부정이나 반대의 뜻을 나타내는 말.
not
An adverb that has the meaning of negation or opposite.

• **좋다 (adjective)** : 신체적 조건이나 건강 상태 등이 보통보다 낫다.
good
Above average in physical condition or health.

• -아 보이다 : 겉으로 볼 때 앞의 말이 나타내는 것처럼 느껴지거나 추측됨을 나타내는 표현.
-a boida (no equivalent expression)
An expression used to indicate that one feels or guesses something by the appearance of something mentioned in the preceding statement.

• -어 : (두루낮춤으로) 어떤 사실을 서술하거나 물음, 명령, 권유를 나타내는 종결 어미.
-eo (no equivalent expression)
(informal addressee-lowering) A sentence-final ending used to **describe** a certain fact, ask a question, give an order, or advise.

배+가 고파(고프)+아서 빵+을 급하+게 먹+었더니 체하+[ㄴ 것 같]+아요.

고파서 **체한 것 같아요**

• **배 (noun)** : 사람이나 동물의 몸에서 음식을 소화시키는 위장, 창자 등의 내장이 있는 곳.
stomach; belly
The place where the digestive organs, such as the stomach and intestines, are located in the human or animal body.

• 가 : 어떤 상태나 상황에 놓인 대상이나 동작의 주체를 나타내는 조사.
ga (no equivalent expression)
A postpositional particle referring to a subject under a certain state or situation, or the subject of an act.

• **고프다 (adjective)** : 뱃속이 비어 음식을 먹고 싶다.
hungry
Wanting to eat food due to an empty stomach.

• -아서 : 이유나 근거를 나타내는 연결 어미.
-aseo (no equivalent expression)
A connective ending used for a reason or cause.

• **빵 (noun)** : 밀가루를 반죽하여 발효시켜 찌거나 구운 음식.
bread
Food made by baking or steaming fermented dough.

• 을 : 동작이 직접적으로 영향을 미치는 대상을 나타내는 조사.
eul (no equivalent expression)
A postpositional particle used to indicate the subject that an action has a direct influence on.

• **급하다 (adjective)** : 시간적 여유 없이 일을 서둘러 매우 빠르다.
hurried
Very quick and in a hurry without time to spare.

• -게 : 앞의 말이 뒤에서 가리키는 일의 목적이나 결과, 방식, 정도 등이 됨을 나타내는 연결 어미.
-ge (no equivalent expression)
A connective ending used when the preceding statement is the purpose, result, method, amount, etc., of something mentioned in the following statement.

• **먹다 (verb)** : 음식 등을 입을 통하여 배 속에 들여보내다.
eat; have; consume; take
To put food into one's mouth and take it in one's stomach.

• -었더니 : 과거의 사실이나 상황이 뒤에 오는 말의 원인이나 이유가 됨을 나타내는 표현.
-eotdeoni (no equivalent expression)
An expression used to indicate that a past incident or situation becomes the cause or reason for the following statement.

• **체하다 (verb)** : 먹은 음식이 잘 소화되지 않아 배 속에 답답하게 남아 있다.
have an upset stomach
To feel heavy on the stomach due to difficulty in digesting food.

• -ㄴ 것 같다 : 추측을 나타내는 표현.
-n geot gatda (no equivalent expression)
An expression used to indicate that the statement is a guess.

• -아요 : (두루높임으로) 어떤 사실을 서술하거나 질문, 명령, 권유함을 나타내는 종결 어미.
-ayo (no equivalent expression)
(informal addressee-raising) A sentence-final ending used to **describe** a certain fact, ask a question, give an order, or advise.

< 대화(dialogue) > - 92

배가 좀 아픈데 우리 잠깐 쉬었다 가자.
배가 좀 아픈데 우리 잠깐 쉬얻따 가자.
baega jom apeunde uri jamkkan swieotda gaja.

음식을 먹은 다음에 바로 운동을 해서 그런가 보다.
음시글 머근 다으메 바로 운동을 해서 그런가 보다.
eumsigeul meogeun daeume baro undongeul haeseo geureonga boda.

< 설명(explanation) / 번역(translation) >

배+가 좀 아프+ㄴ데 우리 잠깐 쉬+었+다 가+자.
아픈데

• **배 (noun)** : 사람이나 동물의 몸에서 음식을 소화시키는 위장, 창자 등의 내장이 있는 곳.
stomach; belly
The place where the digestive organs, such as the stomach and intestines, are located in the human or animal body.

• 가 : 어떤 상태나 상황에 놓인 대상이나 동작의 주체를 나타내는 조사.
ga (no equivalent expression)
A postpositional particle referring to a subject under a certain state or situation, or the subject of an act.

• **좀 (adverb)** : 분량이나 정도가 적게.
a little
In a small quantity or to a small degree.

• **아프다 (adjective)** : 다치거나 병이 생겨 통증이나 괴로움을 느끼다.
hurting; aching
Feeling pain or suffering due to an injury or illness.

• -ㄴ데 : 뒤의 말을 하기 위하여 그 대상과 관련이 있는 상황을 미리 말함을 나타내는 연결 어미.
-nde (no equivalent expression)
A connective ending used to talk in advance about a situation to follow.

• **우리 (pronoun)** : 말하는 사람이 자기와 듣는 사람 또는 이를 포함한 여러 사람들을 가리키는 말.
we
A pronoun used when the speaker refers to himself/herself and the listener or listeners, or a group of people including the speaker and listener or listeners.

• **잠깐 (adverb)** : 아주 짧은 시간 동안에.
for a moment; for an instant; for a while
For a very short time.

• **쉬다 (verb)** : 피로를 없애기 위해 몸을 편안하게 하다.
rest; repose; take a rest
To relax oneself to relieve one's fatigue.

• -었- : 어떤 사건이 과거에 완료되었거나 그 사건의 결과가 현재까지 지속되는 상황을 나타내는 어미.
-eot- (no equivalent expression)
An ending of a word used to indicate that an event was completed in the past or its result continues in the present.

• -다 : 어떤 행동이나 상태 등이 중단되고 다른 행동이나 상태로 바뀜을 나타내는 연결 어미.
-da (no equivalent expression)
A connective ending used when an action or state, etc., is stopped and changed to another action or state.

• **가다 (verb)** : 한 곳에서 다른 곳으로 장소를 이동하다.
go; travel
To move from one place to another place.

• -자 : (아주낮춤으로) 어떤 행동을 함께 하자는 뜻을 나타내는 종결 어미.
-ja (no equivalent expression)
(formal, highly addressee-lowering) A sentence-final ending used to indicate the suggestion to do a certain act together.

음식+을 먹+[은 다음에] 바로 운동+을 하+여서 그렇(그러)+[ㄴ가 보]+다.

해서 그런가 보다

• **음식 (noun)** : 사람이 먹거나 마시는 모든 것.
food
Everything that humans eat or drink.

• 을 : 동작이 직접적으로 영향을 미치는 대상을 나타내는 조사.
eul (no equivalent expression)
A postpositional particle used to indicate the subject that an action has a direct influence on.

• **먹다 (verb)** : 음식 등을 입을 통하여 배 속에 들여보내다.
eat; have; consume; take
To put food into one's mouth and take it in one's stomach.

• -은 다음에 : 앞에 오는 말이 가리키는 일이나 과정이 끝난 뒤임을 나타내는 표현.
-eun daeume (no equivalent expression)
An expression used to indicate that the time being described takes places after the completion of a certain work or process mentioned in the preceding statement.

• **바로 (adverb)** : 시간 차를 두지 않고 곧장.
promptly; right away
Immediately without delay.

• **운동 (noun)** : 몸을 단련하거나 건강을 위하여 몸을 움직이는 일.
exercise
The act of moving one's body in order to train it or improve one's health.

• 을 : 동작이 직접적으로 영향을 미치는 대상을 나타내는 조사.
eul (no equivalent expression)
A postpositional particle used to indicate the subject that an action has a direct influence on.

• **하다 (verb)** : 어떤 행동이나 동작, 활동 등을 행하다.
do; perform
To perform a certain move, action, activity, etc.

• -여서 : 이유나 근거를 나타내는 연결 어미.
-yeoseo (no equivalent expression)
A connective ending used to indicate a reason or cause.

• **그렇다 (adjective)** : 상태, 모양, 성질 등이 그와 같다.
so; as such; like that
A state, appearance, characteristic, etc. being as such.

• -ㄴ가 보다 : 앞의 말이 나타내는 사실을 추측함을 나타내는 표현.
-nga boda (no equivalent expression)
An expression used to guess about a fact mentioned in the preceding statement.

• -다 : (아주낮춤으로) 어떤 사건이나 사실, 상태를 서술함을 나타내는 종결 어미.
-da (no equivalent expression)
(formal, highly addressee-lowering) A sentence-final ending used when describing a certain event, fact, state, etc.

< 대화(dialogue) > - 93

우리 저기 보이는 카페에 가서 같이 커피 마실까요?
우리 저기 보이는 카페에 가서 가치 커피 마실까요?
uri jeogi boineun kapee gaseo gachi keopi masilkkayo?

좋아요. 오늘은 제가 살게요.
조아요. 오느른 제가 살께요.
joayo. oneureun jega salgeyo.

< 설명(explanation) / 번역(translation) >

우리 저기 보이+는 카페+에 가+(아)서 같이 커피 마시+ㄹ까요?
가서 마실까요

• **우리 (pronoun)** : 말하는 사람이 자기와 듣는 사람 또는 이를 포함한 여러 사람들을 가리키는 말.
we
A pronoun used when the speaker refers to himself/herself and the listener or listeners, or a group of people including the speaker and listener or listeners.

• **저기 (pronoun)** : 말하는 사람이나 듣는 사람으로부터 멀리 떨어져 있는 곳을 가리키는 말.
that place
A word used to describe a place that is far away from the speaker or the listener.

• **보이다 (verb)** : 눈으로 대상의 존재나 겉모습을 알게 되다.
be viewed; be visible; be in sight
To come to know the presence or outward appearance of an object by looking at it.

• -는 : 앞의 말이 관형어의 기능을 하게 만들고 사건이나 동작이 현재 일어남을 나타내는 어미.
-neun (no equivalent expression)
An ending of a word that makes the preceding statement function as an adnominal phrase and implies that an event or action is happening in the present.

• **카페 (noun)** : 주로 커피와 차, 가벼운 간식거리 등을 파는 가게.
cafe; coffee shop
A shop where coffee, tea, light snacks, etc., are sold.

• 에 : 앞말이 목적지이거나 어떤 행위의 진행 방향임을 나타내는 조사.
to; at
A postpositional particle to indicate that the preceding statement refers to a destination or the course of a certain action.

• **가다 (verb)** : 한 곳에서 다른 곳으로 장소를 이동하다.
go; travel
To move from one place to another place.

• -아서 : 앞의 말과 뒤의 말이 순차적으로 일어남을 나타내는 연결 어미.
-aseo (no equivalent expression)
A connective ending used to indicate that the preceding event and the following one happened sequentially.

• **같이 (adverb)** : 둘 이상이 함께.
together
With each other.

• **커피 (noun)** : 독특한 향기가 나고 카페인이 들어 있으며 약간 쓴, 커피나무의 열매로 만든 진한 갈색의 차.
coffee
Thick, brown, aromatic brew, tasting a little bitter and containing caffeine, which is made of the fruits of a coffee tree.

• **마시다 (verb)** : 물 등의 액체를 목구멍으로 넘어가게 하다.
drink
To make liquid such as water, etc., pass down one's throat.

• -ㄹ까요 : (두루높임으로) 듣는 사람에게 의견을 묻거나 제안함을 나타내는 표현.
-lkkayo (no equivalent expression)
(informal addressee-raising) An expression used to ask for the listener's opinion or propose something.

좋+아요.

오늘+은 제+가 사+ㄹ게요.
살게요

• **좋다 (adjective)** : 어떤 일이나 대상이 마음에 들고 만족스럽다.
fond of; in love with
Happy about and satisfied with a thing or object.

• -아요 : (두루높임으로) 어떤 사실을 서술하거나 질문, 명령, 권유함을 나타내는 종결 어미.
-ayo (no equivalent expression)
(informal addressee-raising) A sentence-final ending used to **describe** a certain fact, ask a question, give an order, or advise.

• **오늘 (noun)** : 지금 지나가고 있는 이날.
today
The day that is passing at the present time.

• 은 : 어떤 대상이 다른 것과 대조됨을 나타내는 조사.
eun (no equivalent expression)
A postpositional particle used to indicate that a certain subject contrasts with something else.

• **제 (pronoun)** : 말하는 사람이 자신을 낮추어 가리키는 말인 '저'에 조사 '가'가 붙을 때의 형태.
I
A form of '저' (I), the humble form used by the speaker to show humility, when the postpositional particle '가' is attached to it.

• 가 : 어떤 상태나 상황에 놓인 대상이나 동작의 주체를 나타내는 조사.
ga (no equivalent expression)
A postpositional particle referring to a subject under a certain state or situation, or the subject of an act.

• **사다 (verb)** : 다른 사람과 함께 먹은 음식의 값을 치르다.
buy; treat
To pay for someone's food after you both ate together.

• -ㄹ게요 : (두루높임으로) 말하는 사람이 어떤 행동을 할 것을 듣는 사람에게 약속하거나 의지를 나타내는 표현.
-lgeyo (no equivalent expression)
(informal addressee-raising) An expression used when the speaker promises or notifies the listener that he/she will do something.

< 대화(dialogue) > - 94

어떻게 공부를 했길래 하나도 안 틀렸어요?
어떠케 공부를 핻낄래 하나도 안 틀려써요?
eotteoke gongbureul haetgillae hanado an teullyeosseoyo?

전 그저 학교에서 배운 것을 빠짐없이 복습했을 뿐이에요.
전 그저 학꾜에서 배운 거슬 빠짐업씨 복쓰패쓸 뿌니에요.
jeon geujeo hakgyoeseo baeun geoseul ppajimeopsi bokseupaesseul ppunieyo.

< 설명(explanation) / 번역(translation) >

어떻게 공부+를 하+였+길래 하나+도 안 틀리+었+어요?

했길래 **틀렸어요**

• **어떻게 (adverb)** : 어떤 방법으로. 또는 어떤 방식으로.
how
In what method; in what way.

• **공부 (noun)** : 학문이나 기술을 배워서 지식을 얻음.
study
The act of gaining knowledge by learning studies or techniques.

• 를 : 동작이 직접적으로 영향을 미치는 대상을 나타내는 조사.
reul (no equivalent expression)
A postpositional particle used to indicate the subject that an act has a direct influence on.

• **하다 (verb)** : 어떤 행동이나 동작, 활동 등을 행하다.
do; perform
To perform a certain move, action, activity, etc.

• -였- : 어떤 사건이 과거에 완료되었거나 그 사건의 결과가 현재까지 지속되는 상황을 나타내는 어미.
-yeot- (no equivalent expression)
An ending of a word used to indicate that an event was completed in the past or its result continues in the present.

• -길래 : 뒤에 오는 말의 원인이나 근거를 나타내는 연결 어미.
-gillae (no equivalent expression)
A connective ending referring to the cause or reason of the following statement.

• **하나 (noun)** : 전혀, 조금도.
none
Not at all, not in the least.

• 도 : 극단적인 경우를 들어 다른 경우는 말할 것도 없음을 나타내는 조사.
do (no equivalent expression)
A postpositional particle used when giving an extreme case in order to show that it is obvious in another case.

• **안 (adverb)** : 부정이나 반대의 뜻을 나타내는 말.
not
An adverb that has the meaning of negation or opposite.

• **틀리다 (verb)** : 계산이나 답, 사실 등이 맞지 않다.
be wrong; be incorrect
For a calculation, answer, fact, etc., to not be correct.

• -었- : 어떤 사건이 과거에 완료되었거나 그 사건의 결과가 현재까지 지속되는 상황을 나타내는 어미.
-eot- (no equivalent expression)
An ending of a word used to indicate that an event was completed in the past or its result continues in the present.

• -어요 : (두루높임으로) 어떤 사실을 서술하거나 질문, 명령, 권유함을 나타내는 종결 어미.
-eoyo (no equivalent expression)
(informal addressee-raising) A sentence-final ending used to describe a certain fact, **ask a question**, give an order, or advise.

저+는 그저 학교+에서 배우+[ㄴ 것]+을 빠짐없이 복습하+였+[을 뿐이]+에요.
전 배운 것을 복습했을 뿐이에요

• **저 (pronoun)** : 말하는 사람이 듣는 사람에게 자신을 낮추어 가리키는 말.
I; me
The humble form used by the speaker to refer to himself/herself for the purpose of showing humility to the listener.

• 는 : 문장 속에서 어떤 대상이 화제임을 나타내는 조사.
neun (no equivalent expression)
A postpositional particle used to indicate that a certain subject is the topic of a sentence.

• **그저 (adverb)** : 다른 일은 하지 않고 그냥.
just
Without doing anything else.

• **학교 (noun)** : 일정한 목적, 교과 과정, 제도 등에 의하여 교사가 학생을 가르치는 기관.
school
An institution where teachers teach students in accordance with a certain purpose, curriculum, or policy, etc.

• 에서 : 앞말이 행동이 이루어지고 있는 장소임을 나타내는 조사.
eseo (no equivalent expression)
A postpositional particle used to indicate that the preceding word refers to a place where a certain action is being done.

• **배우다 (verb)** : 새로운 지식을 얻다.
learn
To obtain new knowledge.

• -ㄴ 것 : 명사가 아닌 것을 문장에서 명사처럼 쓰이게 하거나 '이다' 앞에 쓰일 수 있게 할 때 쓰는 표현.
-n geot (no equivalent expression)
An expression used to enable a non-noun word to be used as a noun in a sentence or to be used in front of '이다' (be).

• 을 : 동작이 직접적으로 영향을 미치는 대상을 나타내는 조사.
eul (no equivalent expression)
A postpositional particle used to indicate the subject that an action has a direct influence on.

• **빠짐없이 (adverb)** : 하나도 빠뜨리지 않고 다.
everything; all
All without exception.

• **복습하다 (verb)** : 배운 것을 다시 공부하다.
review
To go over what has been learned.

• -였- : 어떤 사건이 과거에 완료되었거나 그 사건의 결과가 현재까지 지속되는 상황을 나타내는 어미.
-yeot- (no equivalent expression)
An ending of a word used to indicate that an event was completed in the past or its result continues in the present.

• -을 뿐이다 : 앞에 오는 말이 나타내는 상태나 상황 이외에 다른 어떤 것도 없음을 나타내는 표현.
-eul ppunida (no equivalent expression)
An expression used to indicate that the state or situation mentioned in the preceding statement is the only option

- -에요 : (두루높임으로) 어떤 사실을 서술하거나 질문함을 나타내는 종결 어미.
  -eyo (no equivalent expression)
  (informal addressee-raising) A sentence-final ending used when **describing** a certain fact or asking a question.

< 대화(dialogue) > - 95

듣기 좋은 노래 좀 추천해 주세요.
듣끼 조은 노래 좀 추천해 주세요.
deutgi joeun norae jom chucheonhae juseyo.

신나는 노래 위주로 듣는다면 이건 어때요?
신나는 조용한 노래 위주로 든는다면 이건 어때요?
sinnaneun norae wijuro deunneundamyeon igeon eottaeyo?

< 설명(explanation) / 번역(translation) >

듣+기 좋+은 노래 좀 추천하+[여 주]+세요.

추천해 주세요

• **듣다 (verb)** : 귀로 소리를 알아차리다.
hear
To sense a sound with ears.

• -기 : 앞의 말이 명사의 기능을 하게 하는 어미.
-gi (no equivalent expression)
An ending of a word used to make the preceding word function as a noun.

• **좋다 (adjective)** : 어떤 것의 성질이나 내용 등이 훌륭하여 만족할 만하다.
good; great; excellent
Excellent and satisfactory in features and content.

• -은 : 앞의 말이 관형어의 기능을 하게 만들고 현재의 상태를 나타내는 어미.
-eun (no equivalent expression)
An ending of a word that makes the preceding word function as an adnominal phrase and refers to the present state.

• **노래 (noun)** : 운율에 맞게 지은 가사에 곡을 붙인 음악. 또는 그런 음악을 소리 내어 부름.
song; music; singing
A composition created by setting rhythmical lyrics to music; or the act of singing such a piece of music.

• **좀 (adverb)** : 주로 부탁이나 동의를 구할 때 부드러운 느낌을 주기 위해 넣는 말.
please
A word chiefly used to soften a request for a favor or agreement.

• **추천하다 (verb)** : 어떤 조건에 알맞은 사람이나 물건을 책임지고 소개하다.
recommend
To responsibly introduce someone or something that meets a certain condition.

• -여 주다 : 남을 위해 앞의 말이 나타내는 행동을 함을 나타내는 표현.
-yeo juda (no equivalent expression)
An expression used to indicate that one does the act mentioned in the preceding statement for someone.

• -세요 : (두루높임으로) 설명, 의문, 명령, 요청의 뜻을 나타내는 종결 어미.
-seyo (no equivalent expression)
(informal addressee-raising) A sentence-final ending used to describe, ask a question, order, and request.

신나+는 노래 위주+로 듣+는다면 이것(이거)+은 어떻+어요?
이건 어때요

• **신나다 (verb)** : 흥이 나고 기분이 아주 좋아지다.
become happy; become delighted; become elated
To get excited and come to feel very good.

• -는 : 앞의 말이 관형어의 기능을 하게 만들고 사건이나 동작이 현재 일어남을 나타내는 어미.
-neun (no equivalent expression)
An ending of a word that makes the preceding statement function as an adnominal phrase and implies that an event or action is happening in the present.

• **노래 (noun)** : 운율에 맞게 지은 가사에 곡을 붙인 음악. 또는 그런 음악을 소리 내어 부름.
song; music; singing
A composition created by setting rhythmical lyrics to music; or the act of singing such a piece of music.

• **위주 (noun)** : 무엇을 가장 중요한 것으로 삼음.
center; focus
The act of regarding something as the most important.

• 로 : 어떤 일의 방법이나 방식을 나타내는 조사.
ro (no equivalent expression)
A postpositional particle that indicates a method or way to do something.

• **듣다 (verb)** : 귀로 소리를 알아차리다.
hear
To sense a sound with ears.

• -는다면 : 어떠한 사실이나 상황을 가정하는 뜻을 나타내는 연결 어미.
-neundamyeon (no equivalent expression)
A connective ending used when assuming a certain fact or situation.

• **이것 (pronoun)** : 말하는 사람에게 가까이 있거나 말하는 사람이 생각하고 있는 것을 가리키는 말.
this
The word that refers to something that is close to the speaker or something that the speaker is thinking of.

• 은 : 문장 속에서 어떤 대상이 화제임을 나타내는 조사.
eun (no equivalent expression)
A postpositional particle used to indicate that a certain subject is the topic of a sentence.

• **어떻다 (adjective)** : 생각, 느낌, 상태, 형편 등이 어찌 되어 있다.
such
Being such in one's thoughts, feelings, state, situation, etc.

• -어요 : (두루높임으로) 어떤 사실을 서술하거나 질문, 명령, 권유함을 나타내는 종결 어미.
-eoyo (no equivalent expression)
(informal addressee-raising) A sentence-final ending used to describe a certain fact, **ask a question**, give an order, or advise.

< 대화(dialogue) > - 96

너 모자를 새로 샀구나. 잘 어울린다.
너 모자를 새로 삳꾸나. 잘 어울린다.
neo mojareul saero satguna. jal eoullinda.

고마워. 가게에서 보자마자 마음에 들어서 바로 사 버렸지.
고마워. 가게에서 보자마자 마으메 드러서 바로 사 버렫찌.
gomawo. gageeseo bojamaja maeume deureoseo baro sa beoryeotji.

< 설명(explanation) / 번역(translation) >

너 모자+를 새로 사+았+구나.

샀구나

잘 어울리+ㄴ다.

어울린다

• **너 (pronoun)** : 듣는 사람이 친구나 아랫사람일 때, 그 사람을 가리키는 말.
no equivalent expression
A pronoun used to indicate the listener when he/she is the same age or younger.

• **모자 (noun)** : 예의를 차리거나 추위나 더위 등을 막기 위해 머리에 쓰는 물건.
hat
An object worn on the head in order to be polite or to keep out the cold or heat, etc.

• 를 : 동작이 직접적으로 영향을 미치는 대상을 나타내는 조사.
reul (no equivalent expression)
A postpositional particle used to indicate the subject that an act has a direct influence on.

• **새로 (adverb)** : 전과 달리 새롭게. 또는 새것으로.
freshly
Newly again, different from the past, or with a new thing.

• **사다 (verb)** : 돈을 주고 어떤 물건이나 권리 등을 자기 것으로 만들다.
buy; purchase; get
To get ownership of an item, right, etc., by paying for it.

• -았- : 어떤 사건이 과거에 완료되었거나 그 사건의 결과가 현재까지 지속되는 상황을 나타내는 어미.
-at- (no equivalent expression)
An ending of a word used to indicate that an event was completed in the past or its result continues in the present.

• -구나 : (아주낮춤으로) 새롭게 알게 된 사실에 어떤 느낌을 실어 말함을 나타내는 종결 어미.
-guna (no equivalent expression)
(formal, highly addressee-lowering) A sentence-final ending used to imply a certain feeling in a newly learned fact.

• **잘 (adverb)** : 아주 멋지고 예쁘게.
well; fashionably
In a very beautiful and pretty manner.

• **어울리다 (verb)** : 자연스럽게 서로 조화를 이루다.
harmonize; be in keeping with; go well with
To be harmonious with each other naturally.

• -ㄴ다 : (아주낮춤으로) 현재 사건이나 사실을 서술함을 나타내는 종결 어미.
-nda (no equivalent expression)
(formal, highly addressee-lowering) A sentence-final ending used to describe an event or fact of the present.

고맙(고마우)+어.
고마워

가게+에서 보+자마자 [마음에 들]+어서 바로 사+[(아) 버리]+었+지.
사 버렸지

• **고맙다 (adjective)** : 남이 자신을 위해 무엇을 해주어서 마음이 흐뭇하고 보답하고 싶다.
thankful; grateful
Pleased and wanting to return a favor to someone.

• -어 : (두루낮춤으로) 어떤 사실을 서술하거나 물음, 명령, 권유를 나타내는 종결 어미.
-eo (no equivalent expression)
(informal addressee-lowering) A sentence-final ending used to **describe** a certain fact, ask a question, give an order, or advise.

• **가게 (noun)** : 작은 규모로 물건을 펼쳐 놓고 파는 집.
shop; store
A place where products are displayed and sold on a small scale.

• 에서 : 앞말이 어떤 일의 출처임을 나타내는 조사.
eseo (no equivalent expression)
A postpositional particle used to indicate that the preceding word refers to the source of something.

• **보다 (verb)** : 눈으로 대상의 존재나 겉모습을 알다.
see; look at; notice
To perceive with eyes the existence or appearance of an object.

• -자마자 : 앞의 말이 나타내는 사건이나 상황이 일어나고 곧바로 뒤의 말이 나타내는 사건이나 상황이 일어남을 나타내는 연결 어미.
-jamaja (no equivalent expression)
A connective ending used to indicate that the following event or situation occurs right after the preceding event or situation.

• 마음에 들다 (idiom) : 자신의 느낌이나 생각과 맞아 좋게 느껴지다.
come in one's mind
To feel good about something as it fits what one feels or thinks.

• -어서 : 이유나 근거를 나타내는 연결 어미.
-eoseo (no equivalent expression)
A connective ending used for a reason or cause.

• **바로 (adverb)** : 시간 차를 두지 않고 곧장.
promptly; right away
Immediately without delay.

• **사다 (verb)** : 돈을 주고 어떤 물건이나 권리 등을 자기 것으로 만들다.
buy; purchase; get
To get ownership of an item, right, etc., by paying for it.

• -아 버리다 : 앞의 말이 나타내는 행동이 완전히 끝났음을 나타내는 표현.
-a beorida (no equivalent expression)
An expression used to indicate that the act mentioned in the preceding statement is completely done.

• -었- : 어떤 사건이 과거에 완료되었거나 그 사건의 결과가 현재까지 지속되는 상황을 나타내는 어미.
-eot- (no equivalent expression)
An ending of a word used to indicate that an event was completed in the past or its result continues in the present.

• -지 : (두루낮춤으로) 말하는 사람이 자신에 대한 이야기나 자신의 생각을 친근하게 말할 때 쓰는 종결 어미.

-ji (no equivalent expression)

(informal addressee-lowering) A sentence-final ending used when the speaker talks about himself/herself or his/her thoughts in a friendly manner.

< 대화(dialogue) > - 97

엄마, 약속 시간에 늦어서 밥 먹을 시간 없어요.
엄마, 약쏙 시가네 느저서 밥 머글 시간 업써요.
eomma, yaksok sigane neujeoseo bap meogeul sigan eopseoyo.

조금 늦더라도 밥은 먹고 가야지.
조금 늗떠라도 바븐 먹꼬 가야지.
jogeum neutdeorado babeun meokgo gayaji.

< 설명(explanation) / 번역(translation) >

엄마, 약속 시간+에 늦+어서 밥 먹+을 시간 없+어요.

• **엄마 (noun)** : 격식을 갖추지 않아도 되는 상황에서 어머니를 이르거나 부르는 말.
mom
A word used to refer to or address one's mother in an informal situation.

• **약속 (noun)** : 다른 사람과 어떤 일을 하기로 미리 정함. 또는 그렇게 정한 내용.
promise; appointment; pledge
An act of agreeing with someone to do a certain thing, or details of such an agreement.

• **시간 (noun)** : 어떤 일을 하도록 정해진 때. 또는 하루 중의 어느 한 때.
time
A time when one is supposed to do something, or a particular time of day.

• 에 : 앞말이 시간이나 때임을 나타내는 조사.
in; at
A postpositional particle to indicate that the preceding statement refers to the time.

• **늦다 (verb)** : 정해진 때보다 지나다.
be late
To be later than the set time.

• -어서 : 이유나 근거를 나타내는 연결 어미.
-eoseo (no equivalent expression)
A connective ending used for a reason or cause.

• **밥 (noun)** : 매일 일정한 때에 먹는 음식.
meal
Food that is eaten at particular times of the day.

• **먹다 (verb)** : 음식 등을 입을 통하여 배 속에 들여보내다.
eat; have; consume; take
To put food into one's mouth and take it in one's stomach.

• -을 : 앞의 말이 관형어의 기능을 하게 만들고 추측, 예정, 의지, 가능성 등을 나타내는 어미.
eul (no equivalent expression)
An ending of a word that makes the preceding statement function as an adnominal phrase and indicates assumption, prearrangement, intention, possibility, etc.

• **시간 (noun)** : 어떤 일을 할 여유.
time
Spare time that one can use to do something.

• **없다 (adjective)** : 어떤 사실이나 현상이 현실로 존재하지 않는 상태이다.
lacking
(for a fact or phenomenon to be) Not existent in reality.

• -어요 : (두루높임으로) 어떤 사실을 서술하거나 질문, 명령, 권유함을 나타내는 종결 어미.
-eoyo (no equivalent expression)
(informal addressee-raising) A sentence-final ending used to **describe** a certain fact, ask a question, give an order, or advise.

조금 늦+더라도 밥+은 먹+고 가+(아)야지.
가야지

• **조금 (adverb)** : 시간이 짧게.
a little
For a short while.

• **늦다 (verb)** : 정해진 때보다 지나다.
be late
To be later than the set time.

• -더라도 : 앞에 오는 말을 가정하거나 인정하지만 뒤에 오는 말에는 관계가 없거나 영향을 끼치지 않음을 나타내는 연결 어미.
-deorado (no equivalent expression)
A connective ending used when assuming or recognizing the truth of the preceding statement, but implying that it is not related to or does not influence the following statement.

• **밥 (noun)** : 매일 일정한 때에 먹는 음식.
meal
Food that is eaten at particular times of the day.

• 은 : 강조의 뜻을 나타내는 조사.
eun (no equivalent expression)
A postpositional particle used to indicate an emphasis.

• **먹다 (verb)** : 음식 등을 입을 통하여 배 속에 들여보내다.
eat; have; consume; take
To put food into one's mouth and take it in one's stomach.

• -고 : 앞의 말과 뒤의 말이 차례대로 일어남을 나타내는 연결 어미.
-go (no equivalent expression)
A connective ending used when the preceding statement and the following statement happen in order.

• **가다 (verb)** : 한 곳에서 다른 곳으로 장소를 이동하다.
go; travel
To move from one place to another place.

• -아야지 : (두루낮춤으로) 듣는 사람이나 다른 사람이 어떤 일을 해야 하거나 어떤 상태여야 함을 나타내는 종결 어미.
-ayaji (no equivalent expression)
(informal addressee-lowering) A sentence-final ending used to indicate that the listener or another person is supposed to do a certain thing or be in a certain state.

< 대화(dialogue) > - 98

너 오늘 많이 피곤해 보인다.
너 오늘 마니 피곤해 보인다.
neo oneul mani pigonhae boinda.

어제 늦게까지 술을 마셔 가지고 컨디션이 안 좋아.
어제 늗께까지 수를 마셔 가지고 컨디셔니 안 조아.
eoje neutgekkaji sureul masyeo gajigo keondisyeoni an joa.

< 설명(explanation) / 번역(translation) >

너 오늘 많이 피곤하+[여 보이]+ㄴ다.
피곤해 보인다

• **너 (pronoun)** : 듣는 사람이 친구나 아랫사람일 때, 그 사람을 가리키는 말.
no equivalent expression
A pronoun used to indicate the listener when he/she is the same age or younger.

• **오늘 (adverb)** : 지금 지나가고 있는 이날에.
today
The day that is passing at the present time.

• **많이 (adverb)** : 수나 양, 정도 등이 일정한 기준보다 넘게.
much; in large numbers; in large amounts
In a state in which a number, amount, degree, etc., are larger than a certain standard.

• **피곤하다 (adjective)** : 몸이나 마음이 지쳐서 힘들다.
tired; exhausted; fatigued
Being tired and worn-out physically or mentally.

• -여 보이다 : 겉으로 볼 때 앞의 말이 나타내는 것처럼 느껴지거나 추측됨을 나타내는 표현.
-yeo boida (no equivalent expression)
An expression used to indicate that one feels or guesses something by appearance as mentioned in the preceding statement.

• -ㄴ다 : (아주낮춤으로) 현재 사건이나 사실을 서술함을 나타내는 종결 어미.
-nda (no equivalent expression)
(formal, highly addressee-lowering) A sentence-final ending used to describe an event or fact of the present.

어제 늦+게+까지 술+을 마시+[어 가지고] 컨디션+이 안 좋+아.
마셔 가지고

• **어제 (adverb)** : 오늘의 하루 전날에.
yesterday
On the day before today.

• **늦다 (adjective)** : 적당한 때를 지나 있다. 또는 시기가 한창인 때를 지나 있다.
late; later
Being past the right time, or being past the peak of something.

• -게 : 앞의 말이 뒤에서 가리키는 일의 목적이나 결과, 방식, 정도 등이 됨을 나타내는 연결 어미.
-ge (no equivalent expression)
A connective ending used when the preceding statement is the purpose, result, method, amount, etc., of something mentioned in the following statement.

• 까지 : 어떤 범위의 끝임을 나타내는 조사.
kkaji (no equivalent expression)
A postpositional particle referring to the end of a certain range.

• **술 (noun)** : 맥주나 소주 등과 같이 알코올 성분이 들어 있어서 마시면 취하는 음료.
alcohol; liquor
A beverage that contains alcoholic ingredients so that one gets drunk if one drinks it, such as beer, soju, Korean distilled liquor, etc.

• 을 : 동작이 직접적으로 영향을 미치는 대상을 나타내는 조사.
eul (no equivalent expression)
A postpositional particle used to indicate the subject that an action has a direct influence on.

• **마시다 (verb)** : 물 등의 액체를 목구멍으로 넘어가게 하다.
drink
To make liquid such as water, etc., pass down one's throat.

• -어 가지고 : 앞의 말이 나타내는 행동이나 상태가 뒤의 말의 원인이나 이유임을 나타내는 표현.
-eo gajigo (no equivalent expression)
An expression used to indicate that the act or state mentioned in the preceding statement is the cause, means, or reason for the following statement.

• **컨디션 (noun)** : 몸이나 건강, 마음 등의 상태.
condition
The state of one's body, health. emotion, etc.

• 이 : 어떤 상태나 상황의 대상이나 동작의 주체를 나타내는 조사.
i (no equivalent expression)
A postpositional particle referring to a subject under a certain state or situation, or the agent of an action.

• **안 (adverb)** : 부정이나 반대의 뜻을 나타내는 말.
not
An adverb that has the meaning of negation or opposite.

• **좋다 (adjective)** : 신체적 조건이나 건강 상태 등이 보통보다 낫다.
good
Above average in physical condition or health.

• -아 : (두루낮춤으로) 어떤 사실을 서술하거나 물음, 명령, 권유를 나타내는 종결 어미.
-a (no equivalent expression)
(informal addressee-lowering) A sentence-final ending used to **describe** a certain fact, ask a question, give an order, or advise.

< 대화(dialogue) > - 99

요리 학원에 가서 수업이라도 들을까 봐.
요리 하궈네 가서 수어비라도 드를까 봐.
yori hagwone gaseo sueobirado deureulkka bwa.

갑자기 왜? 요리를 해야 할 일이 있어?
갑짜기 왜? 요리를 해야 할 이리 이써?
gapjagi wae? yorireul haeya hal iri isseo?

< 설명(explanation) / 번역(translation) >

요리 학원+에 가+(아)서 수업+이라도 듣(들)+[을까 보]+아.
가서 들을까 봐

• **요리 (noun)** : 음식을 만듦.
cooking
An act of making food.

• **학원 (noun)** : 학생을 모집하여 지식, 기술, 예체능 등을 가르치는 사립 교육 기관.
private institute; academy; cram school
A private educational institution that recruits students and then teaches knowledge and skills including art, music, physical education, etc.

• 에 : 앞말이 목적지이거나 어떤 행위의 진행 방향임을 나타내는 조사.
to; at
A postpositional particle to indicate that the preceding statement refers to a destination or the course of a certain action.

• **가다 (verb)** : 한 곳에서 다른 곳으로 장소를 이동하다.
go; travel
To move from one place to another place.

• -아서 : 앞의 말과 뒤의 말이 순차적으로 일어남을 나타내는 연결 어미.
-aseo (no equivalent expression)
A connective ending used to indicate that the preceding event and the following one happened sequentially.

• **수업 (noun)** : 교사가 학생에게 지식이나 기술을 가르쳐 줌.
class; lesson; course
A teacher teaching a student certain studies or skills.

• 이라도 : 그것이 최선은 아니나 여럿 중에서는 그런대로 괜찮음을 나타내는 조사.
irado (no equivalent expression)
A postpositional particle used to indicate that it is not the best option but the most acceptable among many options.

• **듣다 (verb)** : 다른 사람의 말이나 소리 등에 귀를 기울이다.
listen to
To listen carefully with strained ears to others' words or sounds.

• -을까 보다 : 앞에 오는 말이 나타내는 행동을 할 의도가 있음을 나타내는 표현.
-eulkka boda (no equivalent expression)
An expression used to indicate that the speaker has an intention to do the act mentioned in the preceding statement.

• -아 : (두루낮춤으로) 어떤 사실을 서술하거나 물음, 명령, 권유를 나타내는 종결 어미.
-a (no equivalent expression)
(informal addressee-lowering) A sentence-final ending used to **describe** a certain fact, ask a question, give an order, or advise.

갑자기 왜?

요리+를 하+[여야 하]+ㄹ 일+이 있+어?
해야 할

• **갑자기 (adverb)** : 미처 생각할 틈도 없이 빨리.
suddenly; all of a sudden
Quickly, not allowing someone to think.

• **왜 (adverb)** : 무슨 이유로. 또는 어째서.
why
For what reason; how come.

• **요리 (noun)** : 음식을 만듦.
cooking
An act of making food.

• 를 : 동작이 직접적으로 영향을 미치는 대상을 나타내는 조사.
reul (no equivalent expression)
A postpositional particle used to indicate the subject that an act has a direct influence on.

• **하다 (verb)** : 어떤 행동이나 동작, 활동 등을 행하다.
do; perform
To perform a certain move, action, activity, etc.

• -여야 하다 : 앞에 오는 말이 어떤 일을 하거나 어떤 상황에 이르기 위한 의무적인 행동이거나 필수적인 조건임을 나타내는 표현.
-yeoya hada (no equivalent expression)
An expression used to indicate that the preceding statement is the required act or condition to realize a certain incident or situation.

• -ㄹ : 앞의 말이 관형어의 기능을 하게 만들고 추측, 예정, 의지, 가능성 등을 나타내는 어미.
-l (no equivalent expression)
An ending of a word that makes the preceding statement function as an adnominal phrase and refers to assumption, prearrangement, intention, possibility, etc.

• **일 (noun)** : 해결하거나 처리해야 할 문제나 사항.
business; engagement
A problem or thing that one should resolve or deal with.

• 이 : 어떤 상태나 상황의 대상이나 동작의 주체를 나타내는 조사.
i (no equivalent expression)
A postpositional particle referring to a subject under a certain state or situation, or the agent of an action.

• **있다 (adjective)** : 어떤 사람에게 무슨 일이 생긴 상태이다.
no equivalent expression
Something happening to someone.

• -어 : (두루낮춤으로) 어떤 사실을 서술하거나 물음, 명령, 권유를 나타내는 종결 어미.
-eo (no equivalent expression)
(informal addressee-lowering) A sentence-final ending used to describe a certain fact, **ask a question**, give an order, or advise.

< 대화(dialogue) > - 100

이 옷 사이즈도 맞고 너무 예뻐요.
이 옫 사이즈도 맏꼬 너무 예뻐요.
i ot saijeudo matgo neomu yeppeoyo.

다행이네. 너한테 작을까 봐 조금 걱정했는데.
다행이네. 너한테 자글까 봐 조금 걱쩡핸는데.
dahaengine. neohante jageulkka bwa jogeum geokjeonghaenneunde.

< 설명(explanation) / 번역(translation) >

이 옷 사이즈+도 맞+고 너무 예쁘(예ㅃ)+어요.

예뻐요

• **이 (determiner)** : 말하는 사람에게 가까이 있거나 말하는 사람이 생각하고 있는 대상을 가리킬 때 쓰는 말.
this
The word that is used to refer to a person who is close to the speaker or something that the speaker is thinking of.

• **옷 (noun)** : 사람의 몸을 가리고 더위나 추위 등으로부터 보호하며 멋을 내기 위하여 입는 것.
clothes; garment
An item that one wears to cover his/her body, protect himself/herself from cold, heat, etc., and look fashionable.

• **사이즈 (noun)** : 옷이나 신발 등의 크기나 치수.
size; measurement
A size or measurement of clothing, shoes, etc.

• 도 : 이미 있는 어떤 것에 다른 것을 더하거나 포함함을 나타내는 조사.
do (no equivalent expression)
A postpositional particle used to indicate an addition or inclusion of another thing to something that already exists.

• **맞다 (verb)** : 크기나 규격 등이 어떤 것과 일치하다.
fit; be the same as
For a size, specification, etc., to be the same as something.

• -고 : 두 가지 이상의 대등한 사실을 나열할 때 쓰는 연결 어미.
-go (no equivalent expression)
A connective ending used when listing more than two equal facts.

• **너무 (adverb)** : 일정한 정도나 한계를 훨씬 넘어선 상태로.
too
To an excessive degree.

• **예쁘다 (adjective)** : 생긴 모양이 눈으로 보기에 좋을 만큼 아름답다.
pretty; beautiful; comely
The appearance of someone or something looking good and beautiful.

• -어요 : (두루높임으로) 어떤 사실을 서술하거나 질문, 명령, 권유함을 나타내는 종결 어미.
-eoyo (no equivalent expression)
(informal addressee-raising) A sentence-final ending used to **describe** a certain fact, ask a question, give an order, or advise.

다행+이+네.

너+한테 작+[을까 보]+아 조금 걱정하+였+는데.

작을 까봐　　　　　걱정했는데

• **다행 (noun)** : 뜻밖에 운이 좋음.
being fortunate
A state of being lucky beyond expectation.

• 이다 : 주어가 지시하는 대상의 속성이나 부류를 지정하는 뜻을 나타내는 서술격 조사.
ida (no equivalent expression)
A predicate particle indicating the meaning of the attribute or category of the thing that the subject of the sentence refers to.

• -네 : (아주낮춤으로) 지금 깨달은 일에 대하여 말함을 나타내는 종결 어미.
-ne (no equivalent expression)
(formal, highly addressee-lowering) A sentence-final ending used when talking about something that one just learned.

• **너 (pronoun)** : 듣는 사람이 친구나 아랫사람일 때, 그 사람을 가리키는 말.
no equivalent expression
A pronoun used to indicate the listener when he/she is the same age or younger.

• 한테 : 앞말이 기준이 되는 대상이나 단위임을 나타내는 조사.
per; for; against
A postpositional particle to indicate that the preceding statement is a unit or subject that is the standard for something.

• **작다 (adjective)** : 정해진 크기에 모자라서 맞지 아니하다.
small
Not fitting since the size is smaller than required.

• -을까 보다 : 앞에 오는 말이 나타내는 상황이 될 것을 걱정하거나 두려워함을 나타내는 표현.
-eulkka boda (no equivalent expression)
An expression used to indicate that the speaker is worried or afraid that the situation mentioned in the preceding statement may happen.

• -아 : 앞에 오는 말이 뒤에 오는 말에 대한 원인이나 이유임을 나타내는 연결 어미.
-a (no equivalent expression)
A connective ending used when the preceding statement is the cause or reason for the following statement.

• **조금 (adverb)** : 분량이나 정도가 적게.
a little
In a small quantity or to a small degree.

• **걱정하다 (verb)** : 좋지 않은 일이 있을까 봐 두려워하고 불안해하다.
worry; be worried; be concerned
To feel fearful and anxious that something bad might happen.

• -였- : 어떤 사건이 과거에 완료되었거나 그 사건의 결과가 현재까지 지속되는 상황을 나타내는 어미.
-yeot- (no equivalent expression)
An ending of a word used to indicate that an event was completed in the past or its result continues in the present.

• -는데 : (두루낮춤으로) 듣는 사람의 반응을 기대하며 어떤 일에 대해 감탄함을 나타내는 종결 어미.
-neunde (no equivalent expression)
(informal addressee-lowering) A sentence-final ending used to admire something while anticipating the listener's response.

< 참고 문헌 (reference) >

고려대학교 한국어대사전, 고려대학교 민족문화연구원, 2009
우리말샘, 국립국어원, 2016
표준국어대사전, 국립국어원, 1999
한국어교육 문법 자료편, 한글파크, 2016
한국어 교육학 사전, 하우, 2014
한국어기초사전, 국립국어원, 2016
한국어 문법 총론 Ⅰ, 집문당, 2015

대화로 배우는 한국어 English(translation)

발　행 | 2024년 6월 20일
저　자 | 주식회사 한글2119연구소
펴낸이 | 한건희
펴낸곳 | 주식회사 부크크
출판사등록 | 2014.07.15.(제2014-16호)
주　소 | 서울특별시 금천구 가산디지털1로 119 SK트윈타워 A동 305호
전　화 | 1670-8316
이메일 | info@bookk.co.kr

ISBN | 979-11-410-9056-2

www.bookk.co.kr